Environmental Communication and Travel Journalism

Travel journalism about natural attractions is environmental communication at the cusp of consumerism and concern. Countries and regions that market forests, rivers and wildlife to international tourists drive place-of-origin brand recognition that benefits exporters in other sectors. Place-branding in such destinations is not just PR for environmentally sustainable development and consumption, but also a political enterprise.

Environmental Communication and Travel Journalism considers tourism public relations as elite reputation management, and applies models of political conflict and source–media relations to the analysis of the 'soft' genre of travel journalism. The book seeks to understand how, in whose interests and against what odds discourses of cosmopolitanism and place-branding influence the way travel journalists represent vulnerable and contested environments.

Informed by interviews with journalists and their sources, *Environmental Communication and Travel Journalism* identifies and theorises networks, cultures, discursive strategies and multiple loyalties that can assist or interrupt flows of environmental concern in the cosmopolitan public sphere. The book should be of interest to scholars of environmental communication, environmental politics, journalism, tourism, marketing and public relations.

Lyn McGaurr is a Research Associate at the University of Tasmania, Australia, where she completed a PhD in Journalism. She has published internationally in the fields of environmental conflict and concern, mediated climate-change risk, travel journalism, cosmopolitanism and place-branding.

Routledge Studies in Environmental Communication and Media

Culture, Development and Petroleum
An Ethnography of the High North
Edited by Jan-Oddvar Sørnes, Larry Browning and Jan Terje Henriksen

Discourses of Global Climate Change
Apocalyptic framing and political antagonisms
Jonas Anshelm and Martin Hultman

The Troubled Rhetoric and Communication of Climate Change
The argumentative situation
Philip Eubanks

Environmental Communication and Travel Journalism
Consumerism, Conflict and Concern
Lyn McGaurr

Environmental Ethics and Film
Pat Brereton

Environmental Communication and Travel Journalism

Consumerism, conflict and concern

Lyn McGaurr

Routledge
Taylor & Francis Group

LONDON AND NEW YORK

First published 2015
by Routledge
2 Park Square, Milton Park, Abingdon, Oxon OX14 4RN

and by Routledge
711 Third Avenue, New York, NY 10017

First issued in paperback 2017

Routledge is an imprint of the Taylor & Francis Group, an informa business

British Library Cataloguing-in-Publication Data
A catalogue record for this book is available from the British Library

Library of Congress Cataloging-in-Publication Data
McGaurr, Lyn.
Environmental communication and travel journalism consumerism: conflict and concern / Lyn McGaurr.
pages cm. — (Routledge studies in environmental communication and media)
Includes bibliographical references and index.
ISBN 978-1-138-77525-1 (hb) — ISBN 978-1-315-77390-2 (e-book)
1. Communication in the environmental sciences. 2. Travel journalism. 3. Tourism—Environmental aspects. I. Title.
GE25.M44 2015
070.4'493637—dc23
2015004498

ISBN 13: 978-1-138-50689-3 (pbk)
ISBN 13: 978-1-138-77525-1 (hbk)

Typeset in Goudy
by Fish Books Ltd.

Contents

Acknowledgements   vii

1   Introduction   1

PART I
Theoretical foundations   27

2   A cosmopolitan perspective   29

3   Travel journalism and the brands   52

PART II
In the field   77

4   A place-branded discourse   79

5   The authority   93

6   The travel media   116

7   The challengers   135

PART III
In the media   151

8   The distractions and attractions of search   153

9   Running with the lists   166

10 The (travel journalism) environment   178

Index   186

Acknowledgements

My warm thanks to Professor Libby Lester, head of the Journalism, Media and Communications Program at the University of Tasmania, for her encouragement over many years. She supervised the PhD thesis that was the basis for Parts I and II of this book. Her enthusiasm and expertise in the fields of environmental communication and journalism were invaluable. More recently, it has been a privilege to work with Professor Lester and Professor Bruce Tranter on a large research project "Leadership and the construction of environmental concerns in Australia", funded by the Australian Research Council [DP130102154]. A small amount of material from one of our jointly authored journal articles arising from the project appears in this book. The article, entitled "Wilderness and the media politics of place branding", was published in *Environmental Communication: A Journal of Nature and Culture*.

Thank you to the examiners of my PhD thesis, Professor Alison Anderson and Professor Silvio Waisbord, for encouraging me to publish the thesis as a book, and to Professor Anderson for suggesting I include examples beyond Australia. A small writing-up grant from the University of Tasmania's Institute for the Study of Social Change helped me make time to prepare the manuscript for publication.

Dr Folker Hanusch's tireless advocacy and research in the field of travel journalism studies has given me opportunities to publish my own findings. Small sections of this book are drawn from my chapter "Your threat or mine? Travel journalists and environmental problems" in *Travel Journalism: Exploring Production, Impact and Culture*, edited by Dr Hanusch and Associate Professor Elfriede Fürsich, and published by Palgrave Macmillan. I have also drawn from "The devil may care: Travel journalism, cosmopolitan concern, politics and the brand", which was published in a special issue of *Journalism Practice* edited by Dr Hanusch.

A version of part of Chapter 7 was first published in my chapter "Not so soft? Travel journalism, environmental protest, power and the Internet" in *Environmental Conflict and the Media*, edited by Professor Lester and Associate Professor Brett Hutchins and published by Peter Lang, while other small sections of the book have appeared in the article "Travel journalism and environmental conflict: A cosmopolitan perspective", published in *Journalism Studies*.

I am especially grateful to all the interviewees who made time available in their very busy lives to participate in this research.

Dr Ingvar A. Sigurðsson very kindly directed me to information about puffin numbers in Iceland's Westman Islands, while Dr Geo Takach's research into Albertan place-branding and identity published in 2013 and 2014 gave me a wonderful insight into that province.

Finally, thanks to the dear family and friends whose love and support made this book possible: Russell, Kara, Cameron, Josephine, Jeanette and Sam.

1   Introduction

On the night Richard Flanagan won the 2014 Man Booker Prize, the BBC's Kirsty Wark (2014) asked him to comment on a statement by the Australian Prime Minister that coal was good for humanity. Flanagan answered that it made him ashamed to be Australian. Then Wark asked him about the repeal of a hard-won forest peace accord by the new government of his home state of Tasmania. The novelist responded that the island's contested forests were sacred places that the politics of the day wanted to destroy, dividing people unnecessarily. In Tasmania's capital city, Hobart, *The Mercury* newspaper called for unity, reflecting on a time when Flanagan had often been "pilloried by some and defended by few" for criticising the woodchip industry (*The Mercury* 2014). The editorial did not elaborate, but among examples it might have cited in addition to material in its own archive was one that implicated travel journalism. In 2007 Flanagan had told a reporter working for a national magazine that he was being ostracised by a state tourism office intent on ensuring international travel journalists did not cross his path (Fleming 2007). Flanagan had been outspoken in national and international news, essays and opinion pieces, but he had also published a travel feature in *The New York Times* describing Tasmanian logging in apocalyptic terms (Flanagan 2004) and been quoted in an adventure travel piece in United States magazine *Outside* reiterating his concerns (Flanagan in Jenkins 2005).

A week after Flanagan received the Booker Prize, Lonely Planet declared Tasmania the fourth best regional travel destination in the world for 2015 (Zeiher 2014). Within hours the state tourism office had written to tourism businesses explaining how to insert the Lonely Planet accolade into their marketing and public relations (Tourism Tasmania 2014a, 2014b, 2014c). The media release template it suggested they use was a lesson in brand-aligned cross-promotion, with references to "the world's most trusted travel publisher" alongside praise for the state's natural and cultural attractions (Tourism Tasmania 2014d). There was no mention in Tourism Tasmania's communications of Lonely Planet's observation that everyone on the island has a passionate opinion about its logging debate (Zeiher 2014, p. 71). Instead, the tourism office invited businesses to join it in hosting national and international journalists visiting the state (Tourism Tasmania 2014c).

In *The Mercury*, the Lonely Planet accolade was celebrated individually (Glaetzer 2014) and in combination with reports that British travel journalist and restaurant reviewer AA Gill would soon be dining in Tasmania, along with many other food and wine luminaries (Ironside 2014). Forgotten was Gill's 2007 assessment in a travel feature in London's *Sunday Times* that the island's forest was being "rubbed out by special pleading, arm-twisting and back-scratching corruption" (Gill 2007, see Chapter 6). Gill has described journalists as performing on "an invisible stage" and himself as read by "more people than will pick up a Booker Prize-nominated novel in a year" (2005, p. 3). When he attended the gala dinner in November at Hobart's Museum of Old and New Art – the finale of Tourism Australia's $40 million 2014 "Restaurant Australia" campaign – he was introduced in national television coverage as one of the "harshest food critics in the world" (Atkin 2014). But on this occasion he was rhapsodic: "It was fantastic. Amazing food in an amazing room. I mean it really is spectacular" (Gill in Atkin 2014).

A month later Gill published a glowing review in *The Sunday Times* of a Hobart restaurant called Garagistes. In the years since he had last been in the state, a timber company that in 2007 had been planning to build a controversial 1.9 AUD pulp mill in the wine-tourism region of the Tamar Valley had gone into receivership, never having secured the "social licence" it belatedly came to recognise was necessary to attract the financial backing it required to proceed (see Montgomery 2012). Perhaps Gill had concluded environmental conflict in Tasmania had largely abated. Perhaps he believed in the performativity of celebrity suggestion. Whatever the reasons, in his review of Garagistes he did not mention forestry, despite the international attention that had been accorded Flanagan's comments at the Booker Prize ceremony just two months earlier, including a report in *The Times* (see Lagan 2014). Rather, he described the state as "very aware of its clean ecological credentials" (Gill 2014).

If you live in the Northern Hemisphere – in Britain or Western Europe, perhaps, or North America – you may assume my opening anecdote is idiosyncratic and parochial, emerging as it does from a small island at the other end of the world. Yet I have found similarly intense passions and politics when researching Canada and Iceland. I have also interviewed travel journalists from Britain and the United States who describe their experience of Tasmanian tourism public relations as, if anything, more skilled and professional than they are used to. So I have opened with this particular story not because it arises from the subject of my primary case study, Tasmania, but because it spans many of the topics that will emerge in the following chapters as important considerations in the study of environmental communication and travel journalism. These include journalistic agency, professional and personal tastes and interests, tourism marketing and public relations strategies and tactics, competition between sources for media access, place identity, projected image, symbols, brand extensions, celebrity, even the power of accolades in travel lists to submerge political frames. Yet for the most part, travel journalism flies under the radar of academic scrutiny. Too often, it seems to me, its tendency to ignore claims of environmental irresponsibility is disregarded in the scholarly calculation of elite advantage. Perhaps because overtly political frames have traditionally been unusual in travel texts (see, for example, Hill-James 2006), journalism scholars rarely take account of the political advantage to pro-development governments of celebratory travel journalism about natural attractions.

Environmental communication is symbolic action (Cox 2013). In its pragmatic form it provides information that helps us to solve environmental problems. In its constitutive capacity it may "invite us to perceive forests and rivers as natural resources for use or exploitation or as vital life support systems" (Cox 2013, p. 19). It defines some subjects as problems but not others, and associates problems with particular values (Cox 2013). And in the tourism sector, it beckons us to form relationships with brands (see Hansen 2010). Tourism's job-creation potential and capacity to build local pride through affirmative discourses in its products and publicity can attract local goodwill and public support for government destination promotion. This has led to assertions that tourism is "a refreshingly simple and honest business" whose communications have an automatic legitimacy (Anholt 2010, p. 89). Tourism offices frequently portray themselves as contributing to the health of other parts of the economy. They do this by deploying the rhetoric of place-branding to argue that travellers include business people, investors and entrepreneurs from a variety of industries. "The broad benefits that travellers bring to Canada go far beyond supporting our $82-billion dollar tourism industry," writes the Canadian Tourism Commission (CTC), for example. "As these visitors... become acquainted with our country and its high-quality products, they become advocates for Canada, uncovering investment and trade opportunities, identifying business partnerships and creating a foundation for trade" (CTC 2014). In nature-based destinations, landscapes, wildlife and ecotourism that are instrumentalised by tourism offices coincidentally secure access to consumers of travel media for discourses that reflect favourably on government and business. If competition for natural resources leads to controversy, routine celebratory tourism communications can easily become the fulcrum of cross-sectoral brand maintenance or rehabilitation efforts (McGaurr 2010, 2012; McGaurr, Tranter and Lester 2014). Glossy travel journalism that ignores threats to branded nature by extractive industries benefits pro-development interests by presenting target audiences with place-based projections of scenic beauty, natural abundance and social harmony that can function as a form of symbolic annihilation (Shanahan and McComas 1999 in Cox 2013, p. 166) not of the environment per se but of environmental conflict.

According to Chris Ryan and Anne Zahra, jurisdictional tourism offices are usually "quasi-public sector bodies, primarily funded by local and national government" (2004, p. 80). The pivotal role of state, provincial and national tourism offices in reputation-building is evident in public–private and whole-of-government (or multi-agency) approaches to economic development that position the tourism sector at the heart of global marketing initiatives. In Tasmania in the first decade of this century, for example, tourism was described as the most influential sectoral brand under the state's master brand, which in turn was tasked with nationally and internationally aligning the messages of stakeholders who might be "in competition or in conflict with one another" (Department of Premier and Cabinet, Tasmania, 2006). In Iceland, *The Promote Iceland Act 2010* has as its first objective "to strengthen Iceland's image and reputation, enhance the competitive position of Icelandic undertakings on foreign markets and to attract foreign investment and tourists to the country" (Althing 2010). And in 2014 in Alberta, Canada, a framework that aimed to "solidify" the province as "a world centre for resource-based and resource-related industries" also made tourism central to securing it an expanded global presence (Government of Alberta 2014, pp. 4, 6). This is not to suggest that governments supportive of extractive industries allocate public money to government or quasi-public tourism offices with instructions that it be spent on marketing and public relations to counter the claims of environmental organisations. In times of environmental conflict, public funding for tourism communications usually goes unremarked partly because there is no need for such edicts to be issued. Whether or not the tourism industry disagrees with government priorities – whether or not it considers its own competitiveness threatened by policies that encourage logging, mining, drilling or dam-building – we might reasonably expect that tourism offices will continue to represent destinations to travel journalists in a favourable light, because that is their raison d'être.

There is, of course, more to environmental communication in travel texts than the question of whether or not it mediates political conflict. Travel journalism that ignores disputes over natural resources may include less controversial environmental information or concern. As a mainstay of the tourism industry, landscapes and wildlife provide countless opportunities for businesses and governments as well as "places" to represent themselves as responsible global citizens. In a world of more than 1000 million international tourists (United Nations World Tourism Organization (UNWTO) 2014, p. 2), travel media can be conduits for publicising or promoting preservation, conservation or sustainable practices, thereby fulfilling foundational aspirations of the tourism industry by encouraging potential and imaginative travellers to care about distant locations. The sense of attachment created in this manner might inspire people to visit more than once, to the benefit of the local economy, but describing and praising clean, green practices might conceivably also encourage travellers to live their own lives more sustainably. In addition, we must be open to the possibility that financial benefit derived from nature-based tourism publicised through travel journalism will give local communities the motivation to improve their protection and stewardship of the environment (see Hajer 1995).

The legitimacy accorded tourism communications in nature-based destinations often rests, in part, on the qualified endorsement of environmental organisations and green political parties. These actors tend to have an ambivalent or contingent relationship with the travel industry. Overcrowding and demands for roads or commercial developments in national parks and reserves can complicate their engagement with the sector. However, they regularly cite the tourism and brand value of natural attractions in their arguments for conservation (see, for example, McGaurr, Tranter and Lester 2014). "Independent policy advisor on national identity and reputation" (GfK 2013) and co-author of the annual *Nation Brand Index* Simon Anholt may originally have intended the term "brand" to be a *metaphor* for the way places compete for visitors, ideas, investment, products, services and influence in a global marketplace (Anholt 2007), but there is a gap between theory and practice. For example, when Travel Alberta demanded a parody of its branding be removed from YouTube, its CEO defended the action by saying his province's brand was all that distinguished it from competing tourism destinations (Okabe in CBC News 2013). As Celia Lury (2004) observes, brands may be intangible but they are far from immaterial. Environmental groups and green politicians understand this. Their contingent endorsement of tourism facilitates the flow of symbols such as wilderness and iconic animals back and forth between consumerism and activism, allowing them to accumulate salience and power that can be redeployed in times of environmental conflict to argue that government support for extractive industries is damaging the brand (McGaurr, Tranter and Lester 2014).

Even if a general lack of political content in travel journalism suggests an unequal competition in the genre between environmental discourses circulated by elite and challenger media sources, alternative frames do sometimes gain purchase in particular media organisations and occasionally even endure. For example, in January 2014 *Outside* published another travel feature about Tasmania, and on this occasion, the journalist, Stephanie Pearson, predicted that if a conservative government were elected in a forthcoming poll, Tasmania's forests would be the losers (Pearson 2014). Nine years after the *Outside* travel feature quoting Flanagan's concerns (Jenkins 2005, see above), the magazine was still reporting that forest controversies defined and divided Australia's poorest state.

The silences that characterise so many travel texts become eloquent when examined in the light of contemporaneous disputes over natural resources, but the reverse is also true: examples such as *Outside* urge us to be curious about environmental discourses that retain their political edge in "soft" journalism. Cities, regions and countries that deploy natural attractions as brand attributes invoke countless associations, loyalties, expectations, myths, claims and counterclaims about the environment everywhere. In attempting to brand nature, they allow nature to brand them in return, opening the way for environmental organisations, journalists and citizens to hold them to account. When New Zealand attaches the label "100% Pure" to scenes of fjords and glaciers, when Alaska stamps an image of a polar bear and her cub next to the words "Made in Alaska", when Switzerland tells its visitors to "get natural", Alberta says "remember to breathe" and British Columbia calls itself "Super, Natural", an ethics of care (Szerszynski and Urry 2002, p. 480) is as readily to hand as any expectation of holiday magic or product purity. Place-branding particularises physical space but universalises promises in order to penetrate world markets. In so doing, it situates environmental assets within a global discourse. In the tourism sector, a version of that discourse resides in the texts of overseas travel journalists who visit a country, region or city to report their impressions to their readers back home. If they judge that a destination has failed to deliver on a brand promise of exemplary environmental stewardship, they may choose to express disappointment as cosmopolitan concern.

Anthropologist Ulf Hannerz's (2006) approach to cosmopolitanism has explanatory appeal in relation to the interaction of travel journalism and place-branding. Hannerz sees cosmopolitan value in the more narrative forms of transnational journalism. Comparing hard news and features, he attributes to features an ability to convey a broader variety of sentiments, provide a closer approximation of the complexity of distant others, and make those others, their locations and their situations more "durable" (2004, p. 33). He describes cosmopolitanism as having two faces: the happy face of cultural cosmopolitanism associated with an openness to distant cultures evident, for example, in an aesthetic and intellectual appreciation of their food, literature and music, and the worried face of political cosmopolitanism that attempts to deal with concerns such as environmental degradation, species extinction, humanitarian crises, human rights abuses and climate change. Hannerz (2006) entertains the possibility of an intertwining of cultural and political cosmopolitanism arising from "banal cosmopolitanism" – an awareness of diversity resulting from work or recreational travel, cross-border friendships and kinship, encounters with immigrants and refugees, and other lived encounters that at their most positive can lead one to feel "at home in the world" (2004, 2006). Sociologists Bronislaw Szerszynski and John Urry (2002, 2006) go so far as to speculate that the public's everyday encounters with representations of universal connectedness in a world of globalised media may have the capacity to animate both international tourism and the environment movement. By contrast, sociologist Ulrich Beck argues that the media's unveiling of environmental risks that transcend national borders can promote the self-interested formation of imagined communities of global risks and associated interdependencies, and a cosmopolitan "politicization and establishment of norms" (Beck 2011, p. 1353, see Chapter 2).

Travel journalism, then, is a site where eco-friendly messages can be promoted but commodified landscapes and wildlife can also be deployed by antagonists on both sides of environmental disputes. Steeped in the messy complexity of environmental communication at the cusp of consumerism and concern, this book asks in whose interests and against what odds discourses of cosmopolitanism and place-branding influence the way travel journalists represent vulnerable and contested places. In this respect my interests diverge somewhat from those of Folker Hanusch and Thomas Hanitzsch (2013), who include travel journalism among genres they define collectively as lifestyle journalism. Whereas Hanusch and Hanitzsch delineate and theorise lifestyle journalism's role in shaping identities in consumer society, I argue that international travel journalism about nature-based destinations is (also) a cosmopolitan site made politically potent by its soft reputation.

Travel journalism studies

When I began researching international travel journalism and cosmopolitanism in 2008, I found only a small body of scholarly literature on the genre. In marketing and public relations journals there was some discussion of tourism office hosting programs (Dore and Crouch 2003; Mackellar and Fenton 2000; Seligman 1990) and the merits or otherwise of "freebies" (Seligman 1990; Simon 1988). Accounts of travel journalists' views of free travel and accommodation appeared in journals of journalism practice (Gillespie 1988; Moss 2008; Weir Alderson 1988), and in this regard Jeremy Weir Alderson (1988) briefly drew attention to the genre's neglect of the social, economic or political problems of destinations. Some embryonic content analyses and interviews were conducted as early as 1976 in the United States (Wood 1977) and 1986 in Britain, the latter revealing that travel editors considered "knocking pieces" generally out of place (Seaton n.d., p. 11). However, only since the turn of the century has there been any sustained academic interest in the genre. This is largely due to a seminal article by Elfriede Fürsich and Anandam Kavoori published in 2001, which argued that travel journalism deserved greater attention for what it could reveal about "the ideological dimensions of tourism and transcultural encounters, as well as the ongoing dynamics of media globalization" (2001, p. 150). A number of authors soon took up their challenge. A study of travel journalism about Portugal in United States newspapers published in 2004 found little evidence that travel journalists interacted with locals and concluded, in effect, that monopolisation of them by the tourism industry during their visits meant that "readers are provided with representations that serve to reconfirm their own values and beliefs based on marketing strategies aimed at creating an interesting destination and culture for [in this case] Americans to visit" (Santos 2004, p.132). In 2005 Marcella Daye found an apparent "inability to construct a discourse of difference" (2005, p. 23) in British travel articles about the Caribbean. And in 2006, Stamou and Paraskevopoulos, applying critical discourse analysis to a sample of travel journalism texts in a Greek travel magazine, found the magazine failed to integrate environmental and economic discourses in articles about protected areas. In 2010, Folker Hanusch and I called in separate articles for greater academic interest in the genre, and further empirical research has since been undertaken (Cocking, 2009; 2014; Hanusch 2011, 2012a, 2012b, 2014; McGaurr 2012, 2013, 2014; McGaurr, Tranter and Lester 2014). For example, Hanusch (2011) and Candeeda Hill-James (2006) conducted content analyses of Australian travel journalism representations of foreign places, finding, respectively, few interviews with locals other than those in the tourism industry and little discussion of political issues in destinations. Hanusch (2012a, 2012b) also surveyed Australian travel journalists and found they believe they have strong ethical standards.

In 2014, Hanusch and Fürsich published an edited collection that greatly expanded the depth and breadth of international travel journalism scholarship. The collection incorporates welcome chapters on travel blogs and other forms of online travel content (Pirolli 2014; Raman and Choudary 2014). In a revision of their ground-breaking 2001 article, Fürsich and Kavoori added an overview of relevant mobility scholarship, alerting us to the potential in travel journalism studies of research and theory-building around the concept of virtual mobility – "the movement of ideas, images and information in symbolic spheres" (2014, p. 33). Provocatively in terms of my interest in environmental conflict, Hanusch's own content analysis in the edited volume reveals that travel journalists are reluctant to report on destinations experiencing crises or disasters (2014, p. 171). While acknowledging Hanusch's findings, my own research proceeds on the assumption that non-violent environmental conflict does not deter travel journalists from covering tourism destinations in the way that crime, terrorism, war or a natural disaster might. In my experience, travel journalism about nature-based tourism destinations where environmental conflict is rife has been a fertile site for exploring the genre's political potential.

The travel journalism globe

As Hanusch (2014) has found, the world of travel journalism is not the same as the physical world or even the world of corporeal travel. In the first half of 2009, he conducted content analysis of stories about foreign countries and regions in the travel sections of two "quality" newspapers in each of Australia, Britain, Canada and New Zealand (Hanusch 2014). He found that the factors that determined the places covered were very similar to those that determined coverage in foreign news – "regionalism, a focus on powerful nations or big neighbors and cultural proximity" (Hanusch 2014, p.171). The United States was the subject of more than twice as many stories overall as the next most frequently covered country, Australia, even though, as Hanusch pointed out, it was the most popular travel destination only of Canada (Hanusch 2014, p.170). Overall, Europe (32.5 per cent) was the most frequently covered continent, but with few articles about Eastern Europe (1.9 per cent overall). Europe was followed by the Americas (25.9 per cent), but with 16 per cent overall about *North* America. Least covered were countries in Asia (23.3 per cent), Oceania (12.7 per cent, despite Australia's strong performance largely as a result of New Zealand coverage) and Africa (5.7 per cent). Hanusch found that the coverage of countries did not necessarily correlate with those that were the most popular destinations of the citizens where the articles were published, with some highly visited places – "often less proximate or less powerful ones" – featured less frequently than other destinations (2014, p. 172). Hanusch speculated that this may have been due in part to the influence of hosted visits, with tourism offices and businesses in more affluent countries or in closer proximity better positioned to attract travel journalists. As recipients of the greatest amount of publicity from travel journalism, and as jurisdictions ostensibly best placed to give and receive frank travel journalism reviews and respond to any criticisms, Western democracies are the subject of my research in this book.

Empirical research

Primary case study

Background

The research for this book spans travel journalism about Australia, Canada and Iceland, but the majority of texts discussed in depth are about Tasmania. A temperate Australian island state of just half a million people, it is south across Bass Strait from Melbourne and north across the Southern Ocean from Antarctica. It is approximately 17,000 kilometres from Britain and the United States, which until

2014 were its biggest markets for international visitors. In nearly half a century of environmental conflict it has produced the first green political party in the world and arguably the first global environmental campaign (Lester and Hutchins 2009). Despite its geographical isolation, and also because of it, it has been described in travel journalism as "something of a petri dish for the rest of us" (Pearson 2014). Environmental campaigns against old-growth logging that targeted Tasmania's tourism brand with boycotts and billboards (McGaurr 2010, 2012) anticipated similar tactics deployed in 2010 by the "Rethink Alberta" campaign against further development of Canada's Athabasca bituminous sands (see Takach 2014). During the period of my Tasmanian case study – 2000 to 2010 – environmental conflict in the state was extensive. In the following decade, demand for the state's forestry products slumped and the industry declined. State tourism office Tourism Tasmania's Visiting Journalist Program (VJP) was for many years a powerful tool by which the government sought media endorsement for framing of Tasmania as "natural". In the 1990s wilderness and/or nature were repeatedly identified as the state's biggest tourism asset (see Chapter 4 for more details about this period). Further interstate research conducted in 2010 (Tourism Tasmania 2011, p. 6) found "wilderness" was still the biggest motivator for travel to the state, while in 2014 "wilderness and nature" ranked first among the state's most appealing aspects according to qualitative research contracted by Tourism Research Australia and Tourism Tasmania (Tourism Research Australia 2014, p. 4). Although international visitors made up only around 15 per cent of Tasmania's total visitation in the first decade of the 2000s, during that period Tourism Tasmania was funded by the government to engage representatives in Germany, England, the United States, Canada, Japan and Singapore. Successive Tourism Tasmania annual reports record that the VJP has enjoyed considerable success over many years in attracting travel journalists writing for prestigious travel publications in Britain, the United States and many other countries. For many years, Tasmania's most heavily marketed tourism attributes in addition to its natural environment have been cultural heritage, food and wine. In the early 2000s Tourism Tasmania also worked to improve the state's reputation with gay and lesbian tourists, collaborating closely with a community leader who in 1997 had seen homosexuality decriminalised in the state after a nine-year local, national and international campaign involving the United Nations and Amnesty International. In 2011, a wealthy philanthropist opened a new multimillion-dollar private gallery, the Museum of Old and New Art (MONA), which soon become one of the state's most popular individual tourism attraction, gaining valuable attention from travel journalists in Australia and overseas. In 2012, Tourism Tasmania developed a new brand strategy that gave culture increased prominence.

Methods and approach

In 2009 and (in one instance) June 2010, as part of the research for my PhD, I interviewed 11 journalists who had visited Tasmania to research travel articles for publication in the United States or Britain between 2000 and 2010. They didn't always go looking for forests, mountains or beaches, but all were curious about the island's identity. In most cases they spoke as journalists who had written about innumerable destinations in their careers. Some had also worked as news reporters and could comment from their own experience on how news and travel journalism compared. A number had published successful books, and since our conversations at least three have won Lowell Thomas travel journalism awards from the Society of American Travel Writers.

In addition to interviewing travel journalists, I spoke to many of their named sources, as well as tourism public relations practitioners and other relevant member of the Tasmanian community. I also spoke to one Swiss–Australian journalist who had written news and travel journalism about Tasmania for large German-language newspapers in Europe. Before, during and after these conversations I engaged in an iterative textual analysis of interview transcripts, travel journalism and a wide range of other documents such as government strategies and annual reports, marketing material, web pages and news journalism. Combining this with a contextual analysis informed by many of the same texts, I created thick descriptions (Geertz 1973) of the production and, on occasion, subsequent careers of selected articles. Thus, the primary aim of my case study was, as Clifford Geertz would say, "to draw large conclusions from small, but very densely textured facts" (1973, p. 28). The particular qualitative methods I chose helped me inquire into the complexities of professional and social practice – including those aspects that were not on public display – by "gradually allowing the case narrative to unfold from the diverse, complex, and sometimes conflicting stories that people, documents, and other evidence tell" (Flyvbjerg 2001, p. 86). Importantly, in my analysis of interview transcripts I attended to ways in which journalistic agency as well as social structures had influenced the production, content and circulation of published texts. As Simon Cottle reminds us:

> Journalists do what they do for the most part knowingly and purposefully, which is not to say they are on an 'ideological mission' or, in idealist terms, that they somehow escape the structures in which they work. But it is to say that they are more consciously, knowingly and purposefully productive of news texts and output than they have been theoretically given credit for in the past. They are not, in other words, 'unwittingly, unconsciously' serving 'as a support for the reproduction of a dominant ideological discursive field' (Hall 1982, 82).
>
> (Cottle 2007, p. 10)

By interviewing travel journalists and a range of actors who had sought to have their messages publicised in newspaper and magazine articles about Tasmania as a holiday destination in a decade characterised by extended periods of environmental controversy, I was able to combine "internalist" (analysis of media practices and practitioners) and "externalist" (analysis of source practices and practitioners) approaches (Schlesinger 1990) in my investigation. This, in turn, increased the extent to which I was able to immerse myself in the cultures and issues concerned.

I also wanted to be able to ask interviewees to explain in their own words their motives, actions and values in relation to specific issues, if they were comfortable to do so – something that is often not possible when events are unfolding at a rapid pace during participant observation. In the words of Grant McCracken:

> [the long interview] gives us access to individuals without violating their privacy or testing their patience. It allows us to capture the data needed for penetrating qualitative analysis without participant observation, unobtrusive observation, or prolonged contact. It allows us, in other words, to achieve crucial qualitative objectives within a manageable methodological context.
>
> (McCracken 1988, p. 11)

Among the multiple concerns of this case study was to better understand how actors (individuals and institutions) make meaning and to identify and trace the extent to which actors contribute to the social construction of place. For these purposes, I adapted an approach to text analysis advocated by Carvalho (2005, 2008) – an approach to which discursive strategies are central. Discourses are "recurring pattern[s] of speaking or writing" that have developed from multiple sources and "often influence our understanding of how the world works or should work" (Cox 2013, p. 68). Discursive strategies, by contrast, are goal-oriented interventions in public discourse:

> Discursive strategies are forms of discursive manipulation of reality by social actors, including journalists, in order to achieve an effect or goal. Here, manipulation does not have the sense of an illegitimate alteration of a certain reality (cf. van Dijk, 2006). Rather, I use the term to mean, simply, a discursive intervention. This intervention and the procured aim can be more or less conscious
>
> (Carvalho 2008, p. 169)

As Carvalho (2008) notes, the advantage of analysing discursive strategies is that it provides insight into the link between "source strategies" (Anderson 1997; Lester 2007) and media representations. Because of the importance of distinguishing source strategies from journalists' strategies in the analysis of discursive strategies, Carvalho (2008) advocates attempting to trace the evolution of the discourse by examining source documents as well as quotes and indirect speech in the published journalism text. To this list, my case study adds transcripts of interviews with sources and journalists.

The main discursive strategy Carvalho identifies is framing (see Entman 1993), which importantly in terms of the celebratory, subjective genre of travel journalism can involve the exclusion as well as the inclusion of information and opinions (Carvalho 2008, p. 169). Framing also entails composition – "the arrangement of these elements in order to produce a certain meaning" (Carvalho 2008, p. 169). Framing is both fundamental to Carvalho's approach to the analysis of discursive strategies and an element of discourse that Carla Almeida Santos identifies as being of central importance to the mediation of tourism by travel journalists:

> In their constant quest to provide readers with unique, exciting, and undiscovered destinations, authors, working as cultural brokers (Dann 1996), depend on established frames. That is, they do not constantly create new representations but rather fall on previously established organizing narratives…One of the ways to identify the dominant frames of reference tourists carry is by identifying the representational dynamics used within tourism discourse.
>
> (Santos 2004, p. 123)

My approach to discourse was also time sensitive, which allowed me to take into account the media history and "specific events and developments related to the issue under examination [and] wider aspects of the social environment" (Carvalho 2008, p. 164), including the effects of discourse on social and political issues linked to but outside the texts (Carvalho 2008, p. 165).

In the course of my investigation, I compiled three samples of travel journalism about Tasmania published in Britain and the United States between 2000 and 2010 for close textual and contextual consideration. I paid particular attention to headlines, leads, word choice, actors, and institutional and other source presence, but my primary focus was on frames, symbols and meanings associated with the natural environment in relation to both cosmopolitan concern and branding. The first sample comprised 16 travel journalism features written by the 11 interviewed travel journalists. The second sample comprised 11 travel journalism features about the Bay of Fires, which Lonely Planet listed in late 2008 as one of its top destinations in the world for 2009. This sample included three features that were also part of the first sample but only one feature published after the Lonely Planet accolade. A third sample comprised seven features that appeared in *The New York Times* in the case study period and were included in that newspaper's online "Tasmania" travel guide. One of these features was part of the sample of those by interviewed journalists and another was part of the Bay of Fires sample.

Autoethnographic elements

Before I began my post-graduate studies full time at the University of Tasmania in 2008, I was employed full time by Tourism Tasmania, where I worked in corporate communications from mid-2002 to late-2007 and then for some months as a manager in the section responsible for liaising with travel journalists. While working for Tourism Tasmania, I contributed to the production of some of the documents I consulted in my research for this book and worked with some of the people I interviewed for the case study. However, before embarking on my PhD I had not met or corresponded with any of the British, United States or Swiss–Australian journalists I interviewed for my thesis. Prior to working for Tourism Tasmania, I had worked in-house and freelance for the guidebook company Lonely Planet as an editor and had been the sole updating author of the second edition of its *Tasmania* guide, published in 1999. I had no contact with the Tourism Tasmania Visiting Journalist Program while writing for Lonely Planet and accepted no "freebies" during my research for the *Tasmania* guide. Moreover, *Lonely Planet* destination guidebooks are not travel journalism according to the definition I have adopted in this book (see pages 14–17).

Anthropologist Leon Anderson advocates a realist form of autoethnography in which researchers who are part of the community being studied, either by chance or design, are "involved in the construction of meaning and values in the social worlds they investigate" and are reflexively aware of the effects of their participation (Anderson 2006, p. 384). Anderson describes such autoethnography as analytic because it "point[s] to a broad set of data-transcending practices that are directed toward theoretical development, refinement, and extension" (Anderson 2006, p. 387). As I have not approached my research through participant observation, it is not autoethnographic in the way Anderson conceives of it. However, I found it necessary to incorporate elements of his approach retrospectively to account for my past occupations. I did not use my own experiences at Tourism Tasmania or Lonely Planet as data in my Tasmanian case study. Nevertheless, I think it is important to acknowledge that working for Tourism Tasmania afforded me a valuable insight into the world of publicly funded tourism public relations and corporate communications, while updating Lonely Planet's *Tasmania* guide gave me an appreciation of what is involved in researching and writing about a tourist destination for a commercial publisher and an audience of potential tourists. In addition, my exposure to current affairs news culture early in my career informed my engagement with the journalists I interviewed – particularly those who had written news as well as travel articles.

There are, of course, disadvantages to having "witness[ed] the messy business of cultural manufacture" (Deacon et. al. 1999, p. 261) first hand prior to undertaking a case study. For example, I am aware that I may be accused of having sacrificed academic distance by choosing a subject closely related to some of my past occupations. In the words of Deacon et al.:

> [i]f we become too drawn into the view of the world constructed by those we are studying, it may be that we lose distance and analytical detachment. It becomes impossible to arrive at any explanation of the experiences and motives of those we observe other than those they themselves express. Some would argue that this is a good thing, since it allows the "subjects to speak", rather than the researcher speaking on their behalf. However, it is seen by many as a problem which restricts the analytical capacity of the researcher and produces descriptions rather than explanations.
>
> (Deacon et al. 1999, p. 256)

Deacon et al.'s comments quoted here refer to participant observation, but they are also relevant to associations formed between work colleagues. I readily acknowledge that it would have been impossible to purge myself of all residual subjectivity resulting from my past experiences. Instead, I put it reflexively to work, in the spirit of analytic autoethnography. In so doing, I believe I remained appropriately and sufficiently detached while pursuing my research for the results to be academically valid, in part because, to the extent that they do correspond, the occupations I refer to above range across separate categories of case-study interviewee. Indeed, the observations of Deacon et al. add weight to my argument for interviewing both journalists and their sources: not only did this ensure I avoided a media-centric approach (Schlesinger 1990) but it also helped me set the responses of inter-viewees more firmly in their social context. My own professional experiences, in turn, increased my confidence in my ability to grasp their actual rather than potential meanings and strengthened my claims to achieving thick description by facilitating a more nuanced interpretation of the data. In other words, far from resulting in descriptions rather than explanations, I believe my past experiences improved the quality of my explanations.

Additional research

This book includes the results of a year of additional research in 2014 in which I extended the work of my Tasmanian case study and investigated new destinations by conducting content, textual and/or contextual analysis of travel journalism about Iceland and the Canadian provinces of Alberta and British Columbia. Details of my approach are provided in Chapters 8 and 9.

Travel journalism objects of analysis

According to Chris Moss – a British book author and freelance travel writer and editor – the very best travel stories in newspapers and magazines are "a model of journalism" (2008, pp. 38–39):

> They entertain, they educate (occasionally), they illuminate. The main contemporary issues – the environment, the cultural impact of travel, the economics of the tourist dollar, the horrors of globetrotting and the terror of airport and airplane – should all command space among the upbeat copy on boutique hotels, delicious food, beautiful landscapes and unique cultures.
>
> (Moss 2008, pp. 38–39)

Yet Moss wrote his article for the *British Journalism Review* because he believed the comprehensive travel journalism described above was not valued by editors and was not being given sufficient space (2008, p. 39).

Brian McNair divides the purposes of journalism into three areas – surveillance, participation in the public sphere, and "recreational and cultural" (2005, p. 28):

- "Surveillance" refers to journalism's watchdog role – its fourth-estate function of scrutinising governments and institutions in order to alert citizens to abuses of power.
- "Participation in the public sphere" relates to journalism's ability to furnish citizens with information they need to participate effectively in democratic

society and to a view of the collective mass media as a site for informed discussion and debate.

- "Recreational and cultural" encompasses a plethora of categories often described as entertainment, lifestyle or soft journalism.

The three purposes of journalism can be separate or overlap, but McNair finds there is often tension between the first two and the third (2005, p. 28). In the opening paragraph of her investigation of news as a construction of reality, Gaye Tuchman defines news as telling readers what they "want to know, need to know, and should know" (Tuchman 1978, p. 1). While Tuchman here is referring to hard news, these qualities might also be expected of travel journalism. Travel material in what purports to be journalism perhaps does not need to be as timely as traditional news, but it might well give aspiring travellers the information they need to know and should know about a destination they might want to visit. In so doing, it would present the public with the useful, factual information McNair believes journalism prides itself on providing:

> In agreeing to pay [the price of a newspaper or online subscription] we are purchasing what we believe to be a reliable account of the real beyond our immediate experience, mediated through the professional skills of the journalist and the resources of the journalistic organisation. Journalism can be defined, in this sense, as *mediated reality*... The journalist, like the novelist and the historian in their different ways, tells stories, but the former's stories are presented to potential audiences as factual, rather than fictional, artistic, or scientific... To have value as information, journalism has to be accepted as true, or at least an acceptable approximation of the truth.
>
> (McNair 2005, p. 30, original emphasis)

A reasonable understanding of travel journalism might include literary travel writing's defining characteristic of the autobiographical account but would necessarily depart from definitions of travel writing that allow for entertaining fabrication (see, for example, Holland and Huggan 2000). Excluding fabrication, however, is no guarantee of incontestable truthfulness. Bill Kovach and Tom Rosenstiel (2001, p. 43) describe journalists' pursuit of "a practical or functional form of truth" as "a process – or continuing journey toward understanding – which begins with the first-day stories and builds over time". For these authors, journalism is not only about "getting the facts right" but about giving context by making those facts coherent (Kovach and Rosenstiel 2001, p. 41) – an account that implicitly acknowledges, as does Elfriede Fürsich (2002, 2003), that it is possible to be factual without being complete. Fürsich's understanding of travel journalism, thus, pays tribute to an observation by John Hartley that "[t]he most important component of [journalism's] system is the creation of readers as publics, and the connection of these readerships to other systems, such as those of politics, economics and social control" (Hartley 1996, p. 35).

Some media organisations that publish travel journalism – particularly a number of high-profile magazines and large metropolitan newspapers in the United States – do not allow their writers to accept free travel or accommodation, and texts produced without such assistance are an important part of my research. However, many publications do still accept freebies. In these circumstances, tourism offices and operators attempt to gain publicity they consider more credible than advertising by hosting travel journalists so as to capitalise on traditional associations between journalism and objectivity. In the absence of overt control over how these individuals will represent the destination, tourism offices often try to manage their access to information and sources by supplying itineraries and the services of guides. Provided a travel journalist produces a brand-aligned feature, it is in the interests of the tourism industry for readers to regard hosted writers as journalists. For writers who do accept assistance from tourism offices or tourism operators, the moniker "journalist" – whether deployed explicitly or merely implied by their publication in the editorial sections of newspapers and magazines – also serves as a bulwark against assumptions that bias will be an inevitable consequence of freebies. Even if the word "journalist" has come to be attached to certain sorts of travel writing almost by accident, it is laden with meanings that tourism public relations routinely exploit.

In this study, I examine travel journalism about (relatively) affluent democracies published in other affluent democracies. Hanusch's content analysis (see page xxxx) suggests such places will be the beneficiaries of the greatest amount of publicity in travel journalism consumed by rich and influential readers. We might also assume affluent democracies would be best placed economically, politically and socially to respond to any criticisms of their environmental practices. If instead rich democracies seek to hide extractive industries or environmental conflict from the gaze of travel journalists or respond to concern with marketing and public relations rather than action, how can we reasonably expect more progressive behaviour from poor or non-democratic places?

My primary objects of investigation are feature-length by-lined tourism destination reviews that "count as true" (Hartley 1996, p. 35), written by authors who visited the places concerned and were paid for their articles by media organisations as staff members or freelance authors, regardless of how their research trips were funded. I refer to these writers as travel journalists and their related products as travel features (see Chapter 3 for a fuller discussion of the genre). This category of travel journalism can encompass texts in any medium, but I focus on written articles in print or online.

Another form of travel journalism I interrogate is the travel "listicle" – a collection of destination names with text beneath each item. Travel lists are ubiquitous and powerful. Rankings by prestigious travel media organisations regularly feature as accolades on the websites and in the brochures and advertisements of tourism businesses and tourism offices. They are often reported in local and national news, and may even be deemed worthy of a press release from a tourism minister (see Chapter 5). In Ben Cocking's (2014, p. 181) view, travel journalism "must – via narrative formed out of the dynamic interchange between the commercial pressures of both the newspaper and tourism industries – convince its readership to keep reading and keep traveling". Travel lists are signature examples of this symbiotic relationship, simultaneously cross-promoting, and delivering consumers to, travel publications, destinations and commercial tourism operations. Defining lists that contain paragraphs of editorial copy about specific destinations as travel journalism is in keeping with emerging conventions to the extent that the very process of selection and ranking by high-profile newspapers and magazines connotes expectations of "fact, accuracy, truthfulness and ethical conduct" associated with professional notions of journalism and expertise (Hanusch and Fürsich 2014, p. 7). Importantly, it enables me to consider counter-lists of places to see "before they disappear" or "before it's too late" – a category likely to refer to environmental problems (see Chapter 9).

Two kinds of bloggers contribute to our knowledge of tourism destinations: prosumers (Castells 1996), who create culture as they consume it, and produsers, who add to our knowledge but are not part of commercial enterprises (Raman and Choudary 2014, p. 120). Increasingly, state and national tourism offices engage citizen bloggers to create blogs about their destinations, blurring the boundary between the two categories. For example, in 2013 Tourism Australia conducted a "Best jobs in the world" campaign that attracted 330,000 applicants from 196 countries, from whom it funded eight to take six-month working holidays in Australia as tourism bloggers (Tourism Australia n.d.). I categorise the texts of bloggers employed by tourism offices as public relations rather than journalism. However, Bryan Pirolli (2014) observes that blogging independently can also lead to opportunities to blog for traditional travel media organisations. Although, as Pirolli's work demonstrates, there is much of interest in the contribution of independent bloggers, in this book I confine my understanding of travel journalism blogs to those by individuals whose names are clearly associated with a commercial media organisation.

Items listed in publications and on websites as travel news vary enormously. Most are consumer information about travel infrastructure, transport, new holiday deals, visas, or security and safety information related to military conflicts, crime, disease or natural disasters. In some print publications travel news will occasionally include more general information about the destination, while some online travel news sections will aggregate non-travel material as well as traditional travel journalism. These were not generally objects of analysis in my own research.

The output of copy-generating partnerships that are more opaque than travel journalism or advertising – by-lined supplements, brochures, web content and videos produced by media organisations with assistance from tourism businesses, government or quasi-public tourism offices or other non-media corporations – are sometimes difficult to categorise as either editorial or advertising, particularly if the nature of the assistance is not specified. Words such as "partnership" and "joined with" suggest a more prescriptive relationship than is implied by a traditional hosted visit, yet travel media organisations taking advantage of these arrangements may sometimes insist they retain editorial independence. Further complicating attempts to categorise such material is the fact that texts previously published as travel features may reappear in supplements sponsored by tourism offices. To accommodate these ambiguities, I try wherever possible to identify material published by travel media organisations as part of partnership or sponsorship arrangements. Distinguishing between travel features and sponsored or partnered texts in this way allows me greater scope to interrogate the exploitation of, and challenges to, journalistic values posed by the genre's close participation in the tourism industry.

State, provincial and national tourism offices have a long history of targeting food and wine journalists with hosted visits and/or information subsidies. Hunting, farming, fishing, viticulture, cooking and eating traditions and contemporary practices have considerable narrative appeal for journalists and have the added advantage for destinations of enabling industries such as agriculture to benefit from a healthy tourism sector. Travel journalism can accommodate countless special interests, which is one reason why I have chosen to categorise features according to their travel function rather than by their authors' description of their occupation.

Guidebooks are not travel journalism but there is overlap at the margins. For example, guide book company Lonely Planet produces a travel magazine. In addition, I regard its annual "Best in Travel" publication as a travel journalism list, particularly as a condensed version is reproduced in *Lonely Planet Traveller*. Travel narratives in book form are also a separate genre (Hanusch and Fürsich 2014), distinguished from travel journalism by their length, literary style and licence for occasional fabrication (Holland and Huggan 2000; Lisle 2006). However, just as travel journalists sometimes write advertising or marketing copy, authors of travel books sometimes also publish features in newspaper travel sections, travel magazines and even sponsored travel supplements. Moreover, at least one travel feature published in the magazine of an environmental organisation (Teasdale 2012) has had success in the environmental journalism category of the American Society of Travel Writers' Lowell Thomas Travel Journalism Awards. Whatever the term "genre" implies, attempts to define travel journalism are plagued by ambiguities and exceptions. Attending to this in the course of investigation and analysis reveals more than it obscures.

Structure of the book

The book is divided into three sections. Part 1 lays the theoretical foundations of cosmopolitanism, travel journalism and place-branding. In Part 2, I present the Tasmanian case study, directing thick description's cultural analysis towards the "political, economic and stratificatory realities" (Geertz 1973, p. 30) of travel journalism production in the field rather than the newsroom. In Part 3, I consider examples from Iceland, Canada and Australia in their broader media context.

Chapter outline

In Chapter 2 I distinguish the consumerist cosmopolitanism that finds expression in so much travel journalism from other forms of cosmopolitanism, before outlining theoretical debates about the possibility of an intertwining of cultural and political cosmopolitanism. I then attempt to understand travel journalism's failure, on the whole, to mediate distant cultures with cosmopolitan density, before arguing that such a failure does not preclude the mediation of distant environmental conflict and humanity's shared vulnerability to environmental risks.

Chapter 3 situates travel journalism within broad debates about journalism's role in the public sphere, and the challenges to this posed by public relations, place-branding and the increase in soft journalism. This leads to a description of public relations by government tourist offices and their associated programs for assisting travel journalists financially or in kind. Such practices, I argue, privilege government representations of places in travel journalism. The chapter describes how place-branding harnesses but also transcends traditional links between government tourist offices and travel media institutions. The relationship between place-branding and the environment is addressed in detail.

In Chapter 4 I set the scene for subsequent chapters by using a case study to describe the evolution of a place-branded environmental discourse. In Tasmania, a fierce political conflict in the late 1970s and early 1980s brought national and transnational publicity to its natural environment. This resulted in wilderness becoming the foundation of the island's branding when the initial dispute was resolved. In the years that followed, the state tourism office and a joint government and multi-industry Brand Tasmania Council projected an image of Tasmania as "natural" that functioned as both a public relations practice and a set of discursive strategies during subsequent environmental conflicts. A discourse of accessible nature emerged, in which brand-aligned environmental cosmopolitan concern was deployed in the interests of place-branding. In time, however, the environment movement was able to challenge this branding in the national and international media.

When place-branded messages are challenged by the environment movement, government tourism offices may try to regulate the flow of information to potential consumers. For example, they may intensify their control over the itineraries of hosted travel journalists, rely on branding to regulate staff, and exploit blurred boundaries between journalism and advertising in the production of marketing supplements. And as I demonstrate in Chapter 5, even when travel journalists do not accept free accommodation and transport, a combination of elite networks, place-branding and professional judgement can contribute to the exclusion from their texts of environmental communications that are not brand-aligned.

In Chapter 6 I consider travel journalism and environmental conflict from the perspective of publishers. The brands of travel publications can benefit from an association with the brands of tourism products that promote uncontroversial cosmopolitan concern. Yet despite the many advantages enjoyed by government and quasi-public tourism offices, travel publications do not always mediate those offices' branding messages uncritically. In the relationship between the media and antagonists in political conflicts, "[p]ower is a question of relative dependence: who needs whom more at the time of the transaction" (Wolfsfeld 1997, p. 14). A travel publication's brand may occasionally benefit from editorial content praising a destination's natural attractions but containing "constructive" criticism of its policies if, from a media-branding perspective, it is presented as being in the best interests of readers and – in the long run – the destination itself. This framing enables powerful travel media institutions that brand themselves as honest, environmentally responsible and/or discerning an opportunity to circulate politically charged meanings and symbols within a cosmopolitan discourse that is still compatible with their own participation in the tourism industry. Such interventions may be relatively rare, but the audiences they reach can be numerically large and affluent.

In certain circumstances, the environment movement or environmental activists, and sometimes also elite travel journalism sources with challenger sympathies, come together with travel journalists to promote cosmopolitan concern for a natural tourism attribute directly related to a political conflict. In Chapter 7 I draw attention to strategies and tactics of the environment movement, the scope and limits of journalistic agency, and the role of rationality and affect – particularly the strategic effectiveness of deploying celebrity and the voices of passionate locals.

The publication of travel journalism online is changing the world of imaginative travel. In Chapter 8 I consider the influence of digital searches on what travel journalism comes to public attention, and how this constrains or enables the circulation of environmental frames. Then, directing my attention to the hierarchies of travel lists, in Chapter 9 I ask whether the benefits these traditionally bestow on elites can be turned to the advantage of challenger claims-makers.

In my concluding chapter, I use the example of Iceland to draw together the many strands of my inquiry and suggest directions for future research.

References

Althing 2010, *The Promote Iceland Act 2010*, Íslandsstofa Promote Iceland, 29 April, viewed 26 January 2015, www.islandsstofa.is/en/about/the-promote-iceland-act/
Anderson, Alison 1997, *Media, Culture and Environment*, Routledge, London.
Anderson, Leon 2006, "Analytic autoethnography", *Journal of Contemporary Ethnography*, vol. 35, no. 4, pp. 373–395.
Anholt, Simon 2010, *Places: Identity, Image and Reputation*, Palgrave Macmillan, Basingstoke.
Anholt, Simon 2007, *Competitive Identity: The New Brand Management for Nations, Cities and Regions*, Palgrave Macmillan, Basingstoke.
Atkin, Michael 2014, report on Tourism Australia's pitch to international food and wine identities, *7.30*, ABC, 17 November, viewed 18 November 2014, http://iview.abc.net.au/programs/7-30/NC1405H187S00
Beck, Ulrich 2011, "Cosmopolitanism as imagined communities of global risk", *American Behavioral Scientist*, vol. 55, no. 10, pp. 1346–1361.
Beck, Ulrich 2006, *The Cosmopolitan Vision*, trans. Ciaran Cronin, Polity, Cambridge.
Canadian Tourism Commission (CTC) 2014, "News releases: Canadian Tourism Commission publishes 2013 Annual Report", Canadian Tourism Commission, 5 May, viewed 10 September 2014, http://en-corporate.canada.travel/content/news_release/2013-annual-report-helping-tourism-businesses-prosper
Carvalho, Anabela 2008, "Media(ted) discourses and society: Rethinking the framework of critical discourse analysis", *Journalism Studies*, vol. 9, no. 2, pp. 161–177.

Carvalho, Anabela 2005, "Representing the politics of the greenhouse effect: Discursive strategies in the British media", *Critical Discourse Studies*, vol. 2, no. 1, pp. 1–29.

CBC News 2013, "Travel Alberta fights US filmmakers over oilsands spoof", CBC News Edmonton, 27 August 2013, viewed 10 December 2014, www.cbc.ca/news/canada/ edmonton/travel-alberta-fights-u-s-filmmakers-over-oilsands-spoof-1.1379076

Cocking, Ben 2014, "'Out there': Travel journalism and the negotiation of cultural difference", in Folker Hanusch & Elfriede Fürsich (eds), *Travel Journalism: Exploring Production, Impact and Culture*, Palgrave Macmillan, Basingstoke, pp. 176–192.

Cocking, Ben 2009, "Travel journalism", *Journalism Studies*, vol. 10, no. 1, pp. 54–68.

Cottle, Simon 2007, "Ethnography and news production: New(s) developments in the field", *Sociology Compass*, vol. 1, no. 1, pp. 1–16.

Cox, Robert 2013, *Environmental Communication and the Public Sphere*, 3rd edn, Sage, Los Angeles.

Daye, Marcella 2005, "Mediating tourism: An analysis of the Caribbean holiday experience in the UK national press", in David Crouch, Rhona Jackson & Felix Thompson (eds), *The Media and the Tourism Imagination*, Routledge, London, pp. 14–26.

Deacon, David, Pickering, Michael, Golding, Peter, and Murdock, Graham 1999, *Researching communications: A practical guide to the methods in media and cultural analysis*, Hodder Arnold, New York.

Department of Premier and Cabinet, Tasmania 2006, *Tasmanian Brand Guide*, Government of Tasmania, Hobart.

Dore, Lynne and Crouch, Geoffrey I 2003, "Promoting destinations: An exploratory study of publicity programmes used by national tourism organisations", *Journal of Vacation Marketing*, vol. 9, no. 2, pp. 137–151.

Entman, Robert M 1993, "Framing: Toward clarification of a fractured paradigm", *Journal of Communication*, vol. 43, no. 4, pp. 51–58.

Flanagan, Richard 2004, "Tasmania", *New York Times*, 12 September, viewed 3 November 2014, http://travel.nytimes.com/2004/09/12/travel/sophisticated/12ST-TASMANIA. html

Fleming, Katherine 2007, "Gunning for Flanagan", *The Bulletin with Newsweek*, 27 November, p. 12.

Flyvbjerg, Bent 2001, *Making Social Science Matter: Why Social Inquiry Fails and How It Can Succeed Again*, trans. Steven Sampson, Cambridge University Press, Cambridge.

Fürsich, Elfriede 2003, "Between credibility and commodification: Nonfiction entertainment as a global media genre", *International Journal of Cultural Studies*, vol. 6, no. 2, pp. 131–153.

Fürsich, Elfriede 2002, "Packaging culture: The potential and limitations of travel programs on global television", *Communication Quarterly*, vol. 50, no. 2, pp. 204–226.

Fürsich, Elfriede & Kavoori, Anandam P. 2001, "Mapping a critical framework for the study of travel journalism", *International Journal of Cultural Studies*, vol. 4, no. 2, pp. 149–171.

Geertz, Clifford 1973, *The Interpretation of Cultures*, Basic Books Inc., New York.

GfK 2013, "Nation Brand Index: Latest findings: US voted top country for attracting talent and investment – but with a reducing lead", 14 November, viewed 6 January 2014, www.gfk.com/news-and-events/press-room/press-releases/pages/nation-brand-index-2013-latest-findings.aspx

Gill, AA 2014, "Table talk: AA Gill reviews Garagistes, Tasmania", *The Sunday Times*, 14 December, viewed 20 December 2014, www.thesundaytimes.co.uk/sto/Magazine/article1491624.ece

Gill, AA 2007, "The end of the world", *The Sunday Times*, 8 April, pp. 40–47.

Gill, AA 2005, *AA Gill is Away*, Simon & Schuster, New York.

Gillespie, Ian 1988, "The flip side of freebies: Travel writers may get a free ride – but it's often the reader who pays", *Ryerson Review of Journalism*, March, viewed 8 August 2012, www.rrj.ca/m3606/.

Glaetzer, Sally 2014, "Lonely Planet puts Tassie in international top 10 of must-see destinations", *The Mercury*, 21 October, viewed 11 April 2015, www.themercury.com.au/news/lonely-planet-puts-tassie-in-international-top-10-of-mustsee-destinations/story-fnj4f7kx-1227096680114

Government of Alberta 2014, *Building on Alberta's Strengths: Alberta's Economic Development Framework*, June, viewed 6 December 2014, http://eae.alberta.ca/media/416667/building%20on%20our%20strengths%20-%20web-final.pdf

Hajer, Maarten 1997, *The Politics of Environmental Discourse: Ecological Modernization and the Policy Process*, Clarendon Press, Oxford.

Hannerz, Ulf 2006, "Two Faces of Cosmopolitanism: Culture and Politics", Fundació CIDOB, Barcelona.

Hannerz, Ulf 2004, *Foreign News: Exploring the World of Foreign Correspondents*, University of Chicago Press, Chicago.

Hansen, Anders 2010, *Environment, Media and Communication*, Routledge, London.

Hanusch, Folker 2014, "Along similar lines: Does travel content follow foreign news flows?", in Folker Hanusch & Elfriede Fürsich (eds), *Travel Journalism: Exploring Production, Impact and Culture*, Palgrave Macmillan, Basingstoke, pp. 155–175.

Hanusch, Folker 2012a, "A profile of Australian travel journalists' views and ethical standards", *Journalism: Theory, Practice and Criticism*, vol. 13, no. 5, pp. 668–686.

Hanusch, Folker 2012b, "Travel journalists' attitudes toward public relations: Findings from a representative survey", *Public Relations Review: A Global Journal of Research and Comment*, vol. 38, no. 1, pp. 69–75.

Hanusch, Folker 2011, "Representations of foreign places outside the news: An analysis of Australian newspaper travel sections", *Media International Australia*, no. 138, February, pp. 21–35.

Hanusch, Folker 2010, "Dimensions of travel journalism: Exploring new fields for journalism research beyond news", *Journalism Studies*, vol. 11, no. 1, pp. 68–82.

Hanusch, Folker & Fürsich, Elfriede (eds) 2014, *Travel Journalism: Exploring Production, Impact and Culture*, Palgrave Macmillan, Basingstoke.

Hanusch, Folker & Hanitzsch, Thomas 2013, "Mediating orientation and self-expression in the world of consumption: Australian and German lifestyle journalists' professional views", *Media, Culture & Society*, vol. 35, no. 8, pp. 943–959.

Hartley, John 1996, *Popular Reality: Journalism, Modernity, Popular Culture*, Arnold, London.

Hill-James, Candeeda Rennie 2006, "Citizen tourist: Newspaper travel journalism's responsibility to its audience", unpublished master's thesis, Creative Industries Faculty, Queensland Institute of Technology, viewed 7 September 2012, http://eprints.qut.edu.au/16304/

Holland, Patrick & Huggan, Graham 2000, *Tourists with Typewriters: Critical Reflections on Contemporary Travel Writing*, University of Michigan Press, Ann Arbor.

Ironside, Robyn, "Tasmania receives unprecedented wave of international exposure courtesy of Lonely Planet, China and Tourism Australia", *The Mercury*, 21 October 2014, viewed 5 January 2015, www.themercury.com.au/news/tasmania/tasmania-receives-unprecedented-wave-of-international-exposure-courtesy-of-lonely-planet-china-and-tourism-australia/story-fnj4f7k1-1227096476946

Jenkins, Mark 2005, "Bush bashing", *Outside*, June, viewed 31 December 2011, www.outside online.com/adventure-travel/Bush-Bashing.html

Kovach, Bill & Rosenstiel, Tom 2001, *The Elements of Journalism*, Crown Publishers, New York.

Lagan, Bernard 2014, "Booker winner Richard Flanagan 'ashamed to be Australian'", *The Times*, 16 October, viewed 11 January 2015, www.thetimes.co.uk/tto/news/world/ australia-newzealand/article4237748.ece

Lester, Libby 2007, *Giving Ground: Media and Environmental Conflict in Tasmania*, Quintus, Hobart.

Lester, Libby & Hutchins, Brett 2009, "Power games: Environmental protest, news media and the internet", *Media, Culture & Society*, vol. 31, no. 4, pp. 579–595.

Lisle, Debbie 2006, *The Global Politics of Contemporary Travel Writing*, Cambridge University Press, Cambridge.

Lury, Celia 2004, *Brands: The Logos of the Global Economy*, Routledge, Abingdon.

Mackellar, Jo & Fenton, Jane 2000, "Hosting the international travel media – a review of the Australian Tourist Commission's visiting journalist programme", *Journal of Vacation Marketing*, vol. 6, no. 3, pp. 255–264.

McCracken, Grant 1988, *The Long Interview*, Sage, Newbury Park, CA.

McGaurr, Lyn, 2014, "Your threat or mine? Travel journalists and environmental problems", in Folker Hanusch & Elfriede Fürsich (eds), *Travel Journalism: Exploring Production, Impact and Culture*, Palgrave Macmillan, Basingstoke, pp. 231–248.

McGaurr, Lyn 2013, "Not so soft? Travel journalism, environmental protest, power and the internet", in Libby Lester & Brett Hutchins (eds), Peter Lang, New York, pp. 93–104.

McGaurr, Lyn 2012, "The devil may care: Travel journalism, cosmopolitan concern, politics and the brand", *Journalism Practice*, vol. 6, no 1, pp. 42–48.

McGaurr, Lyn 2010, "Travel journalism and environmental conflict: A cosmopolitan perspective", *Journalism Studies*, vol. 11, no. 1, pp. 50–67.

McGaurr, Lyn, Tranter, Bruce & Lester, Libby 2014, "Wilderness and the Politics of Place Branding", *Environmental Communication: A Journal of Nature and Culture*, doi: 10.1080/17524032.2014.919947.

McNair, Brian 2005, "What is journalism?", in Hugo de Burgh (ed.), *Making Journalists: Diverse Models, Global Issues*, Routledge, London, pp. 25–43.

Mercury, The 2014, "Uniting our island home", 16 October, p. 20.

Montgomery, Bruce 2012, "Pulped: Gunns' Tassie pulp mill is finally dead", *Crikey*, 28 September, viewed 20 April 2015, www.crikey.com.au/2012/09/28/pulped-gunns-tassie-mill-is-finally-dead/?wpmp_switcher=mobile

Moss, Chris 2008, "Travel journalism: The road to nowhere", *British Journalism Review*, vol. 19, no. 1, pp. 33–40.

Pearson, Stephanie 2014, "Surviving Tasmania", *Outside*, 20 January, viewed 29 August 2014, www.outsideonline.com/adventure-travel/australia-pacific/australia/The-Devil-Made-Me-Do-It-Travel-Tasmania.html

Pirolli, Bryan 2014, "Travel journalism in flux: New practices in the blogosphere", in Folker Hanusch & Elfriede Fürsich (eds), *Travel Journalism: Exploring Production, Impact and Culture*, Palgrave Macmillan, Basingstoke, pp. 83–98.

Raman, Usha & Choudary, Divya 2014, "Have travelled, will write: User-generated content and new travel journalism", in Folker Hanusch & Elfriede Fürsich (eds), *Travel Journalism: Exploring Production, Impact and Culture*, Palgrave Macmillan, Basingstoke, pp. 116–133.

Ryan, Chris & Zahra, Anne 2004, "The political challenge: The case of New Zealand's tourism organizations", in Nigel Morgan, Annette Pritchard & Roger Pride (eds),

Destination Branding: Creating the Unique Destination Proposition, 2nd edn, Elsevier Butterworth-Heinemann, Oxford, pp. 79–110

Santos, Carla Almeida 2004, "Framing Portugal: Representational dynamics", *Annals of Tourism Research*, vol. 31, no. 1, pp. 122–38.

Schlesinger, Philip 1990, "Rethinking the sociology of journalism: Source strategies and the limits of media centrism", in M Ferguson (ed.), *Public Communication: The New Imperatives*, Sage Publications, London, pp. 61–83.

Seaton, AV n.d., *The Occupational Influences and Ideologies of Travel Writers: Freebies? Puffs? Vade Mecums? Or Belles Lettres?*, Centre for Travel and Tourism in Association with Business Education Publishers, Newcastle upon Tyne.

Seligman, Mac 1990, "Travel writers' expenses: Who should pay?", *The Public Relations Journal*, vol 46, no. 5, pp. 27+.

Simon, Julie 1988, "How to handle travel and tourism freebies", *Public Relations Journal*, June, pp. 33–34.

Stamou, Anastasia G & Paraskevopoulos, Stephanos 2006, "Representing protected areas: A critical discourse analysis of tourism destination building in a Greek travel magazine", *International Journal of Tourism Research*, vol. 8, pp. 431–449.

Szerszynski, Bronislaw & Urry, John 2006, "Visuality, mobility and the cosmopolitan: inhabiting the world from afar", *The British Journal of Sociology*, vol. 57, no. 1, pp. 113–131.

Szerszynski, Bronislaw & Urry, John 2002, "Cultures of cosmopolitanism", *The Sociological Review*, vol. 50, no. 4, pp. 461–481.

Takach, Geo 2014, "Visualizing Alberta: Duelling documentaries and bituminous sands", in Robert Boschman & Mario Tronto (eds), *Found in Alberta: Environmental Themes for the Anthropocene*, Wilfrid Laurier University Press, Waterloo, pp. 85–103.

Teasdale, Aaron 2012, "Sound off: Will the symphony of the Great Bear Rainforest be silenced by tar sands oil tankers?", Sierra Magazine, May/June, viewed 7 August 2014, http://vault.sierraclub.org/sierra/201205/great-bear-rainforest-paddleboarding-155.aspx

Tourism Australia 2013, "Best jobs in the world", viewed 10 February 2014, http://bestjobs.australia.com/

Tourism Research Australia 2014, *Motivators and Satisfaction of Visitors to Tasmania: Executive Summary*, Tourism Research Australia, Sydney, viewed 12 April 2015, http://tra.gov.au/publications/publications-list-Tasmania_Motivators_and_satisfaction.html

Tourism Tasmania 2014a, *Tourism Talk Special Edition*, 21 September, email to subscribers.

Tourism Tasmania 2014b, "Lonely Planet names Tasmania one of the world's top 10 regions to visit in 2015", Tourism Tasmania Corporate, viewed 21 September 2014, www.tourismtasmania.com.au/industry/marketing/lonely-planet-2015

Tourism Tasmania 2014c, "Public relations guide for tourism operators: How to take advantage of Lonely Planet's announcement that Tasmania is one of the world's Top 10 Regions to visit in 2015", viewed 21 September 2014, "www.tourismtasmania.com.au/__data/assets/pdf_file/0017/25235/Public-Relations-Guide-LP.pdf

Tourism Tasmania 2014d, "Ripe for the picking: Tasmania is one of the world's top regions to visit in 2015 (according to Lonely Planet)", press release template, viewed 21 September 2014, via www.tourismtasmania.com.au/industry/marketing/lonely-planet-2015

Tourism Tasmania 2011, *Motivations Research: Appeal Triggers and Motivations for Tourism in Tasmania*, Tourism Tasmania, Hobart, viewed 12 April 2015, www.tourismtasmania.com.au/__data/assets/pdf_file/0004/17356/motivations.pdf

United Nations World Tourism Organization (UNWTO) 2014, *UNWTO World Tourism Highlights: 2014 Edition*, United Nations World Tourism Organization, viewed 24 October 2014, http://dtxtq4w60xqpw.cloudfront.net/sites/all/files/pdf/unwto_highlights 14_en.pdf

Wark, Kirsty, "Man Booker Prize winner Flanagan: 'This was the book I had to write'", BBC, 14 October, video excerpt from television program *Newsnight*, viewed 14 October 2014, www.bbc.com/news/entertainment-arts-29624284

Weir Alderson, Jeremy 1988, "Confessions of a travel writer", *Columbia Journalism Review*, vol. 27, no. 2, pp. 27–28.

Wolfsfeld, Gadi 1997, *Media and Political Conflict: News from the Middle East*, Cambridge UP, Cambridge.

Wood, Larry 1977, "Is Travel writing a growing profession", *Journalism Quarterly*, vol. 54, no. 4, pp. 761–764.

Zeiher, Chris 2014, "Tasmania, Australia", in *Lonely Planet's Best in Travel 2015: The Best Trends, Destinations, Journeys & Experiences for the Year Ahead*, Lonely Planet, Footscray, pp. 68–71.

PART I
Theoretical foundations

2 A cosmopolitan perspective

International relations scholar Peter van Ham (2002, 2008) alludes to a future in which countries become such successfully networked "brand states" that their physical territory becomes irrelevant. There are similarities here with Benedict Anderson (1991) – nations are always to some extent imagined communities – but in terms of its own subject van Ham's observation ignores the pivotal role played by tourism in place-branding, and tourism's reliance on identity and destinations with tangible territories (see Govers and Go 2009). Although Ulrich Beck acknowledges that we live in an age of what Zygmunt Bauman (2000) describes as "liquid modernity", he warns against stream, flow and network metaphors that fail to "thematize the degree to which...processes [of cosmopolitanisation and anti-cosmopolitanisation (see below)] are promoted or inhibited by the agency or impotence of particular groups of actors" (2006, p. 80). His argument is that although boundaries are blurring, social structures have not as yet been fully dissolved by flows, and so mobility should not entirely supersede structure and community as a focus of academic enquiry (2006, p. 80). In Beck's view there is not so much a privileged, mobile, cosmopolitan space of flows and a dominated non-cosmopolitan space of places but an interpenetration of the local, national and global (Holton 2009, p. 53).

Beck's (1992, 1995, 1998, 2006, 2009, 2011; Beck and Levy 2013) approach to cosmopolitanism and his theory of risk society are provocative for the prominence they afford the environment and the media. Many of the environmental risks that populate his books and articles – climate change and radiation, for example – are not limited in time or space, and can be global or catastrophic in their consequences. Risks of this kind are much more difficult to calculate and forecast than earlier risks of industrialisation, such as smog or localised water pollution, meaning that mediated perceptions are increasingly influential in public debate (Beck and Levy 2013, p. 3). The more frequently the media represent these risks in terms of interconnected endangered futures, the more likely it is that a cosmopolitan outlook will become vernacularised, perhaps creating the impetus and conditions for responsive affiliations to form across geographical, cultural and political boundaries (Beck and Levy 2013, pp. 3, 7). Ever present, however, is the potential for anxiety about international events to trigger a retreat into nationalism (Beck 2006). Thus cosmopolitanisation, as Beck envisages it, is a non-linear process whereby the mediated side-effects of global flows slowly coerce individuals into recognising their interdependencies and the need for a collective cosmopolitan response (Beck and Levy 2013).

Beck advocates methodological cosmopolitanism – an analytical approach that requires us to be mindful of the interpenetration of the local, regional, national, transnational and global. He considers transnational environmental communications from non-government organisations (NGOs) an important means by which boundary-crossing risks can be unveiled and refers to civil society movements as "the entrepreneurs of the cosmopolitan commonwealth" (Beck and Levy 2013, p. 15). Yet in Beck's (2011) unsentimental hypothesis, cosmopolitanisation does not necessarily begin with empathy or the desire to make the world a better place but with self-interested recognition of the need for collective responses. With co-author Daniel Levy, he argues that "sociability is not established under conditions of united interpretations but as a result of shared attentiveness to global risks" (Beck and Levy 2013, p. 23). This approach inverts the usual argument that political cosmopolitanism will emerge from the spread of morality-driven cosmopolitanism. Rather, imagined communities of global risks and associated interdependencies are credited with the capacity to promote a cosmopolitan "politicization and establishment of norms" (Beck 2011, p. 1353).

Beck contends that the media can shock people out of their complacency about the risky by-products of industrialisation. In his view, even conflicts over whether distant populations should have a say in the fate of a county's rainforests – which he considers to be global resources – "perform an integrating function in that they make clear that cosmopolitan solutions have to be found" (2006, pp. 23). As Alison Anderson observes, "Beck is right to recognise that perceptions of risk are selective and different environmental issues have varying degrees of cultural potency and mediagenic dying trees and seals, for example, allow us to glimpse the bigger picture" (2000, p. 96). Bronislaw Szerszynski and John Urry have found that multiple mobilities, including imaginative travel via the media, "may provide the context in which the notion of universal rights, relating not only to humans but also to animals and environments, comes to constitute a framing for collective action" (2006, p. 117). Szerszynski speculates that a moral environmental citizenship may be acquired, whereby "the local becomes experienced in a different way, one in which a certain abstraction informs the very perceptions of the particular – an abstraction that makes possible the critical judgment necessary to citizenship" (2006, pp. 86-87). Beck (2006), like Ulf Hannerz (2006) and Szerszynski and Urry (2002, 2006), theorises an intertwining of cultural and political cosmopolitanism. "Consumerist cosmopolitanism" (Calhoun 2002a, p. 889, see below) is a dimension of cultural cosmopolitanism exploited by place-branding and travel media because it is well suited both to places and to flows. Whether it can facilitate or accommodate political content in travel journalism will be explored in Part 2. Meanwhile, in this chapter I set the stage for such an investigation by introducing these three manifestations of cosmopolitanism – cultural, consumerist and political – and examining the role of journalism in Beck's cosmopolitan project. I then consider travel journalism's apparent failure to mediate cultural diversity with cosmopolitan density before arguing that this does not necessarily mean that it cannot play a role in unveiling environmental threats and mediating cosmopolitan concern in ways that can be meaningful for diverse publics.

The faces of cosmopolitanism

Hannerz's worried face of political cosmopolitanism and happy face of cultural cosmopolitanism (2006, see Chapter 1) are useful metaphors in the context of travel journalism studies. They capture something of the distinction Robertson (2010, p. 6) makes between transnational democratic projects and theories of citizenship that transcend the nation-state on the one hand, and the discourses and practices that celebrate and sustain diversity while building the solidarity that can help bring such projects into being on the other. In reality, however, such a range of positive and negative connotations are attached to the term cosmopolitan today (Holton 2009) that it is not always possible to categorise a particular form as exclusively cultural or political, just as it can be difficult sometimes to separate consumerist cosmopolitanism from the forces that might be harnessed to bring about a more just and humane world.

Cosmopolitan theories that acknowledge the strength of non-global commitments and loyalties have resurfaced relatively recently. As Bruce Robbins notes, during the latter decades of the 20th century cosmopolitanism was more often criticised as incompatible with nationalism for promoting a footloose detachment from the responsibilities of citizenship (1998, p. 1). Robert Holton, for example, describes "frequent travellers" (Calhoun 2002a) such as those concerned for the wellbeing of humanity and/or in favour of world citizenship as contributing to a normative intellectual cosmopolitanism that might still conceivably extend to "a disdain for the national, local and parochial, as a less desirable and exciting way of life, with narrow horizons and small-minded prejudices" (2009, p. 9). Yet as an Enlightenment ethic advocating "a universal humanism that transcends regional particularities" (Cheah 1998, p. 22), cosmopolitanism predated the nation-state, and at least as conceived of by Emanuel Kant, its aims of reforming absolutist state rule were similar to those of 19th century nationalist movements (Cheah 1998, pp. 24–25).

While contemporary cosmopolitanism is often differentiated from globalisation as encompassing features other than the economic, it has a long association with international commerce. According to Craig Calhoun, it was originally "a project of empires, of long-distance trade, and of cities" (2002a, p. 871-872). In the great trading hubs of the Ottoman empire it manifested itself as a tolerance of cultural diversity that helped facilitate the exchange of goods (Calhoun 2002a, p. 872). In Kant's writings, international commerce was considered an historical fact of cosmopolitanism and a force for harmony between states (Cheah 1998, p. 23): trade and a "universal culture comprising the fine arts and sciences" (Cheah 1998, p. 23), Kant believed, would contribute to a world in which individuals and states co-existed "in an external relationship of mutual influences" (Kant 1795 cited in Cheah 1998, p. 23).

With so many historical inter-relationships between cosmopolitanism and commerce, it is little wonder that the distinctions between cosmopolitanisation and globalisation are sometimes blurred. Hiro Saito argues that in sociology globalisation and cosmopolitanisation essentially refer to the same thing: "growing flows of economic, political, social, and cultural activities across national borders and corresponding transformations of institutions and practices inside nation-states" (2011, p. 126). Calhoun, however, accuses theorists writing in the 1990s of failing to disentangle cosmopolitanism from neo-liberal capitalism (2002a, p. 892). Implicit in his complaint is an acceptance he shares with Beck (2006) and Hannerz (2004b) that globalisation is generally understood as a top-down economic trend towards a free global market. Stephen Gill goes so far as to argue that globalisation has as its aim the establishment of a "market civilisation" which is associated with perspectives that are "ahistorical, economistic, materialistic, 'me-oriented', short-termist and ecologically myopic" and whose "coordination is achieved by a combination of market discipline and political power" (1995, p. 399). Cosmopolitanisation as described by Calhoun, Beck and Hannerz, by contrast, today refers to those processes that may lead to broader, sometimes bottom-up, cultural, social and political attitudes and responses to a world in which time and space are, to use David Harvey's (1989) term, "compressed".

Centuries before live international television broadcasts and household Internet access, advances in technology were already enabling information and debate to cross geographical, political and cultural boundaries. The printing press was central to the rise of a public sphere whose ideals reflected aspects of cosmopolitanism (Calhoun 2002a; Cheah 1998). In *The Structural Transformation of the Public Sphere* (1989), Habermas not only exhibits a "Kantian orientation" (Calhoun 1992, p. 1) but also "prefigures Anderson's concept of 'print capitalism'" (Calhoun 1992, p. 8) in the extent to which he acknowledges the importance of advances in printing to facilitating rational-critical debate beyond face-to-face contact and expanding markets beyond local communities (Calhoun 1992; Robbins 1998). Linking advances in communications technology with cosmopolitanism may initially seem at odds with Anderson's thesis in *Imagined Communities* (Anderson 1991) that the vernacular of early newspapers provided readers of the day with a sense of shared culture that fostered an enduring *nationalism*. Yet as Bruce Robbins points out, there seems little reason why media cannot just as effectively facilitate *transnational* bonds in the current age of digital capitalism (Robbins 1998, p. 7).

It is not only globalisation that is charged with being a top-down process. Accusations of elitism have been levelled at those who distinguish cosmopolitans from other social types largely on the basis of active cultural competence (see Szerszynski and Urry 2002, p. 469). This is because such cosmopolitans may appear self-indulgent if their attitude "does not involve using those cultural experiences from somewhere else to effect change, except at some private level" (Hannerz 1996, p. 61). Calhoun goes further, drawing a distinction between a cultural cosmopolitanism that might promote cosmopolitan citizenship through symbols and meanings (see Robertson 2010) and a cultural cosmopolitanism that is merely aesthetic and, as he describes it, "consumerist" (Calhoun 2002a, p. 889): "Food, tourism, music, literature, and clothes are all easy faces of cosmopolitanism. They are indeed broadening, literally after a fashion, but they are not hard tests for the relationship between local solidarity and international civil society" (Calhoun 2002a, p. 889).

Travel of itself does not guarantee that individuals will acquire cultural competence: it is all too easy to travel internationally and inhabit an environment of material and cultural sameness (Calhoun 2002a; Urry 2002; Woodward, Skrbis and Bean 2008). "Aided by the frequent-flyer lounges (and their extensions in 'international standard' hotels)," writes Calhoun, "contemporary cosmopolitans meet others of different backgrounds in spaces that retain familiarity" (2002a, p. 888). By Hannerz's measure, the "soft" cosmopolitans Calhoun criticises here are not cosmopolitans at all. But even if an individual travelling internationally "surrenders" to cultures as "package deals" rather than mastering only those aspects that suit his or her own perspective, "the surrender is of course only conditional… All the time he [or she] knows where the exit is" (Hannerz 1996, p. 104).

Groups like Ethical Traveler in the United States (established in 2002) and Tourism Concern in the United Kingdom (established in 1988) are playing a part in raising awareness of, respectively, political issues of concern in tourist destinations, and exploitative or destructive tourism practices. Nevertheless, scholars are sceptical of claims that tourists generally are prepared to take political action in respect of destinations they have visited (Bianchi 2006; Higgins-Desbiolles 2006, p. 1201; Urry 1995). Although the United Nations World Tourism Organization (UNWTO) pays tribute to the potential for tourism to have positive social and cultural effects, its focus is overwhelmingly on tourism's economic benefits to communities. To this end it promotes environmentally responsible and accessible tourism to drive social and economic progress, particularly in developing countries (UNWTO n.d.a, n.d.b). Between 2005 and 2013, the average annual growth in people travelling to emerging countries outstripped the growth in those travelling to advanced economies by 1.8 per cent (UNWTO 2014). In 2013 emerging economies had 46.6 per cent of the market, and this is forecast to reach 57 per cent in 2030 (UNWTO 2014). Today the citizens of non-western countries are also travelling internationally in increasing numbers: between 1990 and 2004, outbound tourism from Asia and the pacific increased by close to 150 per cent, and tourism from Africa almost doubled (UNWTO 2005). Between 2005 and 2013 the annual average increase from Asia and the Pacific was 6.3 per cent, and from Africa 7.1 per cent – much higher than the rate of growth in those travelling from Europe and the Americas (UNWTO 2014). At the macro level, the economic value of tourism to emerging economies is undeniable. With 1087 million international tourists in 2013 (UNWTO 2014), the scope for promoting cosmopolitan awareness through corporeal travel has never been greater. Even so, there is concern among some scholars that a pervasive preoccupation with tourism as industry distracts governments from giving due attention to its potential as a transformative social force (Higgins-Desbiolles 2006).

If cosmopolitanism is "a characteristic within and of individuals" (Szerszynski and Urry 2002, p. 468), many theorists would agree that cosmopolitans must demonstrate, at the very least:

> a cultural disposition involving an intellectual and aesthetic stance of "openness" towards peoples, places and experiences from different cultures, especially those from different "nations"...Cosmopolitanism involves the search for, and delight in, the contrasts between societies rather than a longing for superiority or for uniformity.
>
> (Szerszynski and Urry 2002, p. 468)

This egalitarian description comes at a cost, however, for it is notoriously difficult to identify empirically a single group that exhibits such a cosmopolitan predisposition (Woodward, Skrbis and Bean 2008, p. 223). Furthermore, it is far from evident that even the kind of cosmopolitanism described by either Szerszynski and Urry or Hannerz fosters enduring personal commitment to other cultures. Indeed, Manuel Castells uses the term "cosmopolitans" to label elites pursuing their own interests in the network society's space of flows (1996, p. 415). As noted in Chapter 1, however, there is an alternative view, or mechanism perhaps. Hannerz describes the lived experience of diversity arising from people's day-to-day encounters with migrants and refugees as a form of banal cosmopolitanism that may promote a sense of being "at home in the world" (2006, p. 14), while Szerszynski and Urry (2002, p. 477) refer to banal globalism – the public's everyday encounters with the world from afar via images and narratives of connectedness in the mass media. These authors speculate that when combined with an "ethics of care", banal globalism might contribute to the formation of a cosmopolitan civil society, helping to transform the public sphere into a "cosmopolitan public stage" for the "visual and narrative 'staging' of contemporary life" (2002, p. 478). Hannerz, for his part, holds out hope for a form of bottom-up cosmopolitics resulting from "having a similar range of experiences out there, of others and of oneself, personally or vicariously, as one has closer at hand, in a local community or in a nation" (2006, p. 26). In his view, cosmopolitans have an important role whether or not their pursuit of cultural diversity is self-indulgent, for they provide coherence to a world of distinct cultures, and their advocacy of cultural diversity contributes to its preservation (1996, p. 111). And while access to a more globalised culture can empower groups marginalised or otherwise disadvantaged by dominant traditions (Jeong and Santos 2004), the preservation of cultural diversity can help maintain "a reserve of improvements and alternatives to what is at any one time immediately available in one's own culture, and of solutions to its problems" (Hannerz 1996, p. 62).

Cosmopolitanism and the environment

In the social sciences, nature is typically viewed as mediated and constructed rather than separate from culture. Phil Macnaghten and John Urry explain that as "nature and culture dissolve into one another" the terminology changes and we begin to talk instead of the environment – "a particular way of representing space as sets of observable and measurable dimensions and forces" (Macnaghten and Urry, 1998, p. 30). Indeed some scholars speculate that "abstract and mediated kinds of knowledge and experience" (Heise 2008, p. 62) might even be capable of facilitating an eco-cosmopolitanism in which not only distant humans but also non-human groups are envisioned as part of imagined communities (Heise 2008, p.61).

In her work on travel journalism, Marcella Daye draws attention to links between culture and environment by citing Stephen Bourassa when she points out that landscape is "one form through which cultural groups seek to create and preserve their identities" (Bourassa 1991, in Daye 2005, p. 24). Since the 1800s, associations have been apparent between national identity and romanticised nature (Hansen 2010, p. 152), but there is also evidence that constructions and interpretations of nature are culturally specific (Hansen 2010, p. 153). Anders Hansen is sceptical of claims that there is "some universality of nature as a sign and metaphor", suspecting that any similarities are likely to have arisen from the homogenising effects of advertising (2010, p. 153). No matter how much nature is entangled with social practices and cultural representations, the commodification of landscape as spectacle inevitably sees it divorced to some extent from its social context (Macnaghten and Urry, 1998). This carries the risk that each place will become no more than "a particular combination of abstract characteristics, which mark it out as similar or different, as more or less scenic or characterful than other places", but it is also possible that the "aesthetic judgement" of landscape produced by mobility, including imaginative travel, will contribute to the acquisition of cosmopolitan dispositions (Szerszynski and Urry 2006, pp. 126–127).

The environment is intimately connected with tourism not only because tourist destinations are places but also because pleasure-seeking tourists pursuing "the natural" in a range of destinations acquire the cultural capital to distinguish aesthetically between the natural and the damaged. This may lead to nothing more than demands for satisfaction as consumers of nature but there are additional possibilities associated with thin and thick forms of cosmopolitanism. In the former, corporeal or imaginative travellers may acquire the ability to identify with others as members of a common humanity, whereas in the latter they may come to consider themselves global citizens capable of bringing about structural change. Andrew Dobson (2006) argues that a sense of causal responsibility for the effects of, for example, climate change might create the sense of nearness to physically distant others that compassion alone cannot achieve, thereby creating the conditions necessary for thick cosmopolitanism.

Holton identifies what might be described as an affective cosmopolitics already evident in modern environmentalism, "which has arisen as a response to environmental challenges that cannot be resolved on a national basis within single countries, and which draws emotional power from images of Planet Earth under imminent threat of ecological crisis" (2009, p. 5). Indeed, Macnaghten and Urry have found evidence of this among some of the groups they researched, as the media, new technologies and the activities of environmental groups made it possible for citizens to dwell in both local and faraway places. However, they have also identified a pervasive sense of powerlessness partly associated with a mistrust of government, corporations and environmental organisations. These authors speculate that this may initiate a form of cosmopolitanism from below "endlessly resistant, forever opposing states and corporations…a cosmopolitan civil society which frees itself from the overarching structures of the contemporary world, an immensely heterogeneous and cosmopolitan civil society which the globe needs instantaneously, in order possibly to survive in glacial time" (Macnaghten and Urry 1998, p. 276).

Of course, particular environmental problems and the individuals who suffer their consequences may be physically distant from the readers of travel journalism, but it is highly likely that wherever that journalism is consumed different cultures will be living side by side. The kind of cosmopolitics envisioned by Hannerz need not go so far as advocating the construction of a world society but does emphasise "that human beings are not only to be seen as a labor force or as consumers" (Hannerz 2004a, p. 21). Thus, in Hannerz's view, cosmopolitanism from below might turn out to be as much about learning that one can at least cope with multiculturalism as about "delighting" in that cultural diversity (Hannerz 2006). In Beck's view, if the incidental or forced "mixing" with other cultures that results from the cross-border flows of capital, labour and commodities associated with globalisation is "passively or unwillingly suffered" it is merely "*deformed*" cosmopolitanism (2006, p. 20, original emphasis). Non-deformed cosmopolitanism emerging out of the reflexive cosmopolitan outlook, by contrast, is chosen rather than suffered: "A non-deformed cosmopolitanism…results from a sense of partaking in the great human experiment in civilization – with one's own language and cultural symbols and the means to counter global threats – and hence of making a contribution to world culture" (Beck 2006, p. 21). Cosmopolitanism, thus conceived, is neither an alternative to nationalism nor a utopian vision but a pragmatic response (Smith 2008, p. 258). "In a world of global crises and dangers produced by civilization," Beck writes, "the old differentiations between internal and external, national and international, us and them, lose their validity and a new cosmopolitan realism becomes essential to survival" (2006, p. 14). This "world risk society" to which Beck (2009) refers is the result of "bad" connections in the form of threats generated by globalisation "that can make or break cosmopolitanism by testing the limit of openness to foreign others and cultures" generated by aesthetic and ethical cosmopolitanism (Saito 2011, p. 139). In view of this and the many references noted above to an environmental component of cosmopolitanism, it seems reasonable to follow the lead of Ian Woodward, Zlatko Skrbis and Clive Bean and include among dispositions considered to be cosmopolitan "feelings toward the link between globalization and…global environmental protection" (2008, p. 214).

Cosmopolitanism and journalism

Vital to the emergence of the cosmopolitan outlook, from Beck's perspective, are media that both represent and service the cultural needs of transnationals (Beck

2006): "the framework of the nation is not overcome. But the foundations of the industries and cultures of the mass media have changed dramatically and concomitantly all kinds of transnational connections and confrontations have emerged" (Beck 2006, pp. 6-7). Beck believes that, because transnationals are both native and non-native (Beck 2006, p. 65), media attention to their presence can help populations overcome "us and them" dichotomies (2006, p. 63) by conceptualising difference in terms of "both/and" rather than "either/or" (Beck 2006, p. 62) – both German and Jewish, for example. "What is new," he contends, "is not forced mixing but awareness of it, its self-conscious political affirmation, its reflection and recognition before a global public via the mass media" (Beck 2006, p. 21). Beck includes tourists in his definition of transnationals (2006, p. 90) and asks whether they and other transnationals such as migrants and members of nongovernment organisations are merely tolerated by local communities or may ultimately be encouraged to participate in local politics, thereby contributing to a culture of openness (2006, pp.90-91). Perhaps most provocative of all, from the perspective of tourism stakeholders, he asks whether there might actually be marketing advantages to localities in being seen as politically cosmopolitan because they cooperate with international NGOs and foster global connections (Beck 2006, p. 91).

In addition to servicing the cultural needs of transnationals and bringing attention to their presence, it is possible that some sectors of the media may themselves be considered transnational cultures. Hannerz includes journalism among the occupational cultures he describes as such, thereby attributing to some of its practitioners privileged access to the meanings of cultures other than their own and an associated role as cultural mediators (1996, pp. 108).

Here, then, is scope for something more than banal cosmopolitanism, whereby journalists make their contribution by mediating diverse cultures and global environmental threats with greater depth and competence than may be inherent in the more consumer-oriented global vernacular. In *Cosmopolitan Vision* (2006) Beck invests the media with a key role in facilitating social reflexivity by unveiling manufactured global hazards and risks (hazards and risks that are unintended by-products of industrialisation, such as anthropogenic climate change), explaining their causes and connecting dispersed publics affected by them. "The more ubiquitous the threat as represented in the mass media," he writes, "the greater the political power to explode borders generated by the perception of risk" (2006, p. 35).

There are, of course, counterarguments to Beck's faith in media coverage to contribute to cosmopolitanisation. A number of scholars have criticised Beck's media analysis as underdeveloped and lacking an awareness of media theory, cultural distinctions among news organisation occupying different media niches, cultural and political differences between countries, and the processes of news production (Anderson 2014; Cottle 1998). Beck has addressed the first of these criticisms to some extent in his collaboration with Levy, which introduces to his work concepts such as agenda-setting – the idea that media might not tell us what to think but can influence what we choose to think about or ignore. In this regard,

Beck focusses on the potential for people to become habituated to reports of disasters as global media events, where "the degree of habituation is not the result of shared interpretations of global risks but rather the shared exposure and consumption of media events themselves" (Beck and Levy 2013, p. 21).

There is also limited evidence of a connection between journalistic representations of political, social or environmental problems and public action (especially sustained action) related to those problems. Research (Livingstone and Markham 2008, p. 367) indicates that news consumption and news engagement, while positively influencing an individual's propensity to vote, make virtually no difference to the likelihood that he or she will take any other action on a matter of concern (cf. Cottle and Lester 2011). The globalisation of trade, communication and threats has seen political struggles shift from fixed regions to a world economy in territorial flux (Harvey 2009, p. 275). Compassion fatigue is an acknowledged risk of saturation coverage of human misery (Moeller 1999), while dramatic reports of conflict in distant lands or global environmental threats can provoke an anxious withdrawal into nationalism and isolationism (Beck 2006; Bourdieu 1998, p. 8; Hannerz 2004b, p. 29). Indeed two additional indicators of Beck's own dialectical cosmopolitanisation are recognition of "the cosmopolitan conflict character" and a "compulsion to redraw old boundaries" (2006, p. 7) – tendencies elsewhere described as "anti-cosmopolitanism" (Woodward, Skrbis and Bean 2008, p. 210).

Beck acknowledges that media representations of the side-effects of industrialisation and globalisation may result in a backlash against cosmopolitanism, but he also believes that representations demonstrating cosmopolitan values present opportunities for "cosmopolitan pioneers" to "exploit the growing perception of global risks in their efforts to promote more extensive…cooperation and integration" (Smith 2008, p. 257). In contrast to those who engage in lengthy debate about the mass media's capacity for cultural homogenisation, in *Cosmopolitan Vision* Beck draws attention to the media's pluralist potential. As such, he differs from those who see plurality resulting from postmodern attributes of the mass media (for example, Mowforth and Munt 1998, p. 27): for Beck, postmodern culture is only a shallow imitation of the cosmopolitan outlook because, as montage, it cannot adequately accommodate the historical depth and specificity of different cultures (2006, p. 29). Here he appears to be challenging journalists to do more than merely extend global connectedness through the "brands, icons and narratives" (Szerszynski and Urry 2006, p. 477) so characteristic of banal globalism. Hannerz seems to agree, noting that some foreign correspondents believe that more portrayals of everyday life in the communities to which they are assigned can help counter the possibility of an anti-cosmopolitan backlash to media representations of distant conflict, trauma and catastrophe (Hannerz 2004b, p. 29). In arguing in favour of foreign correspondents writing features to complement their news reports, he warns against trivialising other cultures (2004b, pp. 36–37). Although Hannerz is referring to foreign correspondents when he suggests they should be held to account for any "biases, gaps and misrepresentations" in their accounts of distant cultures, it seems reasonable to ask the converse – that is, why travel journalists should not be expected to report relevant political issues in tourist destinations fully and accurately. Whatever else might motivate travel journalists to take up this challenge, engagement with "place" is likely to be central.

Cosmopolitanism and travel journalists

Tourism public relations practitioners and travel journalists are cultural mediators who help shape the consumption patterns of tourists by positioning knowledge about, and experience of, distant places as a sign of social distinction (Ateljevic and Doorne 2002, p. 663; Hannerz 2004a, p. 74).

Cultural capital (Bourdieu 1984) is that form of power derived from one's habitus, whereby upbringing, education and professional experience imbue one with certain "predispositions, assumptions, judgements and behaviours" that, though not unchangeable, tend to shape the practices and experiences that follow throughout one's life (Benson and Neveu 2005, p. 3). Cultural capital is distinct from economic capital but valued within one's workplace and among one's colleagues. For international travel journalists, an aesthetic appreciation of distant cultures and the ability to be, or appear to be, "at home in the world" (Hannerz 2004b, 2006) might reasonably be considered a form of cultural capital bestowing status among peers and credibility with readers. It is surprising, therefore, that to date there is little scholarly evidence that travel journalism makes a significant contribution to cross-cultural understanding. In fact, in academia travel journalism is more likely to be accused of misrepresenting distant cultures. Such misrepresentations are often attributed to journalists' tendency to portray host cultures in terms of reader expectations rather than in their actual context. In a qualitative study of United States newspaper travel journalists' representations of Portugal, for example, Santos finds no reported communication with "ordinary" Portuguese (2004, p. 132) and concludes that the frames of the articles are "anchored in the socio-cultural paradigm of the writer and reader" (2004, p. 135). This romanticised view, she concludes, provides tourists with enchanting but irrelevant representations that simply bind host cultures to tourists' expectations (2004, p. 135). Ben Cocking (2009, 2014) finds that European travel journalism about the Middle East and British travel journalism about Africa perpetuate the outdated preconceptions of the writers' audiences about the host culture. And Richard Voase (2006) believes travel journalists' failure to interact with "ordinary locals" may be responsible for instances in which they overstate cultural interest as their search for novelty leads them to write articles conveying a misleadingly heightened sense of a destination's cultural diversity. In British travel articles about the Caribbean, Marcella Daye, by contrast, finds an apparent "inability to construct a discourse of difference" (2005, p. 23). Far from indicating cultural competence, this array of journalistic confusion may be an example of cultural incompetence (Voase 2006). Unsurprisingly, however, such a judgement does not accord with travel journalists' self-perceptions: a recent survey by Folker Hanusch found that

Australian travel journalists regard "the inclusion of locals in stories as much more important than ethnocentric approaches" (2012a, p. 675). In addition, despite travel journalists giving cultural mediation a low priority, Hanusch's survey results suggest that the more time they spend travelling, the greater the importance they are likely to attach to their role as cultural mediators. Nevertheless, Hanusch's related content analysis (2011) supports the conclusions of Santos and Cocking, finding few quotes from locals and little engagement with local culture.

For marketers, cosmopolitans who conform to Calhoun's description of "consumerist" do not *necessarily* have a desire to enter into other cultures to the extent of acquiring cultural competence; consumerist cosmopolitans are of interest to marketers as a distinctive demographic simply because they are likely to be more sophisticated, independent, objective and, therefore, demanding consumers (Cannon and Yaprak 2002). It is possible that, compared to foreign correspondents (Hannerz 2004b), travel journalists generally do not spend enough time in individual distant destinations to acquire a comprehensive understanding of local culture. This does not, however, preclude them from having cosmopolitical predispositions. Calhoun considers cosmopolitanism elitist and thin (2002a, p. 879), but even when it is exercised in association with the consumerist cosmopolitanism one would expect to find in much tourism and travel journalism, it may still be capable of producing unexpected outcomes at the intersection between places and flows. Moreover, Beck (2011) suggests that the addition of knowledge of global risks acquired via media reports may be the initiating force that finally leads to a thickening of cosmopolitics:

> The "bonds" that characterize cosmopolitan communities should not, therefore, be misunderstood as the fleeting lightness of fluid human interests, unable to bear any strain – "thin cosmopolitanism," so to speak. They are based, rather, on the combination of particular national and individual interests with the materiality of causal chains of effect. They establish a link between the most fundamental interests of nations (and individuals) and the new, unbounded spaces and duties of a responsibility for the survival of all. The community-initiating power of risk depends on realism and not simply on sympathy, regret, and pity for the suffering of others – that is what is meant by "thick cosmopolitanism."
>
> (Beck 2011, p. 1352)

The tourist gaze and staged authenticity

A distinction Urry (2002) makes between the romantic and collective tourist gazes might offer some insights into the dearth of travel journalism demonstrating cultural competence. Urry attributes any desire among tourists for authenticity in their tourism experiences primarily to those pursing the romantic tourist gaze (1995, p. 140). As the alternative to the collective tourist gaze, its emphasis is on "solitude, privacy and a personal, semi-spiritual relationship with the object of the gaze" (Urry 2002, p. 43). Urry links such a predilection for solitary consumption of tourism objects to Bourdieu's discussion of good taste (2002, pp. 43, 79–81). Consistent with a concept of aesthetic cosmopolitanism from above, Urry perceives those who value the romantic gaze to be middle-class proselytisers who undermine their own solitude as more and more tourists seek the experiences they praise so highly (2002, p. 44). Even when the romantic tourist gaze is that of a flâneur and the search for authenticity is taken as far as the "dark, seamy corners" of crowded cities (Urry 2002, p. 127), he considers the objective of the traveller to be observation not interaction (Urry 2002, p. 126).

In contrast with the romantic tourist gaze is MacCannell's concept of "staged authenticity" – a response to tourists' desire to find authenticity by going behind the scenes of tourism offerings (1999). These back regions of tourism attractions and destinations are, necessarily, contrived so as to protect the locals being observed from too much intrusion. As such, they may satisfy the tourist's yearning for an intimate experience of difference (1999) but do not necessarily engender cultural competence. This is because tourists, in MacCannell's view, are not so much *participants* in foreign cultures as people attracted by difference – *witnesses* of difference who must be protected from the consequences of their own misunderstandings (MacCannell 2011, p. 228). An additional explanation for the frequent failure of travel journalists to mediate distant cultures with cosmopolitan density, therefore, may be that however high their cultural capital – however much they may believe themselves to be culturally competent enough and sufficiently "at home in the world" (Hannerz, 2004b, 2006) to contribute reliably to a discourse of cultural diversity – they may rarely do more than witness cultural difference on behalf of their readers. Here MacCannell's (2011) idea of a reflexive "second gaze" offers an insight. The second gaze does not leave responsibility for its own construction to "the corporation, the state and the apparatus of tourism representations" (2011, p. 210). Rather, aware that something is being concealed, it "looks for the unexpected, not the extraordinary...to open a window in structure" (2011, p. 210). One such "gap in the cultural unconscious" enabling travel journalists to "glimpse the symbolic in action" (2011, p. 210) might be the unexpectedly familiar – evidence that those in distant lands are facing the same problems as the travel journalist's readers at home. Thus, while a "polygamy of place" (Beck 2006, p. 43) "intimately connected with consumption" (Beck 2006, p. 41) may lead to cosmopolitanism being worn as a badge of elite consumerism (via the consumption of foreign movies, food, travel etc.), it could conceivably also make travel journalism a forum for the mediation not only of concerns of global significance but also of more localised concerns in instances where distant audiences are grappling with similar issues. In such circumstances, either a common environmental threat or a common type of threat might create bonds between distant publics via the mediation of travel journalists even when their representations of foreign cultures lack cultural density. During times of environmental risk or conflict in tourist destinations, travel journalists with high cultural or symbolic capital might sometimes be prepared to look beyond the constructions of destinations projected by "the corporation, the state, and the apparatus of tourism represen-tation" (MacCannell 2011, p. 210) and self-reflexively enter the debate.

Associated theoretical interests

The public sphere

In view of the scope of my research outlined in Chapter 1, it will be helpful at this point briefly to introduce notions of the public sphere, publicity and the relation-ship between the media and sources that inform the following chapters. In the above sections, I refer to "publics", which Calhoun describes as "self-organizing fields of discourse in which participation is not based primarily on personal connections and is always in principle open to strangers" (2002b, p. 162). This raises the question of why I have chosen to research travel journalism in terms of cosmopolitan theory rather than public-sphere theory. My answer is that a discussion of the former in respect of journalism will necessarily encompass discussion of the latter. The public sphere, as conceived of by Jürgen Habermas in *The Structural Transformation of the Public Sphere* (1989), is a metaphorical space in which individuals come together as equals to engage in rational-critical debate about their common affairs. Although Habermas was at the time primarily concerned with national public spheres, considerable debate about the possibility and/or emergence of transnational public spheres has been conducted in the light of globalisation (see, for example, Calhoun 2002b; Fraser 2007; Köhler 1998). Many of these debates have been concerned with questions of governance and legitimacy, but Calhoun has also considered the associated need for social solidarity derived in part from "engagement in shared projects of imagining a better future" (2002b, p. 171). Within this, he has questioned Habermas's identification of voluntary public life entirely with rational-critical debate, arguing that the former is also "a process involving modes of cultural creativity and communication not the less valuable for being incompletely rational" (2002b, p. 155). To take this into account, a cosmopolitan public sphere would need to be "a global realm of cultural creativity as well as rational discourse, and a realm of mutual engagement" (Calhoun 2002b, p. 171).

As noted earlier, Beck (2011) argues that the mediation of global risks may be an impetus for the emergence of cosmopolitan imagined communities, here recasting Anderson's (1991) thesis that the printing press made it possible for citizens to imagine themselves as members of a community comprising other citizens they would never meet. In terms of what environmental and humanitarian interest groups might expect as members of such a community, Martin Köhler envisages a cosmopolitan public sphere within which those who are not the citizens of the society that is the object of concern can still exert influence:

> The specific novelty of the cosmopolitan public sphere is that it envisages the possibility for interest aggregation across different groups of people and

states. Directly, through financial support, or indirectly, as a result of easier international contacts, state actors may choose to side with civil society actors in other states to obtain changes in the policies in the latter. Likewise, civil society actors may choose to side with other states in order to obtain changes in their own state's policies.

(Köhler 1998, p. 233)

Today, many of these actors are non-government organisations, and Köhler is interested in formal mechanisms for including their views in global politics. However this neglects the intersections between activism and what Habermas (1989) describes as the refeudalization of the public sphere in response to the promotion of consumption associated with the rise of corporate capitalism, with its emphasis on public displays of status and tendency towards "affirmative rather than critical discourse" (Knight 2010, p. 176).

Graham Knight argues that refeudalization began as groups excluded from the Bourgeois public sphere such as women and the working class started to gain access: "The public sphere was not only transformed into an arena of economic or corporate promotionalism, it was also opened up to new political issues, problems, and perspectives in the form of collective action" (2010, pp. 176-7). Habermas never fully resolves the tension between his democratic aims and his concern about the public sphere's expansion into the realm of popular culture. As Libby Lester cautions:

> Today's public sphere may not be the space where a rational public achieves consensus only through deliberative discussion but rather a space where public involvement is achieved via a yet largely undescribed combination of communicative acts, including deliberative discussion, but also spectacle, entertainment, symbols, affect, image. Nevertheless, Habermas's concerns about refeudalisation and staged publicness cannot be rejected just yet. We must look across history before we can understand how voices, particularly those of alternatives and the non-elite, can achieve sustained involvement in public debate.
>
> (Lester 2007, p. 24)

In his theorisation of rational-critical debate devoid of domination and leading to consensus, Habermas's metaphorical public sphere is utopian not only because it cannot easily accommodate spectacle but also, in Bent Flyvbjerg's (2001) view, because it leaves little space for "forms of public life that are practical, committed, and ready for conflict" (Flyvbjerg 2001, p. 109).

Source–media relations

As public debate has become competitive rather than cooperative, Habermas's distinction between communicative and strategic action has broken down (Knight 2010, p. 180). Through textual analysis Fairclough (2003) shows how texts that appear to be communicative action providing knowledge can actually be strategic action aimed at achieving specific results by way, for example, of covert evaluation. Fairclough offers promotion as a concrete example of the way in which what appears to be communicative action can in fact be strategic. Again using textual analysis, he demonstrates Wernick's understanding of contemporary "promotional culture" (Wernick 1991 in Fairclough 2003) by showing how traditional sources of information from what Hall et al. (1978) would describe as accredited sources (university publications, company annual reports etc.) often simultaneously promote by representing, advocating and anticipating the desired outcome in what appear to be factual statements. As Fairclough observes of this blurring of fact and prediction, "We can connect this to what Bourdieu and Wacquant (2001) have identified as one significant feature of the texts of capitalism: their 'performative power' in bringing into being what they purport to (merely) describe" (2003, p. 113).

Knight identifies branding as strategic promotional action. In the promotional public sphere, branding functions as a short-hand, affective way to "re-anchor identity and manage uncertainty while pursuing comparative advantage and competitive success", and also provides "a way to associate with an imagined community of like-minded people" (Knight 2010, p. 182). When activists target a brand, they challenge the validity of corporate promotional strategies, exposing hypocrisy as well as the damaging practices at issue, although increasingly they find themselves forced to adopt branding strategies themselves in the contest for the identity-dependent, belief-driven credibility so often necessary to achieve media access (Knight 2010). Many political cosmopolitans and Habermas share a faith in the ability of the right sort of democratic procedures, constitutions and institutions to ensure freedom. Foucault, by contrast, believes no institutional arrangements can guarantee freedom and it is, therefore, imperative to continually challenge those that exist (Flyvbjerg 2001). For Foucault, "[r]estistance, struggle, and conflict, in contrast to consensus, are…the most solid bases for the practice of freedom" (Flyvbjerg 2001, p. 102).

In order to be a useful theoretical tool for research about struggles for publicity in times of environmental conflict, the public sphere as it is understood in this book must allow for strategic action and the possibility that consensus may not be its only objective or outcome. For example, Knight's argument in regard to the promotional public sphere (see above) is aligned in part with empirical studies of journalists and sources confirming that governments and corporations enjoy a considerable but not unassailable advantage in the public sphere. In the 1970s, powerful, often institutionalised groups were identified as having a primary role in the definition of issues and representations of social problems in the media, and alternative voices were considered largely ineffective in any attempt they might make to influence debate in a meaningful and lasting way (Hall et al 1978; Molotch and Lester 1974). Hall et al. argued that the media were usually not primary definers of social problems but rather transmitted the definitions of the powerful as a result of their quest for "objective", "authoritative" information from "accredited" sources, thereby assuming the role of secondary definers.

Although the requirement for journalistic balance often ensured that alternative views were heard, Hall et al. concluded that, having already determined the nature of the issue, primary definers were largely free to set the terms of debate (Hall et al. 1978, p. 58). Empirical studies conducted around the same time by pluralists confirmed that elite sources did indeed enjoy considerable advantage over non-elite sources but argued that accounts of dominance failed to pay due attention to source negotiations and conflict prior to media access (Schlesinger 1990). Over time researchers increasingly discussed the interaction of powerful sources with the media as strategic political action (Ericson, Baranek and Chan 1989; Schlesinger 1990; Miller 1994), in some cases finding circumstances in which non-institutional sources could successfully challenge the definitional advantages of elite sources (Anderson 1997; Davis 2002; Lester 2007; Miller 2004; Wolfsfeld 1997). Of particular interest in terms of this book is Gadi Wolfsfeld's (1997) political contest model, which has also been influential in Lester's (2007) study of the media and environmental conflict in Tasmania. Wolfsfeld describes source battles for media access and meaning in news journalism as parts of larger political struggles in which the media fall into categories on a continuum of influence, from those who align themselves closely with the most powerful antagonists in the conflict, to those who champion their opponents (Wolfsfeld, 1997, p. 69). Wolfsfeld describes the more powerful antagonist in a political conflict as the authority and the weaker antagonist as the challenger – terminology I adopt in this book. In the political contest model, antagonists compete for media attention on the basis of their status; control over resources and the flow of information (including the provision of information subsidies); ability to stage events or produce exceptional behaviour; and control over the political environment. Wolfsfeld's research and the other more recent empirical studies noted above demonstrate a comprehensive and nuanced appreciation of the role of source–media relations in the production of news but have largely neglected issues that arise in soft journalism, where the dominance of elite sources as a result of advertising and "pressures to increase audiences through the creation of populist and apolitical 'newszak'" (Davis 2002, p. 7; see also comments on the refeudalization of the public sphere above) seems to be taken for granted. This is surprising, because empirical research has already shown how hallmarks of popular culture such as spectacle and celebrity have been harnessed by non-elite sources to attract news media attention and have also produced media scepticism (Hutchins and Lester 2006; Lester 2006, 2007; Lester and Hutchins 2009). The question of whether source strategies might contribute to what, after all, may sometimes be only ostensibly apolitical outcomes in soft journalism is, to my knowledge, rarely asked, much less answered, and examples of the mediation of political conflict in such genres go largely unremarked and unexplained. Addressing these silences in scholarly journalism research requires empirical work that attends just as closely as empirical studies of more-serious journalism to the actions of conscious agents and the role of "invisible" public relations (see Davis 2002, p. 13).

The network society

One thing that has surprised me in my research is how many articles about Tasmania in publications with very high circulations – some from as long ago as 2000 – are still available online. These are feature-length articles about a small island of just 500,000 people 17,000 kilometres from the two markets in which the articles are published. In view of the opportunities information technology offers to those wishing to exploit the informational capital (Arvidsson 2006) brands deliver as new media objects (Lury 2004) and explore the marketing possibilities offered by virtual reality, it is perhaps not surprising that the network society theories of Manuel Castells (1996) have received attention from scholars of place-branding concerned with where place identity may be located in an increasingly globalised and virtual world (Govers and Go 2009).

According to Castells, in the network society culture and power are, in significant ways, becoming detached from geographical space via the operation of the networked technologies that today underpin the globalised space of flows. The space of flows is defined as "the material organization of time-sharing social practices that work through flows" (1996, p. 412), wherein "domination is not purely structural [but] is enacted...by social actors" (1996, p. 415). The space of places, by contrast, is where most people live: "A place is a locale whose form, function and meaning are self-contained within the boundaries of physical contiguity" (Castells 1996, p. 423). Govers and Go (2009) believe that in the network society the images that place-branding actors project are in greater danger than they once were of becoming victims of power struggles, but their interest is primarily in what this means for tourism rather than for the public sphere. Whereas Govers and Go argue that "there is a desire within the cultural community and public sector to project imagery that represents an authentic identity of place, whereas commercial actors are keen to stage authenticity" (2009, p. 9), I am interested in pressures on the public sector as part of government to construct an identity purged of environmental conflict. The "structural logic" of the network society is towards decentred networks largely unfettered by national boundaries (Hutchins 2004), but destinations (Govers and Go 2009) and location-based environmental organisations (Hutchins and Lester 2006) seek, respectively and in varying degrees, to commodify or protect place by engaging with global flows. In considering regional media as a site that not only resists the domination of these flows but also reaffirms local identity, Brett Hutchins has noted that the "interface between the space of flows and the space of places is not about consistency; it is about unpredictable outcomes, decentred power relations and culture in the act of becoming" (2004, p. 588). Thus, in this book I am alert to the fact that travel journalism, like local/regional news, operates at the interface of places and flows, speaking of distant places to its own local, regional, national or transnational audiences, and that this might produce unpredictable outcomes. Nevertheless, I am mindful of Anderson's assessment that neither network theory nor Beck's theory of risk society take sufficient account of "back-stage, less visible aspects of power" (2014, p. 36) – a deficiency my ethnographic approach goes some way to addressing.

Conclusion

By considering consumerist cosmopolitanism as a distinct form of cultural cosmopolitanism this chapter has presented a view of travel journalists and travel journalism that can be positioned within Beck's explanation of cosmopolitanisation. If travel journalists spend only small amounts of time in most of the destinations they cover, their lived experience of those distant cultures may be closer to what Hannerz (2006) describes as banal cosmopolitanism than cultural competence, and their texts – at the very least those in newspapers or freely available on the internet – may contribute to a banal globalism that equips their readers with the kind of abstraction that Szerszynski (2006) believes can give rise to "the possibility of an enlarged form of citizenship" (2006, p. 86). However, by reflexively mediating environmental risks for their own national, regional or local audiences of wholly or partly consumerist cosmopolitans, cosmopolitical travel journalists' more telling contribution may be to a process of cosmopolitanisation whereby it becomes increasingly apparent to publics that, regardless of whether they wish to engage deeply with distant cultures, "the global other is in our midst. Everybody is connected and confronted with everybody – even if global risks afflict different countries, states and cultures differently" (Beck 2011, p. 1348). In this scenario, the willingness and/or ability of travel journalists to include cosmopolitical discourses and frames in their texts will depend on their level of cultural or symbolic capital, their personal political beliefs and the decisions of sub-editors and publishers. Importantly, however, the strategic actions of elite and non-elite sources – including place branding and responses to place branding – are also likely to be influential.

Beck's argument in favour of the concept of imagined communities of global risks reveals the "dependency (power) and interdependency (mutual dependency)" of risk communities by covering crises in real time for multiple publics (2011, p. 1351). In my view, the "community-shaping power of global risks" (Beck 2011, p. 1352) is, nevertheless, inherent in travel journalism that exposes what Beck describes as "distant decisions" that may cause "collateral damage" (Beck 2011, p. 1352) by – again, in my view – contributing to a worldwide accumulation of environmental degradation via specific instances of, for example, deforestation or species extinction. Such travel journalism may help initiate a "thickening" of political cosmopolitanism in a similar manner to news reports of global risks.

References

Anderson, Alison 2014, *Media, Environment and the Network Society*, Palgrave Macmillan, London.
Anderson, Alison 1997, *Media, Culture and Environment*, Routledge, London.
Anderson, Benedict 1991, *Imagined Communities*, Verso, London.
Arvidsson, Adam 2006, *Brands: Meaning and Value in Media Culture*, Routledge, Abingdon.
Ateljevic, Irena & Doorne, Stephen 2002, "Representing New Zealand: Tourism imagery and ideology", *Annals of Tourism Research*, vol. 29, no. 3, pp. 648–667.
Bauman, Zygmunt 2000, *Liquid Modernity*, Polity Press, Cambridge.

Beck, Ulrich 2011, "Cosmopolitanism as imagined communities of global risk", *American Behavioral Scientist*, vol. 55, no. 10, pp. 1346–1361.

Beck, Ulrich 2009, *World at Risk*, trans. Ciaran Cronin, Polity, Cambridge.

Beck, Ulrich 2006, *The Cosmopolitan Vision*, trans. Ciaran Cronin, Polity, Cambridge.

Beck, Ulrich 1998, "Politics of Risk Society", in Jane Franklin (ed.), *The Politics of Risk Society*, Polity, Cambridge.

Beck, Ulrich 1995, *Ecological Politics in an Age of Risk*, Trans. A. Weisz, Polity, Cambridge.

Beck, Ulrich 1992, *Risk Society: Towards a New Modernity*, trans. M Ritter, Sage Publications, London.

Beck, Ulrich & Levy, David 2013, "Cosmopolitanized nations: Re-imagining collectivity in world risk society", *Theory, Culture & Society*, vol. 30, no. 2, pp. 3–31.

Benson, Rodney & Neveu, Erik 2005, "Introduction: Field theory as a work in progress", in Rodney Benson & Erik Neveu (eds), *Bourdieu and the Journalistic Field*, Polity, Cambridge, pp.1–25.

Bianchi, Raoul 2006, "Tourism and the globalisation of fear: Analysing the politics of risk and (in)security in global travel", *Tourism and Hospitality Research*, vol. 7, no. 1, pp. 64–74.

Bourdieu, Pierre 1984, *Distinction*, Routledge and Kegan Paul, London.

Bourdieu, Pierre 1998, *On Television and Journalism*, Pluto, London.

Cannon, Hugh M & Yaprak, Attila 2002, "Will the real-world citizen please stand up! The many faces of cosmopolitan consumer behavior", *Journal of International Marketing*, vol. 10, no. 4, pp. 30–52.

Calhoun, Craig 2002a, "The class consciousness of frequent travelers: Toward a critique of actually existing cosmopolitanism", *The South Atlantic Quarterly*, vol. 101, no. 4, pp. 869–897.

Calhoun, Craig 2002b, "Imagining solidarity: Cosmopolitanism, constitutional patriotism, and the public sphere", *Public Culture*, vol. 14, no. 1, pp. 147–171.

Calhoun, Craig 1992, "Introduction: Habermas and the public sphere", in Craig Calhoun (ed.), *Habermas and the Public Sphere*, MIT, Cambridge, pp. 1–48.

Castells, Manuel 1996, *The Rise of the Network Society*, Blackwell, Massachusetts.

Cheah, Pheng 1998, "Introduction Part II: The cosmopolitical – today", in Pheng Cheah & Bruce Robbins (eds), *Cosmopolitics: Thinking and Feeling Beyond the Nation*, University of Minnesota Press, Minneapolis, pp. 20–41.

Cocking, Ben 2014, "'Out there': Travel journalism and the negotiation of cultural difference", in Folker Hanusch & Elfriede Fürsich (eds), *Travel Journalism: Exploring Production, Impact and Culture*, Palgrave Macmillan, Basingstoke, pp. 176–192.

Cocking, Ben 2009, "Travel journalism", *Journalism Studies*, vol. 10, no. 1, pp. 54–68.

Cottle, Simon 1998, "Ulrich Beck, 'Risk Society' and the Media: A Catastrophic View?" *European Journal of Communication* vol. 13, no. 1, pp. 5–32.

Cottle, Simon & Lester, Libby (eds) 2011, *Transnational Protest and the Media*, Peter Lang, New York.

Daye, Marcella 2005, "Mediating tourism: An analysis of the Caribbean holiday experience in the UK national press", in David Crouch, Rhona Jackson & Felix Thompson (eds), *The Media and the Tourism Imagination*, Routledge, London, pp. 14–26.

Davis, Aeron 2002, *Public Relations Democracy: Public Relations, Politics and the Mass Media in Britain*, Manchester University Press, New York.

Dobson, Andrew 2006, "Thick cosmopolitanism", *Political Studies*, vol. 54, pp. 165–184.

Ericson, Richard V, Baranek, Patricia M & Chan, Janet BL 1989, *Negotiating Control: A Study of News Sources*, Open University, Milton Keyes.

Fairclough, Norman 2003, *Analysing Discourse: Textual Analysis for Social Research*, Routledge, London.

Flyvbjerg, Bent 2001, *Making Social Science Matter: Why Social Inquiry Fails and How It Can Succeed Again*, trans. Steven Sampson, Cambridge University Press, Cambridge.
Fraser, Nancy 2007, "Transnationalizing the public sphere: On the legitimacy and efficacy of public opinion in a post-Westphalian world", *Theory Culture Society*, vol. 24, no. 4, pp. 7–30.
Gill, Stephen 1995, Globalisation, market civilisation, and disciplinary neoliberalism", *Millennium: Journal of International Studies*, vol. 24, no. 3, pp. 399–423.
Govers, Robert & Go, Frank 2009, *Place Branding: Glocal, Virtual and Physical Identities, Constructed, Imagined and Experienced*, Palgrave Macmillan, Basingstoke.
Habermas, Jürgen 1989, *The Structural Transformation of the Public Sphere: An Inquiry into a Category of Bourgeois Society*, trans. Thomas Burger and Frederick Lawrence, Polity, Cambridge.
Hall, Stuart, Critcher, Chas, Jefferson, Tony, Clarke, John & Roberts, Brian 1978, *Policing the Crisis: Mugging, the State, and Law and Order*, Holmes and Meier, New York.
Hannerz, Ulf 2006, *Two Faces of Cosmopolitanism: Culture and Politics*, Fundació CIDOB, Barcelona.
Hannerz, Ulf 2004a, "Cosmopolitanism", in David Nugent & Joan Vincent (eds), *A Companion to the Anthropology of Politics*, Blackwell, Oxford, pp. 69–85.
Hannerz, Ulf 2004b, *Foreign News: Exploring the World of Foreign Correspondents*, University of Chicago Press, Chicago.
Hannerz, Ulf 1996, *Transnational Connections: Culture, People, Places*, Routledge, London.
Hansen, Anders 2010, *Environment, Media and Communication*, Routledge, London.
Harvey, David 1989, The *Condition of Postmodernity: An Enquiry into the Origins of Cultural Change*, Blackwell, Oxford.
Heise, Ursula 2008, *Sense of Place and Sense of Planet*, Oxford University Press, Oxford.
Higgins-Desbiolles, Freya 2006, "More than an 'industry': The forgotten power of tourism as a social force", *Tourism Management*, vol. 27, pp. 1192–1208.
Holton, Robert J 2009, *Cosmopolitanisms: New Thinking and New Directions*, Palgrave Macmillan, Basingstoke.
Hutchins, Brett 2004, "Castells, regional news media and the information age", *Continuum*, vol. 18, no. 4, pp. 577–590.
Hutchins, Brett & Lester, Libby 2006, "Environmental protest and tap-dancing with the media in the information age", *Media, Culture & Society*, vol. 28, no. 3, pp. 433–51.
Jeong, Sunny & Santos, Carla Almeida 2004, "Cultural politics and contested place identity", *Annals of Tourism Research: A Social Sciences Journal*, vol. 31, no. 3, pp. 640–656.
Knight, Graham 2010, "Activism, branding, and the promotional public sphere", in Melissa Aronczyk & Devon Powers (eds), *Blowing Up the Brand: Critical Perspectives on Promotional Culture*, Peter Lang, London, pp. 173–193.
Köhler, Martin 1998, "From the national to the cosmopolitan public sphere", in Daniele Archibugi, David Held & Martin Köhler (eds), *Reimagining Political Community: Studies in Cosmopolitan Democracy*, Stanford University Press, Stanford.
Lester, Libby 2007, *Giving Ground: Media and Environmental Conflict in Tasmania*, Quintus, Hobart.
Lester, Libby 2006, "Lost in the wilderness? Celebrity, protest and the news", *Journalism Studies*, vol. 7, no. 6, pp. 907–921.
Lester, Libby & Hutchins, Brett 2009, "Power games: Environmental protest, news media and the internet", *Media, Culture & Society*, vol. 31, no. 4, pp. 579–595.
Livingstone, Sonia & Markham, Tim 2008, "The contribution of media consumption to civic participation", *British Journal of Sociology*, vol. 59, pp. 351–371.

Lury, Celia 2004, *Brands: The Logos of the Global Economy*, Routledge, Abingdon

MacCannell, Dean 2011, *The Ethics of Sightseeing*, University of California Press, Berkeley.

MacCannell, Dean 1999, *The Tourist: A New Theory of the Leisure Class*, University of California Press, Berkeley.

Macnaghten, Phil & Urry, John 1998, *Contested Natures*, Sage Publications, London.

Miller, David 1994, *Don't Mention the War: Northern Ireland, Propaganda and the Media*, Pluto Press, London.

Moeller, Susan D 1999, *Compassion Fatigue: How the Media Sell Disease, Famine, War and Death*, Routledge, New York.

Molotch, Harvey & Lester, Marilyn 1974, "News as purposive behavior: On the strategic use of routine events, accidents and scandals", *American Sociological Review*, vol. 39, no. 1, pp. 101–12.

Mowforth, Martin & Munt, Ian 1998, *Tourism and Sustainability: Development and New Tourism in the Third World*, 2nd edn, Routledge, London.

Robertson, Alexa 2010, *Mediated Cosmopolitanism: The World of Television News*, Polity, Cambridge.

Saito, Hiro 2011, "An actor-network theory of cosmopolitanism", *Sociological Theory*, vol. 29, no. 2, pp. 124–149.

Santos, Carla Almeida 2004, "Framing Portugal: Representational dynamics", *Annals of Tourism Research*, vol. 31, no. 1, pp. 122–38.

Schlesinger, Philip 1990, "Rethinking the sociology of journalism: Source strategies and the limits of media centrism", in M Ferguson (ed.), *Public Communication: The New Imperatives*, Sage Publications, London, pp. 61–83.

Smith, William 2008, "A cosmopolitan sociology: Ulrich Beck's trilogy on the global age", *Global Networks*, vol. 8, no. 2, pp. 253–259.

Szerszynski, Bronislaw 2006, "Local landscapes and global belonging: Toward a situated citizenship of the environment", in Andrew Dobson & Derek Bell (eds), *Environmental Citizenship*, Massachusetts Institute of Technology, Cambridge, MA, pp. 75–100.

Szerszynski, Bronislaw & Urry, John 2006, "Visuality, mobility and the cosmopolitan: Inhabiting the world from afar", *The British Journal of Sociology*, vol. 57, no. 1, pp. 113–131.

Szerszynski, Bronislaw & Urry, John 2002, "Cultures of cosmopolitanism", *The Sociological Review*, vol. 50, no. 4, pp. 461–481.

United Nations World Tourism Organization (UNWTO) 2014, *UNWTO Tourism Highlights: 2014 Edition*, viewed 24 October 2014, http://dtxtq4w60xqpw.cloudfront.net/sites/all/files/pdf/unwto_highlights14_en.pdf

United Nations World Tourism Organization (UNWTO) 2005, "Outbound tourism by generating region", "Facts and figures", World Tourism Organization UNWTO, World Tourism Organization, 5 December, viewed 1 July 2011, http://unwto.org/facts/menu.html.

United Nations World Tourism Organization (UNWTO) n.d. "About UNWTO", UNWTO, viewed 16 March 2015, www.unwto.org/aboutwto/index.php.

United Nations World Tourism Organization (UNWTO) n.d. "Why tourism", UNWTO, viewed 16 March 2015, www.unwto.org/aboutwto/why/en/why.php?op=1.

Urry, John 2002, *The Tourist Gaze*, 2nd edn, Sage Publications, London.

Van Ham, Peter 2002, "Branding territory: Inside the wonderful worlds of PR and IR theory", *Millennium – Journal of International Studies* vol. 31. no. 2, pp. 249–269.

Van Ham, Peter 2008, "Place branding: The state of the art", *The Annals of the American Academy of Political and Social Science*, no. 616, pp. 126–149

Voase, Richard 2006, "Creating the tourist destination: Narrating the 'undiscovered' and the paradox of consumption", in Kevin Meethan, Alison Anderson & Steve Miles (eds), *Tourism Consumption and Representation: Narratives of Place and Self*, CABI, Wallingford, pp. 284–299.

Wolfsfeld, Gadi 1997, *Media and Political Conflict: News from the Middle East*, Cambridge UP, Cambridge.

Woodward, Ian, Skrbis, Zlatko & Bean, Clive 2008, "Attitudes towards globalization and cosmopolitanism: Cultural diversity, personal consumption and the national economy", *British Journal of Sociology*, vol. 59, no. 2, pp. 207–226.

3 Travel journalism and the brands

In 2009 an Australian Broadcasting Corporation foreign correspondent expelled from Fiji during political unrest pointedly excluded travel journalists from the fellowship of serious news reporting. "Well," he said, "it's probably open season in Fiji for travel writers but no one else is going to get in" (Dorney in Ritchi 2009). Perhaps we should not be surprised at this newsman's assessment. Decades earlier, in 1988, the chairman of the Canadian chapter of the Society of American Travel Writers had decreed: "We are not qualified, as travel journalists, to take a political or an economic stand. The bottom line is that travel articles are selling tools. They should make people want to go to those places" (Loverseed in Gillespie 1988).

Much of the scepticism directed towards claims that travel journalists might contribute to the public sphere arises from the knowledge that many do their research in the field at the expense of tourism offices or commercial tourism businesses. For this reason it is important for me to reiterate here that some publications do not allow their journalists to accept free travel and accommodation. A number of interviewees in Part 2 travelled to and around Tasmania at the expense of their employing publisher or funded themselves from their freelance payments. Nevertheless, some United States publications do still accept hosted visits, while freebies are common among the British and Australian travel press (in regard to the Australian press, see Hanusch 2012b). In these circumstances, tourism offices and tourism businesses attempt to gain publicity they consider more credible than advertising by hosting travel journalists, hoping to capitalise on traditional associations between journalism and objectivity while simultaneously working to manage the journalists' access to information and sources. When hosted writers produce brand-aligned texts, there is a strategic advantage to the tourism industry for those writers to be regarded as journalists by their readers. For the writers who accept such assistance from tourism offices or tourism operators, the moniker "journalist" – whether explicit or merely implied by their publication in the editorial sections of newspapers and magazines – can also serve as a bulwark against assumptions that bias will be an inevitable consequence of freebies. Even if the word journalist has come to be attached to certain sorts of travel writing almost by accident, it is laden with meanings that tourism public relations routinely exploit.

In this chapter I consider debates about government media management and the influence of public relations on hard journalism in order to contextualise the symbiotic relationship between tourism and travel media, before looking more closely at the role of government and quasi-public tourism offices in attracting travel journalists to destinations. This leads into a discussion of sociological brand theory, which offers insights into some aspects of place-branding. From here, I return to a more detailed discussion of the attributes of place-branding that distinguish it from corporate branding and tourism-only branding but also make it vulnerable to political pressure. Using New Zealand's "100% Pure" campaign as an example, I consider ways in which environments can be branded, before focussing on the uses of branding in broader government media management. Finally, I explain place-branding itself as a public relations practice and a set of discursive strategies intended to secure access to travel journalism and control over meanings in both the space of places and the space of flows.

The ubiquity of free travel and accommodation

A strong growth in travel journalism in the second half of last century (Fürsich and Kavoori 2001; Seaton n.d.; Wood 1997) is unlikely to have been possible without the support of tourism public relations. The often-prohibitive expense of travelling to a destination to report on it has resulted in the evolution of comprehensive national, regional and tourism-operator programs "to entice media to visit a destination and maximise the publicity that can be gained" (Mackellar and Fenton 2000, p. 255). In 2003, survey responses from 10 national tourism organisations were reported as rating such programs as the most important part of their publicity and public relations arsenal (Dore and Crouch 2003, p. 142). In a recent survey of Australian travel journalists, 64.3 per cent said at least 75 per cent of their work was based on free trips and accommodation, and only 2.3 per cent said they never accepted freebies (Hanusch 2012b).

Tourism public relations practitioners' structural ties to travel journalism give them an extremely high level of access. As Fürsich and Kavoori observe, acceptance of, or reliance on, free or subsidised travel "places many travel writers in a difficult position between major interest groups" (2001, p. 154). Visiting Journalist Program (VJP) tours offered by government and quasi-public tourism organisations often take the form of all-expenses-paid hosted tours of a destination provided to selected media representatives (Dore and Crouch 2003; Mackellar and Fenton 2000). The media representatives may travel singly or in groups and will often be accompanied by a guide (Mackellar and Fenton 2000). "Although industry participants in the programme contribute in-kind support/costs," write Lynne Dore and Geoffrey Crouch, "the NTO [national tourism organisation] normally maintains firm control on the overall management and operation of the programme as the central point of control" (2003, p. 145). The stated intention of the tourism organisations that influence, subsidise or entirely fund so much of the research for travel reviews published in newspapers and magazines is to gain favourable coverage of a destination or product (Dore and Crouch 2003; Mackellar and Fenton 2000; Tourism Tasmania 2011).

In recent years, journalism scholar Folker Hanusch (2011, 2012a, 2012b) has compiled empirical evidence that tests practitioner anecdotes and the scholarly conclusions drawn from text analyses of small samples of travel journalism. His quantitative findings indicate "the most important role perceptions [of travel journalists] relate to providing true accounts, discovering new and unique travel experiences, as well as providing specific as well as interesting and entertaining information for audiences" (2012a, p. 674). Hanusch writes that "the Critic role, usually associated most with 'hard news', is not regarded highly by travel journalists at all" (2012a, p. 683). He finds that those with formal journalism training are less likely to consider that free travel and gifts will influence their writing. Despite agreement among respondents that free trips should always be disclosed, those who have been in the business for some time do not see disclosure as particularly important and have faith in their ability to make ethical decisions according to the situation. In addition, most feel that "travel journalists should always tell the truth about an experience, even if it means upsetting the travel sponsor" (2012a, p. 683). Yet, as Hanusch points out, content analyses have shown that travel journalism is "suspiciously devoid" of any negative issues" (2012a, p. 683). Additional analysis by Hanusch (2012b) of travel journalists' perceptions of public relations have led him to conclude that the more financially secure travel journalists are and the stronger their background in mainstream journalism, the more confident they are likely to be of their ability to remain independent of public relations; conversely, "[t]hose who do not have such a background and work as freelancers, which goes hand in hand with a relatively low income…are more likely to be critical of PR and wary of its influence" (2012b, p. 73). Hanusch's results indicate that the ways in which public relations practitioners working for elite sources seek to exert influence over travel journalists, the reasons for their successes and failures, and the motivations of those travel journalists who adopt the role of the critic warrant further attention.

Although the travel journalist creates a text for consumption by potential tourists, it's important for discussions of place-branding and cosmopolitanism to acknowledge that it may be read by anyone who can gain access, from other kinds of travellers to people with an interest in the destination that is unrelated to travel. Furthermore, distribution through the mass media means the actual audience for travel journalism in our online era can be boundless in space and time. Online distribution also means that a feature that might have appeared in a generalist printed newspaper weekend magazine can be given a more explicitly tourism-oriented purpose in its online life by being included in lists of previously published articles under the banner of the newspaper's destination travel guide. That is, the article will appear with a "travel" URL and banner when visitors to the website search for the name of the destination.

Journalism and public relations: Cooperation or contestation?

Later in this chapter I consider the journalistic consequences of the close association between the travel media and tourism offices. First, however, I will give a brief overview of the broader relationship between public relations and journalists, with a particular focus on government public relations.

Media commentators and public relations practitioners tell a similar story about today's newspaper newsrooms (Beecher 2005; Burton 2007; Davies 2008; Lewis et al. 2008; White and Hobsbawm 2007): newspaper journalists in many Western countries are under extreme pressure; competition from online sources, citizen journalists and television is leading newspaper executives to cut staff and adjust their content mix in an effort to find a business model that can ensure their long-term survival; the result is individual journalists who increasingly must work in any combination of print, online, video, audio and photography and who have less time for initiating stories, pursuing sources and checking facts. In such a stressful environment, the temptation to use readymade copy provided by public relations practitioners is often irresistible. Lewis et al. (2008) describe how this apparent rise in the use of public relations material by journalists, together with the increase in their workloads and changes in work practices, has been perceived by some as changing the relationship between journalists and public relations practitioners to one of exchange rather than conflict (Lewis et al. 2008, p. 5).

At least since the 1970s both Marxists and pluralists have generally found that elite sources enjoy considerable advantage over non-elites in their access to journalists and their ability to have their messages delivered in terms they as sources consider accurate (see, for example, Curran et al. 1982; Ericson et al. 1989; Gans 1979; Hall et al. 1978; Schlesinger 1990). As Michael Schudson notes, "[o]ne study after another agrees that the center of news generation is the link between reporter and official" (2005, p. 181). As the public relations industry has matured, however, interest groups have increased their own public relations expertise and, correspondingly, their access to the media (Davis 2002, p. 176). Thus, regardless of how much journalists' use of public relations material might be increasing, and despite the advantages enjoyed by elite sources, institutional public relation practitioners are not *assured* of gaining coverage in today's news media that meets their desired outcomes (Davis 2002).

Although Aeron Davis finds that both journalists and public relations practitioners believe journalists are still in control of the news agenda (Davis 2002, p. 31), "[n]ews predominantly starts with source supply rather than media investigation, and PR is far more part of news production than journalists have hitherto admitted" (Davis 2002, p. 32). In a survey of Australian travel journalists that included some who were desk-bound, Hanusch (2012b) found that nearly two-thirds found public relations material a useful starting point for new story ideas. Davis's thesis is that not all types of elite sources automatically have the same advantages in all categories of journalism. While he sees government sources enjoying huge advantages in news reporting because of their power, influence and ability to provide expert or otherwise authoritative comment (2002, p. 175), he finds the relationship between the media and elite sources less straightforward in the corporate sector. Using case studies of financial sector public relations, Davis reveals that corporate elites, unlike governments, have little "media affinity" with mainstream news journalists but considerable affinity and media capital in specialist news sectors – in this case business news. In fact, Davis finds that "the advantages of large corporate elites in business news…appear far greater than for political elites in mainstream news" (2002, p. 175). His conclusion that business journalism is, in many respects, "captured" by "elite discourse networks" (2002, p. 175) raises serious concerns about ubiquitous public relations. Lewis et al. (2008) have found a large disparity between the media success of businesses and that of nongovernment organisations, while Davis's interviews with journalists have led him to estimate that up to 50 per cent of public relations activity in Britain *blocks* journalists' access to information (2002, p. 179). He concludes that "the liberal description of fourth estate media, based on an image of independent, autonomous journalists seeking out news, has been severely undermined…the dividing line between public relations, advertising and entertainment will thus become increasingly blurred" (Davis 2002, p. 173). Davis's findings are of particular relevance to tourism public relations because they suggest that a government or quasi-public tourism office enjoys the double advantage of being both an elite government and, by association,[1] an elite industry source in its relationship with travel journalists and travel publishers.

To a familiarity with a mix of government and industry public relations advantages and practices, scholars with an interest in travel journalism in destinations with contested environments must add an awareness of strategies developed by governments to manage the media in times of political conflict. In military conflicts, a common way governments restrict journalists' access to information is by insisting that they travel with authorised personnel. Discussing news management techniques adopted by the United States and Britain in conflicts following the Vietnam War, Lewis et al. describe the use of "minders" or "escorts" to "keep reporters under constant supervision" (2006, p. 8):

> The system has ensured that the ability of journalists to do their jobs depends heavily on their individual minder. Minders have had the power to provide information or withhold it; to escort journalists to where the action is or, by contrast, to restrict them to locations where nothing is happening; to interpret ground rules in whatever way they see fit; and to help journalists get their stories back, or to hinder or even block them.
>
> (Lewis et al. 2006, pp. 8–9)

A more recent trend is to embed journalists with troops. In 2003, the United Kingdom and United States reduced their level of censorship in favour of embedding journalists with frontline troops in the hope that the "largely complicit" (Lewis et al. 2006, p. 69) coverage they produced would foster public sympathy for troops, support for the war and tolerance of any mistakes. From the perspective of the Pentagon, "embedding is a mutually beneficial system that gives the journalists what they need (access, stories) whilst enabling the military to get their point of view across" (Lewis et al. 2006, pp. 3–4). Its success in Iraq in 2003 was achieved by "putting a human face on combat operations" (Lewis et al. 2006, p. 37), facilitating a huge volume of dramatic embedded coverage overall, and ensuring there were no gaps in embedded content throughout the 24 hour news cycle that news editors might have been tempted to fill with material less sympathetic to the coalition (Lewis et al. 2006). Such strategies and tactics can severely limit the ability of challengers to gain access to the media, but the obstacles are not insurmountable. Wolfsfeld's extensive 1997 study of the role of the media in a variety of Middle East conflicts found that the media did not always transmit elite framing of conflicts and sometimes even helped construct meaning themselves (Gamson and Wolfsfeld 1993; Wolfsfeld 1997): the extent to which the more powerful antagonist in a conflict had power over the media depended in large part on its power over the political environment and the ability of challengers to mobilise support from within the ranks of the elite (Wolfsfeld 1997).

It is also important to note that today challengers in all kinds of conflicts are increasingly putting new media to work tactically to gain the attention of media that traditionally privilege the messages of elites (Garcia and Lovink 1997; Lester and Hutchins 2009; Lovink 2005; Meikle 2002). Events such as the Arab Spring have highlighted the opportunities offered by new media in "coalescing broad-based, non-hierarchical political movements and coordinating and channelling their demographic weight into real democratic power" and "alerting international news media to growing opposition and dissent events" (Cottle 2011, p. 298). In both new and traditional media, symbols mobilised by social movements through protest, imagery, rhetoric or celebrity (Lester 2006, 2007) can be a potent force in battles for social change, but they must be used with discretion or risk being discredited by a cynical media or simply ignored by a bored public (Hilgartner and Bosk 1988; Lester 2006, 2007). In a genre such as travel journalism, where the advantages enjoyed by government and industry would initially appear to be overwhelming, evidence of the successful deployment of media strategies and tactics by antagonists on both sides of a conflict has the potential to reveal aspects of the interaction between journalists and sources hitherto overlooked by journalism scholars.

Government public relations and travel journalism

Although it is widely suspected that much government public relations activity remains invisible in the hard news it influences (Lewis et al. 2008), little consideration has been given to covert government public relations influence on entertainment and lifestyle coverage – sectors of journalism Angela McRobbie notes have traditionally relied heavily on corporate public relations (2000). In tourism public relations, governments play perhaps an even larger role than business, at least in terms of promoting the destination in its entirety. Tourism offices make no secret of the fact that their VJPs are designed to achieve positive coverage of their destinations by providing journalists with various combinations of logistical support, information subsidies, free accommodation, free travel and guiding services, and that these programs are linked to marketing and public relations efforts in international tourism markets. As described by Mackellar and Fenton's 2000 case study of the VJPs run by the Australian Tourism Commission

(ATC), journalists initially targeted by that organisation's in-market public relations staff were those whose audiences were most similar to people likely to travel to Australia (2000, p. 261). In 1998–99, the ATC hosted 1,500 international print and television "journalists". By the ATC's own reckoning, the value of the publicity generated was more than one billion Australian dollars, calculated by multiplying the cost of buying advertising of an equivalent length or duration by three, based on a belief that journalists' copy is three times as effective as advertising (Mackellar and Fenton 2000, p. 263; cf. Barwise and Styler (2003) for an interesting counterargument to the assumption of such a multiplier effect). The ATC's successor, Tourism Australia, hosts between 800 and 1,000 international media representatives from around 30 countries annually (Tourism Australia 2012) and in 2009 introduced a scheme to host "new media opinion leaders, such as bloggers with extremely high traffic and an audience who is often spread across several of our markets" (Tourism Australia 2009).

VJPs are inundated with requests for assistance from middle ranking and lower ranking national media, but now that, as Dore and Crouch note, these programs have become "critically important elements" of the destination promotion strategies of quasi-public tourism offices around the world (2003, p. 140), competition among them for the most powerful international travel journalists and publications is fierce. Tourism offices work hard to devise itineraries that meet their own objectives and the needs of journalists and tourism operators. As a result, the experiences of international travel journalists they host are far removed from those of most tourists: not only are the tourism operators they visit usually vetted by government tourism public relations staff to ensure they offer a high-quality product, but these operators have an established relationship with the tourism office and are forewarned that they will be hosting a visiting journalist who will be writing about the destination and may include comment on their product (Dore and Crouch 2003; Mackellar and Fenton 2000). Yet for all the resources at their disposal, some destination marketing organisations question the value of VJPs because they cannot control the content of the final article (Dore and Crouch 2003, p. 140). This suggests that government tourism public relations staff have an intuitive understanding of the negativity effect. This is a finding in the "impression formulation literature" that those who are uncommitted to a product (such as, I would suggest, readers of travel journalism who have never visited the destination being reviewed) place far more weight on negative information than positive information about a product, using it "diagnostically" in their purchasing decisions (Ahluwalia, Burnkrant and Unnava 2000). Dore and Crouch downplay this possibility of negative coverage with the reassurance that hosted journalists are unlikely to "bite the hand that feeds them" (2003, p. 148), but there appears to be more strategy involved than merely the anticipation of a quid pro quo. Marketing studies, including place-branding literature, refer to journalists and other opinion-makers as agents and categorise promotion as "autonomous" (such as independent reviews), "covert induced" (such as positive editorial coverage arising from a hosted visit) and "induced" (such as advertising) (Gartner 1993, pp. 200–201; Govers and Go 2009). Rather than clear demarcations between these categories, there is a continuum, with positive "covert induced" image formation considered the most valuable public relations outcome after positive "autonomous" image formation. All the while that VJPs seek to gain publicity that is more credible than advertising by capitalising on traditional associations between journalism and objectivity, they also work to restrict the flow of information to hosted visiting journalists by managing their itineraries and sometimes assigning them trained guides full time during their visits. Itineraries and guides are designed to ensure visiting journalists see the best destinations have to offer, but the converse is also true, in that they tend to avoid experiences tourism offices believe do not showcase the destination to its best advantage. Comparisons with media management in times of military conflict are – purely in terms of illustrating government public relations practices and objectives – hard to ignore:

> The most favourable situation from the authority's point of view is to have the conflict scene in an area that is as isolated as possible. This puts journalists at a serious disadvantage not only because they have to invest a good deal of ingenuity and resources into gaining access, but their lack of knowledge of the area increases their dependence on official sources. The worst case scenario for authorities, on the other hand, is a fight that takes place close to home in an area such as a major city, such as London, which is impossible to seal off from the press…There have been countless studies that emphasize the normative aspects of government "censorship" during wars and far too little about the situational circumstances that either enhance or diminish the ability of authorities to control the flow of information…I take as given that authorities prefer to have a monopoly on the information available to journalists and that journalists would like to break that monopoly. The question, then, is not so much whether governments should restrict inform-ation in the midst of a conflict but whether they can.
>
> (Wolfsfeld 1997, p. 28)

In addition to establishing relationships whereby public relations practitioners and guides can attempt strategically to influence the discourses and framing of travel journalists, VJPs may be viewed as a way of incorporating travel journalists into the networks of government and quasi-public tourism organisations, and of media institutions establishing connections with a range of networks within destinations, including these tourism organisations. Actor-network theory offers one way of understanding such networks. ANT (Latour 2005) "conceptualises both humans and nonhumans as actors, studies connection-making as coterminous with meaning-making, and represents networks from a participant's viewpoint" (Saito 2011, p. 128). Nick Couldry argues that "ANT can be an important part of the panoply of media theory" (2004, p. 6), notably as a way of analysing "how particular people are 'systematically overaccessed' in the production of media narratives, while others by the same token are systematically underaccessed" (2004, p. 9). One of its limitations, however, as Couldry (2004) notes has been argued by Roger Silverstone, is that "the existence of networks does not explain, or even address, agents' *interpretations* of those networks and their resulting possibilities for action" following a network's establishment (Couldry 2004, p. 3, original emphasis). Scholars have traditionally sought evidence of public relations influence through content analyses revealing the presence of public relations material in journalism texts (Lewis et al. 2008; Macnamara, cited in Johnston 2000). As Davis notes, however, results of such content analyses vary wildly precisely because the covert nature of so much public relations means that "the ability to determine what is news and what is PR in any single publication is virtually impossible" (2002, p. 26).

Place-branding

Place-branding exponent Simon Anholt (2010), who addresses much of his advice to governments and the public sector, equates place brands with strong or weak reputations. In her analysis of place-branding as it relates to national identity, Melissa Aronczyk, (2013, p. 16) provisionally defines nation-branding as "the result of the interpenetration of commercial and public sector interests to communicate national priorities among domestic and international populations for a variety of interrelated purposes". Branded places may be countries, states, provinces or cities, but the term can also be applied to the tourism-related branding of localities, elsewhere referred to as destination branding. For tourism scholars Robert Govers and Frank Go (2009), place-branding attempts to "build a coherent product offering (which includes tourism, trade, temporary employment and investment opportunities), communicated in the right way in order to guarantee the emotion-laden place experience that consumers are seeking" (Govers and Go 2009, p. 17).

In this book, when I write of place-branding I am usually referring to destination branding as it contributes to the jurisdictional branding of a state, province or country. In place-branding literature aimed at tourism marketers, the brand is likely to be defined as a discursive asset. Govers and Go, for example, describe a place brand as "a representation of identity, building a favourable internal (with those who deliver the experience) and external (with visitors) image" (2009, p. 17). By defining place brands as positive, these authors imply that negative elements of a place's identity can somehow be excised or rendered impotent in the process of representation. Thus, while I don't believe theirs would be an acceptable definition of a place brand by Anholt's measure, for my purposes it affords a useful way of understanding the *practice* of place-branding in tourism public relations – that is, as an attempt to manage representations of place so that only positive ones circulate or gain a foothold in local and global imaginaries. To this extent, place-branding is characterised by the deployment of discursive strategies (see chapter 1). Like all branding, however, it also directs and informs public relations practice and manages staff (see Lury 2004). Hosting travel journalists is one way in which tourism public relations practitioners help the destination gain access to the travel media. However, just as the discursive strategies of place-branding are not entirely the creation of tourism offices, they also are not the sole preserve of tourism hosting programs. This is one reason why place-branding rather than hosting alone should be a focus of research into travel journalism. A second reason is that place-branding is a political as well as a commercial and cultural project. According to Anholt, "[p]lace branding is the consequence of a realisation that public opinion is an essential component of achieving a political end. It is, one might say, a necessary consequence of democracy and the globalisation of the media" (Anholt 2004, p. 9). External communication is only a small part of his transformative equation. Through public policy and innovation as well as internal communication, place-branding is intended to shape local identity in ways that ensure it deserves the better reputation its external communications attempt to secure (Anholt 2010; van Ham 2008). In applying the brand metaphor to nations, Anholt refers to its ability to differentiate the nation from its international competitors while simultaneously creating a "spirit of benign nationalism... notwithstanding its cultural, social, ethnic, linguistic, economic, political, territorial and historical divisions" (Anholt, 2007, p. 16). Anholt sometimes prefers to call place-branding "competitive identity", arguing that it should not be considered "some form of marketing discipline" but rather "a new approach to statecraft, to economic development and international relations" (2010, p. 8). In practice, however, governments spend large sums of public money projecting a place image to foreign publics through marketing communications and public relations. In this respect, the outcome of attempts by governments to shape local identity as well as international reputation can be influenced by the way local media reflect the external reception of the brand back to their readers. Thus, international travel journalism has the potential to function as one form of feedback to governments and publics. For this reason it is critical to understand both how that feedback is determined and how it circulates in the public sphere.

While Anholt states that national reputations cannot be constructed but can only be earned (2010, p. 6), the process he describes for earning a good reputation is one in which social construction plays an important role. Governments are advised to collaborate with business and civil society to agree upon a national narrative – "the 'story' of who the nation is, where it is going and how it is going to get there – which honestly reflects the skills, the genius and the will of the people", after which it should prove through its actions, policies and products "the country's right to the reputation its people and government desire to acquire" (2010, p. 7). Govers and Go (2009), for their part, argue that place-branding operates by using experience and communication to bridge the gap between a place's identity and the way it is perceived in external markets.

In focusing on brands in her analysis of the economic and social implications of contemporary uses of information, image and media, Lury (2004) conceptualises the brand as a new media object (Manovich 2001 in Lury 2004). Such an approach is possible because brands act as an interface that is a site of interactivity facilitating dynamic, two-way but asymmetrical and selective communication between producers and consumers and also separating them from each other (Lury 2004, pp. 8–9, 131–33). Because in Lury's model elements of the brand are self-organising, the brand itself is considered to be greater than the sum of the purposive actions or activities of marketers, designers and consumers (2004, p. 51). Using the example of brand extensions, whereby the kinds of products available under the brand are extended to attract new kinds of customers, Lury argues that it is the relations between products – "specific system effects" – as much as the actions of any individual or team in the production process that enable a new category of product to leverage off the success of the brand to forge enduring emotional bonds with customers (2004, pp. 61–62, 87). This is especially common in lifestyle brands (2004, pp. 61–62), of which tourism is a prime example. Brands blur the distinction between production and consumption (Lash and Lury 2007; Arvidsson 2006; Lury 2004), at least in part because they are informational capital derived from the networked labour of consumers who engage with the brand in the creation of their own identities and meanings (Arvidsson 2006; see also Chapter 8). While the brand simultaneously delivers information to customers and extracts information from customers to be used in marketing, design, production and distribution, it can also severely limit the ability of customers to interact with it (Lury 2004, p. 137). In other words, the interactivity that brand managers encourage as a source of information about consumers does not necessarily result in consumers having equitable interaction with producers (Aronczyk and Powers 2010; Lury 2004). Arvidsson explains that the informational capital of brands depends on consumers producing a "common sociality" that can be appropriated, then filtered and polished before being redeployed (2006, p. 94).

There are ways in which dissatisfied consumers and staff can challenge producers' ability to use the brand to shield themselves from their environment. Through leaks, protests, consumer organisations and consumer magazines they can, in effect, assert their right to interaction with the brand rather than settle for interactivity. Arvidsson (2006) and Lury (2004) point to the success of the anti-branding movement in subverting attempts by brand managers to direct consumer preferences from below by "programming" the "freedom" of consumers so that it develops in a particular direction (Arvidsson 2006, p. 74). Nevertheless, Lury is pessimistic about the ability of the brand to function as more than "an object of contemporary capitalism" (2004, p. 163). Central to her argument is a tension she perceives between the brand's potential to be open and its tendency to be closed, depending on its degree of indeterminacy and the willingness or otherwise of brand managers to act on all of the information they receive (2004, p. 162). However, in their capacity as both consumer–producers and consumer–mediators of destination brands, travel journalists are well placed to "talk back" (Lury 2004) to place-branding practitioners, policymakers and governments during their visits and through the travel journalism they produce.

Place-branding, tourism and public diplomacy

Anholt sees tourism's communications as having a legitimacy that makes the sector the most powerful place-branding "booster rocket" (2007, p. 88). Yet the very importance attributed to tourism by place-branding is evidence that tourism also "reflects and reinforces social, cultural and economic divisions rooted outside the tourism experience itself" (Morgan and Pritchard 1998, p. 6). As noted by Morgan et al. as recently as 2011, there is still very little academic knowledge about how vested interests intersect in place-branding, particularly when those interests conflict (2011, p. 354) – something this book will go some way to addressing. Tourism as an industry is described as "politically weak" because its business base is fragmented and includes many small commercial operators and public institutions such as national parks that may not be motivated solely or largely by economics (Ryan and Zahra 2004). This has led, on occasion, to high levels of government funding for tourism organisations, governments wielding political power in tourism politics, and direct political interference (Ryan and Zahra 2004). Anholt contends that place-branding will only succeed if its communications are honest, ethical and founded on policy-making that incorporates serious consideration of "market feedback" from public diplomacy (2007, p. 14) – implicit acknowledgement that the integrity of a place's brand will inevitably be challenged from time to time by stakeholders acting in their own interests rather than the interests of the broader community. Govers and Go point to the obvious implications of this for local identity and local politics:

> It raises questions about decision-making processes and power struggles at the local level, as it needs to be determined where and how place identity should be positioned in the global flows of images dominated by the media, and who should be responsible. As Castells (1996, p. 476) argues, in the network society "image-making is power-making".
>
> (Govers and Go 2009, p. 7)

When governments take "a wider perspective of a tourism strategy beyond issues of promotion, and also an extended view of who are the stakeholders within tourism" (Ryan and Zahra 2004) – as Chris Ryan and Anne Zahra have found they do in New Zealand and I would argue is the case whenever tourism is folded into place-branding – there seems little reason to assume that tourism's communications will always be agnostic in a party-political sense.

Geographers Irena Ateljevic and Stephen Doorne (2002) see the power, ideology and discourses of place in terms of hegemony. In recent years, Ateljevic has approached the study of tourism from the perspective of "worldmaking" – a concept in critical tourism studies that theorises and investigates the way tourism can be used positively by groups and communities to advance new visions or negatively to silence unwanted interpretations of place (Hollinshead , Alteljevic and Alie 2009).[2] Margaret Byrne Swain considers worldmaking to be complementary to a hopeful cosmopolitanism that sees tourism at its most progressive offering opportunities "to transform differences into equity" (Byrne Swain 2009, p. 505) – an assessment that resonates with the rhetoric of place-branding. In the view of international relations scholar Peter van Ham, however, place-branding warrants the critical attention of others in his discipline because it is more than "rhetorical window-dressing and intellectual tap-dancing" (van Ham 2002, p. 252):

> It implies a shift in political paradigms, a shift from the modern world of geopolitics and power to the postmodern world of images and influence. If this trend continues, it will have a pronounced impact on the nature of international politics.
>
> (van Ham 2002, p. 252)

For van Ham, what distinguishes place-branding from historical forms of image management in international relations is its "mediagenic creation of emotional ties between the citizen-cum-consumer and the (place) brand" (2008, p. 134).

Place-branding and environmental attractions

Landscape and wildlife are also mediagenic and a source of strong emotional ties between places, residents and visitors. When branding is proposed for publicly owned places such as national parks, the goals in addition to establishing recognition and identity are likely to be some combination of "attracting and educating various stakeholders, building trust and relationships, and offering diverse programs" (Gross et al. 2009, p. 276). In one place-branding analysis of the United States and Canadian national parks systems, for example, the problems the researchers defined and attempted to resolve were associated with multiple stakeholders, objectives and jurisdictions. While their analysis recognised the complexity of different use-values and perspectives, and particularly those of people other than tourists, the solution proposed was communication and marketing, including "'soft power diplomacy', reaching out to their various stakeholders with appropriate messages and through relevant media" (Gross et al. 2009, p. 287). The objective of such communication appears to be the discursive integration of environmental and economic sustainability (see also Stamou and Paraskevopoulos (2006), who espouse a similar objective for communication about Greek national parks in the course of their discourse analysis of travel journalism) – integration that increases the marketing advantages that can be derived from landscape.

One important way that national parks can gain the kind of international recognition that gives them immense power as tourism public relations tools is through inscription on the World Heritage List, which was inaugurated in 1978 and now contains many hundreds of physical and cultural sites (Ryan and Silvanto 2009). Established as a conservation measure by the United Nations, the list has become "a coveted brand and seal of approval" that attracts a constant stream of nominations of natural sites from governments around the world (Ryan and Silvanto 2009, p. 291). Independently, or in combination with a place's existing reputation for natural attractions, World Heritage endorsement of natural phenomena or landscapes as being of global significance contributes not only to their preservation but also to their commodification and – building on successful tourism publicity – to their governments' ability to transform landscapes into branding messages that attribute natural qualities or purity to innumerable products and cultural characteristics. In New Zealand, where the place-branding campaign "100 % Pure New Zealand" has enjoyed outstanding success in its own terms for more than a decade, it has been argued that landscape, nature and "greenness" are a "powerful identity 'myth'" (Ryan 2002, p. 68) that disguises or ignores historical and contemporary environmental mismanagement (Dürr 2007; Ryan 2002): "Both national identity and international reputation are intertwined, and constitute and reproduce each other. Therefore, the '100% Pure' representation also plays a role in constructing New Zealand's identity at home, just as it does work abroad" (Dürr 2007, p. 6).

Another physical quality that can contribute to a place's ability to market itself as exotic and environmentally responsible is the *"island factor"* (Reitsma and Little 2010, original emphasis). In New Zealand, for example the "100% Pure" campaign has turned the country's isolation into an asset by constructing its islands as untouched by population pressures and distant from the polluting effects of northern-hemisphere industrialisation (Dürr 2007). Tasmania makes similar claims (Department of Premier and Cabinet 2006).

National identity and romanticised nature are often linked, but there is also evidence that nature is culturally specific in the way it is constructed and interpreted (Hansen 2010). This reminds us of the perennial challenge of place-branding – how to differentiate a place from all others while simultaneously ensuring the particular can speak to the universal. One mechanism is the visual image – an endemic or charismatic animal, a mountain range etc. As Anders Hansen explains, "the elevation to iconic or representative status, and the public identification of these images as belonging to a particular discourse, requires visual signification 'work'" (Hansen 2010, pp. 2–3).

Although British Columbia and Alberta share a border that traverses the Rocky Mountains, these Canadian provinces differentiate themselves from each other in marketing that represents that grandeur in very different ways. Destination British Columbia anchors visual images of spectacular landscapes mostly devoid of people with an elevated commentary solemnly delivered and the branding slogan "Super, Natural British Columbia" (Destination British Columbia 2014), whereas Travel Alberta presses home nature's use-value with action sequences and close-ups of people in the landscape cut to a lively soundtrack and anchored with the branding slogan "remember to breathe" (Travel Alberta 2011). Perhaps the CEO of Travel Alberta (Okabe in CBC News 2013, see Chapter 1) was thinking about British Columbia and their shared mountains when he said Alberta's brand was all that distinguished it from its tourism competitors. As Geo Takach (2014) demonstrates, however, images of environmental damage from development of the Athabasca bituminous sands may be acquiring sufficient symbolic power from the signification work being done by documentary-makers concerned about this form of oil production to be formidable contenders in a "visual battle to brand Alberta in the international public consciousness" (Takach 2014, p. 98).

Place-branding and the media

Anholt devotes a chapter in *Places* (2010) to the media. In addressing the subject of negative media coverage he advises countries not to try to avoid the issue in question but not to be dominated by it either. A reputation based on a complex identity, he believes, will be better able to withstand negative publicity related to one specific issue than a reputation for a small number of attributes. Nevertheless, he recommends having a national media centre that plans and coordinates visits by journalists to ensure that "proper information, hospitality, access and resources are provided" and to help "coordinate the messaging of the country's major communicators (tourist board, investment promotion agency, main exporters, Ministry of Foreign Affairs etc)" (2010, p. 133). Journalists, as he represents them, are willing allies in the hands of astute public relations practitioners:

> [M]uch international journalism is simply a process of rehearsing, playing with, sometimes examining and very occasionally challenging those national brand images. A lot of journalism is basically a matter of endlessly redeploying such clichés.
>
> (Anholt 2010, p. 142)

> The good news is that journalists are, always and forever, short of good content, and will act as a highly effective (and highly cost-effective) conduit for reputation if only one can provide them with the quantity, consistent quality and professionalism that they require.
>
> (Anholt 2010, p. 143)

Offering an alternative to Anholt's view that public diplomacy should be subsumed in place-branding or, at the very least, fused with it (see above), van Ham considers that "the theory and practice of place-branding is part of a wider discourse that involves propaganda at one end of the spectrum, and public diplomacy at the other" (2008, p. 135). Public diplomacy, he writes, is "the strategy of appealing to the core values of foreign audiences by using new techniques that are frequently directly derived from commercial practice" (2008, p. 135). Public diplomacy differs from traditional diplomacy in that it is government communication aimed at foreign publics rather than at foreign governments and their diplomats. The difference between place-branding and public diplomacy, according to van Ham (2008), is that the latter is not concerned with shaping local identity. However, they both in principle rely on the power of attraction rather than coercion: "For both place-branding and public diplomacy, a key element is to build personal and institutional relationships and dialogue with foreign audiences by focusing on *values*, setting them apart from classical diplomacy, which primarily deals with *issues* (van Ham 2008, p. 135, original emphasis). Issues, therefore – the kinds of issues that result in political conflict, for example – are likely to be problematic for place-branding managers. Yet there are high-profile examples of branding becoming intermeshed with public diplomacy in government issues management. In an attempt to influence the way the Muslim world viewed the United States immediately after the World Trade Center was attacked in 2001 a public relations expert in branding was appointed United States Undersecretary of Public Diplomacy (Lewis et al. 2006, p. 25; van Ham 2002, 2008). And in the lead-up to the 2003 Iraq war "what once would have been the distinct agendas of military/media strategy (truth), image control abroad (selective selling and branding), and psychological operations (manipulation of truth for reasons of national security)" became blurred both institutionally and discursively in the United States and the United Kingdom (Lewis et al. 2006, p. 26).

Public relations, politics, travel Journalism and the brand

As we have seen, VJPs run by government and quasi-public tourism offices enable destination brands to gain greater access to travel journalists than they otherwise might and thus achieve media coverage for less than the cost of advertising. Tourism New Zealand's description of the importance of international media to its "100% Pure" campaign is instructive:

> Despite a new brand and a lot of enthusiasm, Tourism New Zealand didn't have a lot of money. One way of making its marketing dollar go further was to attract high-quality international media to New Zealand with the aim of generating positive coverage for the country as a destination…
>
> Tourism New Zealand worked to attract international media to events, took care of them while they were there and encouraged them to promote New Zealand as part of the event coverage.
>
> Take the America's Cup: an excuse to highlight images of sky and sea and outdoor experiences, and a perfect opportunity to extend the interest of visiting media beyond sailing to trout fishing in the hinterland or environmental themes.
>
> (Tourism New Zealand 2009d)

Once access to media is achieved, tourism office VJPs attempt to ensure the identity of the place that travel journalists encounter during their visit accords with the image of the place the tourism office has projected through its marketing. As elite travel journalism sources, government tourism public relations practitioners are central to how tourist destinations are perceived by the media (MacKellar and Fenton 2000; Dore and Crouch 2003), yet in some cases the offices for which they work are vulnerable to party-political pressure (Morgan and Pritchard 2004; Ryan and Zahra 2004), including the "short-termism of the tourism organizations' political masters" (Morgan and Pritchard 2004, p. 63). In brand-management terms, not only must government tourism public relations practitioners manage journalists to achieve positive publicity for the destination and deal with issues that might impact negatively on the brand (Morgan and Pritchard, 2004) but they must also "produce the identity of the organization, and at the same time produce themselves as members of the organization" (Arvidsson 2006, p. 85). According to Lury, although in today's markets employees are often expected to see their work as a way of adding value to themselves, "the management of brands increasingly has implications for who gets hired or not, who gets promoted or not, and thus who prospers or not" (2004, p. 35). According to Lury, brands are "one of a growing number of devices to monitor and control the performance of the employee" (2004, p. 33). In its manifestation as an overarching government strategy, therefore, place-branding can be expected to guide how public relations practitioners organise itineraries, and direct and conduct tours, but also to be evident in their professional discourse – both in the public relations material they write and in their interactions with travel journalists, colleagues, stakeholders and publics.

In Chapter 2, I began my summary of scholarly debates about source–media relations with a discussion of Hall et al.'s theory of primary definition, whereby journalists seek out institutional sources because they believe them to be authoritative and objective, and as a result these sources are able to set the terms of the debate. While later studies that took into account strategic action by elites and non-elites demonstrated that institutional sources were not entirely dominant, they confirmed that such sources did have a considerable advantage. In travel journalism, that advantage is increased by the ability of state, provincial and national tourism offices in many instances to, in effect, buy editorial *access* for their destinations by hosting travel journalists (remembering that gaining access does not necessarily guarantee that a source's *meanings* will prevail – see below). However, place-branding discourses may gain access *and* be faithfully mediated in the absence of any interaction between government public relations practitioners and travel journalists. Here critical tourism studies provides an insight into the way tourism discourses such as, I would argue, those of place-branding become naturalised not only in tourism publicity material but also in the talk of individuals in the industry and – if place-branding succeeds by its own measure in shaping local identity – the broader community. Specifically, "worldmaking" in critical tourism studies (see above) conceives of place as a discursive construction and expression of power in a manner that is directly applicable to the way place-branding functions:

> the naturalization or normalisation of meaning is an expression of "power", and, nominally, of the power of ascendant groups who have – over time – not only classified the place or space, but standardized the "talk" and "text" in currency about it, and reciprocally "disciplined" the training of those who work in tourism to match those very categorizations (consciously recognized or not), of and about "the world".
>
> (Hollinshead, Ateljevic and Ali 2009, p. 434)

Tourism New Zealand's "100% Pure" campaign was considered so successful that it was still in operation 10 years after its 1999 launch and in 2005 was ranked the

21st global corporate or consumer brand in the world (Tourism New Zealand 2009a, based on calculations by Interbrand). When the campaign encountered media criticism for contradictions between its place-branding and, for example, the way it handled agricultural waste or its promotion of carbon-intensive long-haul flights (Tourism New Zealand 2009b), it took measures to make its tourism industry more environmentally sustainable and used this in its marketing. According to WWF (2012), however, freshwater quality continued to decline as a result of agricultural practices. In 2009 the national tourism office's CEO recast the meaning of a brand promise. Instead of a brand being a guarantee, "100% Pure" was described as "something that New Zealand can aspire to in its environmental performance…a promise we believe the country can and should live up to, for New Zealanders and visitors alike" (Tourism New Zealand 2009c). In the same media release, he defended the "100% Pure" campaign's success and integrity in terms that illustrate how the affirmations so often inherent in place-branded framings lend them the suppleness and resilience they require in order to be effective when deployed within the branded destinations themselves:

> The 100% Pure New Zealand campaign still provides potential visitors with an enduring message of New Zealand. The reason the campaign has been so successful is not just because it's a great catchphrase but because it's true and the people of New Zealand give it that truth.
>
> (George Hickton in Tourism New Zealand 2009c)

The "100% Pure New Zealand" example demonstrates that even place brands have a degree of the object-ness attributed to product brands by Lury (2004) and as such are interfaces between tourism production and consumption that tend to be more closed than open. If governments do not heed Anholt's (2010) advice that communication without action is not enough to secure a place's strong external reputation, there is a risk that in times of environmental conflict place-brand managers will attempt to deploy the brand as a "wall or a shield" (Lury 2004, p. 159) between the place's "true identity" (Govers and Go 2009, p. 71), and foreign markets and publics. There is a sense of this in the New Zealand tourism CEO's insistence that "100% Pure" is "true".

The Interface between places and flows

While actor-network theory provides a useful way of conceptualising non-humans such as brands as actors in a network, another theory of networks – Castells' influential 1996 thesis of the network society (see Chapter 2) – has been invoked by place-branding scholars Govers and Go as being "of prime interest" in "the sense of local landscapes versus global ethnoscapes, mediascapes, technoscapes, financescapes, and ideoscapes" (2009, p. 57). In terms of the relationship between places and flows, Hutchins notes that it is not what separates them that is most significant but what happens where they meet:

The space of flows expresses dominant forms of social power, as represented by global managerial elites and the seemingly unstoppable march of information technology, but the important issue is what happens when these flows interact with actual places.

(Hutchins 2004, p. 580–81)

Hutchins identifies regional newspapers as one site in which global flows meet actual places: regional newspapers not only speak *for* places but also speak *to* places about global flows (2004, p. 587). Thus he finds that regional newspapers are engaged in processes of enabling as well as resistance, but also that the "interface between the space of flows and the space of places is not about consistency; it is about unpredictable outcomes, decentred power relations and culture in the act of becoming" (2004, p. 588). While place-branding defines itself as speaking *for* and *of* places to global and international audiences (for example, via travel journalism), it also sometimes attempts to speak *to* places ostensibly on behalf of global or international audiences via regional media mediation of positive brand reception.

Meanwhile, the environment movement occupies the space of places by choice but can assign place a value in the space of media flows (Hutchins and Lester 2006) through appeals to cosmopolitan concern:

In seeking to protect place, many environmental organizations operate and organize themselves in networked formations, helping to create widespread awareness of issues, disseminate information and coordinate actions. In other words, to generate knowledge of grassroots politics, a concerted effort must be made to engage with and move within the space of flows and, more specifically, the space of media flows.

(Hutchins and Lester 2006, p. 437)

Just as place-branding seeks to shape local identity as well as its global reception, so even when an environment movement seeks to use "universally understood dramatic frames" to rally support from distant publics it must also "manage meanings of its actions within local and particular contexts" (Lester and Cottle 2011, p. 289). When both place-branding and environment movements attempt to use international travel journalism and local or regional media to publicise and manage universal and local environmental meanings, the unpredictability of outcomes is likely to be especially pronounced.

Conclusion

It would be a mistake to believe that the ubiquity of hosted travel means tourism public relations is transparent. Theories and ethnographic studies of source–media relations in news journalism provide important insights into the way meanings are negotiated, contested and mediated – insights that can be applied to the study of travel journalists' reporting on destinations where environmental conflict is rife. But a study of travel journalism directed only at uncovering the influence of hosting on the production of travel journalism would fail to account for examples in which travel journalists who have not been hosted also ignore environmental conflict in their texts. Place-branding has the potential to be a more productive field of inquiry than VJPs per se because it is a comprehensive approach to public relations that simultaneously directs practice (including the public relations practice of those managing VJPs), integrates disparate sectors of the economy, activates networks and deploys discursive strategies to shape meanings in places, markets and the media.

As Tourism New Zealand chief executive George Hickton's assurance that "100% Pure New Zealand" is "true" (see above) suggests, one of the ambitions of place-branding is "to find consensus – and, more importantly, inspiration and stimulation – in a…narrative that is based on a shared dream for the future rather than a shared interpretation of the past or the present" (Anholt 2010, p. 34). Attempts to achieve this are through place-based institutions and structures (both material and cultural). Among those institutions are local and regional media – "mediators and interpreters of global networks of power and information" (Hutchins 2004, p. 588). The point here is that whenever discourses in international travel journalism that endorse or challenge place-branding cycle back into local or regional media reports, they have the potential to influence the course of environmental conflicts. To whatever extent it is possible to say that the geographical landscape is where place-based communities dwell (Harvey 2009, p. 250), that objects of dwelling travel (Lury 1997; see also Appadurai 1986), and that the nature-based place brand is an object (see Lury 2004), international travel journalists are implicated in the construction of the environment for publics in the destinations they review as well as for their publishers' readers. But if place-branding is being promoted by its advocates as a way of reconciling places and flows (see Anholt 2007, 2010; Govers and Go 2009), it will be wise to ask whose interests this might serve. Because international travel journalists are targets of place-branding, and place brands must be positioned within the space of flows, the travel journalism genre lends itself to the kind of analysis that might shed light on some of the complex processes Beck implicates in cosmopolitanisation, including the role of the media in unveiling global risks and the possibility of multiperspectival outlooks that incorporate the local, national, transnational and cosmopolitan. What might motivate travel journalists to include political discourses and frames in their texts, what forms might such comments take, and how might publishers and places respond? These are some of the questions that will be considered in the following chapters.

Notes

1   Industry representatives often sit on government and quasi-public tourism office boards and tourism offices often "partner" with commercial tourism operators, travel agents and transport corporations in their marketing.
2   This approach to "worldmaking" is distinct from the political philosophy interest in world-making (see, for example, Karagiannis and Wagner 2007), although both draw on the work of 20th century American philosopher of art and science Nelson Goodman.

References

Ahluwalia, Rohini, Burnkrant, Robert E & Unnava, H Rao 2000, "Consumer response to negative publicity: The moderating role of commitment", *Journal of Marketing Research*, vol. 37, no. 2, pp. 203–214.

Anholt, Simon 2010, *Places: Identity, Image and Reputation*, Palgrave Macmillan, Basingstoke.

Anholt, Simon 2007, *Competitive Identity: The New Brand Management for Nations, Cities and Regions*, Palgrave Macmillan, Basingstoke.

Anholt, Simon 2004, "Editors foreword to the first issue", *Place Branding*, vol. 1, no. 1, pp. 4–11.

Appadurai, Arjun (ed.) 1986, *The Social Life of Things: Commodities in Social Perspective*, Cambridge University Press, Cambridge.

Aronczyk, Melissa 2014, *Branding the Nation: The Global Business of National Identity*, Oxford University Press, Oxford.

Aronczyk, Melissa & Powers, Devon 2010, "Blowing up the brand: 'New branded world' redux", in Melissa Aronczyk & Devon Powers (eds), *Blowing Up the Brand: Critical Perspectives on Promotional Culture*, Peter Lang, London, pp. 1–26.

Arvidsson, Adam 2006, *Brands: Meaning and Value in Media Culture*, Routledge, Abingdon.

Ateljevic, Irena & Doorne, Stephen 2002,"Representing New Zealand: Tourism imagery and ideology", *Annals of Tourism Research*, vol. 29, no. 3, pp. 648–667.

Barwise, Patrick & Styler, Alan 2003, The Met Report 2003: Marketing expenditure trends 2001–04, London Business School, viewed 8 July 2008, www.london.edu/marketing/reports.html#Marketing%20Expenditure%20Trends

Beecher, Eric 2005, "The decline of the quality press", in Robert Mann (ed.), *Do Not Disturb: Is the Media Failing Australia*, Black Inc., Melbourne, pp. 7–27.

Burton, Bob 2007, *Inside Spin: The Dark Underbelly of the PR Industry*, Allen & Unwin, Crows Nest.

Byrne Swain, Margaret 2009, "The cosmopolitan hope of tourism: Critical action and worldmaking vistas", *Tourism Geographies*, vol. 11, no. 4, pp. 505–525.

Castells, Manuel 1996, *The Rise of the Network Society*, Blackwell, Massachusetts.

Cottle, Simon 2011, "Afterword: Media and the Arab uprisings of 2011", in Simon Cottle & Libby Lester (eds), *Transnational Protest and the Media*, Peter Lang, New York, pp. 293–304.

Couldry, Nick 2004, "Actor network theory and media: Do they connect and on what terms?", December, viewed 7 October 2011, www.andredeak.com.br/pdf/Couldry_ActorNetworkTheoryMedia.pdf

Curran, James, Gurevitch, Michael & Woollacott, Janet 1982, "The study of the media: Theoretical approaches", in Michael Gurevitch, Tony Bennett, James Curran & Janet Woollacott (eds), *Culture, Society and the Media*, Methuen, London, pp. 11–29.

Davies, Nick 2008, *Flat Earth News: An Award-winning Reporter Exposes Falsehood, Distortion and Propaganda in the Global Media*, Chatto & Windus, London.

Davis, Aeron 2002, *Public Relations Democracy: Public Relations, Politics and the Mass Media in Britain*, Manchester University Press, New York.

Destination British Columbia 2014, *The Wild Within*, "Brand Story" video, viewed 23 November 2014, www.destinationbc.ca/

Dore, Lynne & Crouch, Geoffrey I 2003, "Promoting destinations: An exploratory study of publicity programmes used by national tourism organisations", *Journal of Vacation Marketing*, vol. 9, no. 2, pp. 137–151.

Dürr, Eveline 2007, "Island purity as global imaginary: New Zealand and German perspectives", *Working Papers in Culture, Discourse and Communication, vol. 3, Languages and Identities*, Auckland University of Technology, viewed 27 August 2012, www.aut.ac.nz/resources/research/research_institutes/ccr/evelyn_durr.pdf

Ericson, Richard V, Baranek, Patricia M & Chan, Janet BL 1989, *Negotiating Control: A Study of News Sources*, Open University, Milton Keyes.

Fürsich, Elfriede & Kavoori, Anandam P 2001, "Mapping a critical framework for the study of travel journalism", *International Journal of Cultural Studies*, vol. 4, no. 2, pp. 149–171.

Gamson, William & Wolfsfeld, Gadi 1993, "Movements and media as interacting systems", *Annals of the American Academy* vol. 528, no. 93, pp. 114–25.

Gans, Herbert J 1979, *Deciding What's News: A Study of CBS Evening News, NBC Nightly News, Newsweek, and Time*, Pantheon, New York.

Garcia, David & Lovink, Geert, 1997, "The ABC of tactical media", viewed 16 March 2015, www.nettime.org/Lists-Archives/nettime-l-9705/msg00096.html

Gartner, William C 1993, "Image formation process", in Muzzafer Uysal & Daniel R Fesenmaier (eds), *Communication and Channel Systems in Tourism Marketing*, Haworth, Binghamton, pp. 191–215.

Gillespie, Ian 1988, "The flip side of freebies: Travel writers may get a free ride – but it's often the reader who pays", *Ryerson Review of Journalism*, March, viewed 18 December 2014, http://rrj.ca/the-flip-side-of-freebies/

Govers, Robert & Go, Frank 2009, *Place Branding: Glocal, Virtual and Physical Identities, Constructed, Imagined and Experienced*, Palgrave Macmillan, Basingstoke.

Gross, Andrew C, Poor, Jozsef, Sipos, Zoltan & Solymossy, Emeric 2009, "The multiple mandates of national park systems", *Place Branding and Public Diplomacy*, vol. 5, no. 4, pp. 276–289.

Hall, Stuart, Critcher, Chas, Jefferson, Tony, Clarke, John & Roberts, Brian 1978, *Policing the Crisis: Mugging, the State, and Law and Order*, Holmes and Meier, New York.

Hansen, Anders 2010, *Environment, Media and Communication*, Routledge, London.

Hanusch, Folker 2012a, "A profile of Australian travel journalists' views and ethical standards", *Journalism: Theory, Practice and Criticism*, vol. 13, no. 5, pp. 668–686.

Hanusch, Folker 2012b, "Travel journalists' attitudes toward public relations: Findings from a representative survey", *Public Relations Review: A Global Journal of Research and Comment*, vol. 38, no. 1, pp.69–75.

Hanusch, Folker 2011, "Representations of foreign places outside the news: An analysis of Australian newspaper travel sections", *Media International Australia*, no. 138, February, pp. 21–35.

Harvey, David 2009, *Cosmopolitanism and the Geographies of Freedom*, Columbia University Press, New York.

Hilgartner, Stephen & Bosk, Charles L 1988, "The rise and fall of social problems: A public arenas model", *American Journal of Sociology*, vol. 94, no.1, pp. 53–78.

Hutchins, Brett 2004, "Castells, regional news media and the information age", *Continuum*, vol. 18, no. 4, pp. 577–590.

Hutchins, Brett & Lester, Libby 2006, "Environmental protest and tap-dancing with the media in the information age", *Media, Culture & Society*, vol. 28, no. 3, pp. 433–51.

Johnston, Jane 2000, "Media relations", *Public Relations: Theory and Practice*, Jane Johnston & Clara Zawawi (eds), Allen & Unwin, St Leonards, pp. 205–234.

Karagiannis, Nathalie & Wagner, Peter 2007, *Varieties of World-making: Beyond Globalization*, Liverpool University Press, Liverpool.

Lagan, Bernard 1999, "Staring down a gift horse", *The Sydney Morning Herald*, 24 July, p. 41.

Lash, Scott & Lury, Celia 2007, *Global Culture Industry: The Mediation of Things*, Polity, Cambridge.

Latour, Bruno 2005, *Reassembling the Social: An Introduction to Actor-Network-Theory*, Oxford University Press, Oxford.

Lester, Libby 2007, *Giving Ground: Media and Environmental Conflict in Tasmania*, Quintus, Hobart.

Lester, Libby 2006, "Lost in the wilderness? Celebrity, protest and the news", *Journalism Studies*, vol. 7, no. 6, pp. 907–921.

Lester, Libby & Cottle, Simon 2011, "Transnational protests and the media: Toward a global civil society?", in Simon Cottle & Libby Lester (eds), *Transnational Protest and the Media*, Peter Lang, New York, pp. 287–291.

Lester, Libby & Hutchins, Brett 2009, "Power games: Environmental protest, news media and the internet", *Media, Culture & Society*, vol. 31, no. 4, pp. 579–595.

Lewis, Justin, Brookes, Rod, Mosdell, Nick & Threadgold, Terry 2006, *Shoot First and Ask Questions Later: Media Coverage of the 2003 Iraq War*, Peter Lang, New York.

Lewis, Justin, Williams, Andrew, Franklin, Bob, James, Thomas & Mosdell, Nick 2008, *The Quality and Independence of British Journalism: Tracking the Changes Over 20 Years*, MediaWise Journalism and Public Trust Project and Cardiff University, viewed 22 June 2008, www.mediawise.org.uk/display_page.php?id=999

Lovink, Geert 2005, "Tactical media, the second decade", viewed 15 March 2013, http://geertlovink.org/texts/tactical-media-the-second-decade/.

Lury, Celia 2004, *Brands: The Logos of the Global Economy*, Routledge, Abingdon.

Lury, Celia 1997, "The objects of travel", in Chris Rojek & John Urry (eds), *Touring Cultures: Transformations of Travel and Theory*, Routledge, London, pp. 75–95.

Mackellar, Jo & Fenton, Jane 2000, "Hosting the international travel media – a review of the Australian Tourist Commission's Visiting Journalist Programme", *Journal of Vacation Marketing*, vol. 6, no. 3, pp. 255–264.

McRobbie, Angela 2000, "The return to cultural production", in James Curran & Michael Gurevitch (eds), *Mass Media and Society*, 3rd edn, Arnold, London, pp. 255–267.

Meikle, Graham 2002, *Future Active: Media Activism and the Internet*, Pluto Press, Annandale.

Ryan, Chris 2002, "The politics of branding cities and regions: The case of New Zealand", in Nigel Morgan, Annette Pritchard & Roger Pride (eds), *Destination Branding: Creating the Unique Destination Proposition*, Butterworth-Heinemann, Oxford, pp. 66–86.

Ryan, Chris & Zahra, Anne 2004, "The political challenge: The case of New Zealand's tourism organizations", in Nigel Morgan, Annette Pritchard & Roger Pride (eds), *Destination Branding: Creating the Unique Destination Proposition*, 2nd edn, Elsevier Butterworth-Heinemann, Oxford, pp. 79–110

Ryan, Jason & Silvanto, Sari 2009, "The World Heritage List: The making and management of a brand", *Place Branding and Public Diplomacy*, vol. 5, no. 4, pp. 290–300.

Saito, Hiro 2011, "An actor-network theory of cosmopolitanism", *Sociological Theory*, vol. 29, no. 2, pp. 124–149.

Schlesinger, Philip 1990, "Rethinking the sociology of journalism: Source strategies and the limits of media centrism", in M Ferguson (ed.), *Public Communication: The New Imperatives*, Sage Publications, London, pp. 61–83.

Schudson, Michael 2005, "Four approaches to the sociology of news", in James Curran & Michael Gurevitch (eds), *Mass Media and Society*, 4th edn, Hodder Arnold, London, pp. 172–197.

Seaton, AV n.d., *The occupational influences and ideologies of travel writers: Freebies? Puffs? Vade Mecums? Or Belles Lettres?*, Centre for Travel and Tourism in Association with Business Education Publishers, Newcastle upon Tyne.

Takach, Geo 2014, "Visualizing Alberta: Duelling documentaries and bituminous sands", in Robert Boschman & Mario Tronto (eds), *Found in Alberta: Environmental Themes for the Anthropocene*, Wilfrid Laurier University Press, Waterloo, pp. 85–103.

Tourism Australia 2012, "International media program", Tourism Australia, 2 July, viewed 22 September 2012, www.media.australia.com/en-au/mediahosting/default_908.aspx

Tourism Australia 2009, "Visiting opinion leaders program", Tourism Australia, 6 June, viewed 15 January 2012, www.media.australia.com/en-au/mediahosting/default_1931. aspx

Tourism New Zealand 2009a, "100% Pure New Zealand facts and figures", viewed 17 February 2010, http://10yearsyoung.tourismnewzealand.com/files/10%20year%20anni versary%20of%20100%20Pure%20New%20Zealand%20campaign%20-%20Fact %20Sheet.pdf

Tourism New Zealand 2009b, "The birth of an icon: Brand evolution: The environmental promise: Kissing the shadow", *10 Years Young: 100% Pure New Zealand*, viewed 28 August 2012, http://10yearsyoung.tourismnewzealand.com/

Tourism New Zealand 2009c, "100% Pure New Zealand turns 10 years young", Media Release, 31 July, viewed 28 August 2012, www.newzealand.com/travel/media/press-releases/2009/7/tourism-news_100-pure-anniversary_press-release.cfm

Tourism New Zealand 2009d, "1+1=3", *10 years young: 100% Pure New Zealand*, viewed 28 August 2012, http://10yearsyoung.tourismnewzealand.com/

Tourism Tasmania 2011, "Visiting Journalist Program", *Tourism Tasmania Corporate*, viewed 19 August 2011, www.tourismtasmania.com.au/media/vjp

Travel Alberta 2011, *(remember to breathe) – Travel Alberta, Canada*, YouTube, 23 October, viewed 6 December 2014, www.youtube.com/watch?v=ThFCg0tBDck

van Ham, Peter 2008, "Place branding: The state of the art", *The Annals of the American Academy of Political and Social Science*, no. 616, pp. 126–149.

van Ham, Peter 2002, "Branding territory: Inside the wonderful worlds of PR and IR theory", *Millennium – Journal of International Studies* vol. 31. no. 2, pp. 249–269.

White, Jon & Hobsbawm, Julia 2007, "Public relations and journalism: The unquiet relationship – a view from the United Kingdom", *Journalism Practice*, vol. 1, no. 2, pp. 283–292.

Wolfsfeld, Gadi 1997, *Media and Political Conflict: News from the Middle East*, Cambridge UP, Cambridge.

Wood, Larry 1977, "Is Travel writing a growing profession", *Journalism Quarterly*, vol. 54, no.4, pp. 761–764.

WWF 2012, *Beyond Rio: New Zealand's environmental record since the original Earth Summit*, WWF, Wellington, viewed 3 September 2012, http://awsassets.wwfnz.panda.org/downloads/earth_summit_2012_v3.pdf

PART II
In the field

4   A place-branded discourse

When travel journalist Stephanie Pearson (2014) wrote in *Outside* magazine that Tasmania is something of a petri dish for the rest of the world, she probably had in mind its small size, clearly demarcated island geography, well-documented history of intense and protracted environmental conflict, and development or refinement of campaigning tactics that have become mainstays of environmental activism around the world. In combination with its very early adoption of place-branding, they are the same factors that make Tasmanian tourism an ideal case study for investigating the political operation of discursive strategies in jurisdictional reputation management during times of environmental conflict. A history of the evolution of Tasmania's place-branded discourse of accessible nature will facilitate a more nuanced analysis of the production of travel journalism in the rest of the case study.

Tasmania's "natural" branding can be traced back to tourism development and destination marketing by a state tourism office that attempted to capitalise on national and international publicity attracted to the island's wilderness by a campaign to save the wild Franklin River. In the 1980s and 1990s, the state's attempts to harness wilderness as a brand asset found its government struggling to subordinate expectations of *preservation* to its own desire for something closer to ideas of *conservation* as "the wise and efficient use of natural resources" (Merchant 2005 in Cox 2013, p. 44). This eventually led to a lexical shift in government discourse from "wilderness" to "nature". By representing tourism in World Heritage Areas and national parks as promoting environmental protection, then subsuming wilderness in a discourse of accessible nature that also embraced state forests using a frame I call "compatible sectors", the government constructed wilderness, ecotourism and recreational forestry as complementary people-centred projects. Such manoeuvring cast the government's tourism office and forestry corporation as colleagues in concern for the environment rather than adversaries in the fight for its protection. Over the long run, however, the tourism office disrupted the public–private, cross-sectoral and whole-of-government discourse of accessible nature by simultaneously continuing to capitalise on the marketing advantages of wilderness in the interests of its industry stakeholders. Thus, even as Tourism Tasmania and Forestry Tasmania were bound by place-branding, they were divided by wilderness. Ultimately, Tourism Tasmania's reluctance to relinquish the marketing advantages of wilderness would contribute to that symbol's continuing salience and set the stage for its re-politicisation in the first decade of the new century.

Accessible wilderness: Harnessing the PR power of protection

Tasmania – originally called Van Diemen's Land – is Australia's smallest state, a temperate island about the size of Ireland 240 kilometres off the continent's south-eastern corner separated from the mainland by a rough stretch of ocean called Bass Strait. It is reasonably decentralised but most of its 500,000 residents live in one of two population centres – the capital, Hobart, on the Derwent River close to the south-eastern coast, and Launceston, on the Tamar River close to the mid-north coast. The island's Aboriginal inhabitants arrived between 35,000 and 40,000 years ago. In the 1800s they suffered terribly at the hands of the British, who established Hobart – Australia's second-oldest city – as a penal settlement in 1804. Despite murders, dispossession, introduced disease and forced removal of children from their parents, a small Aboriginal community of mixed heritage survived and today actively promotes its culture and political interests. Nevertheless, a myth of total Tasmanian Aboriginal annihilation – originating partly out of recognition of white culpability and expressions of remorse – was for a long time incorporated into the island's international mediated identity.

Tasmania's dramatic and beautiful landscape has attracted international tourists since the 1870s (Emmett n.d.), leading to strong links between public sector tourism and national parks agencies from very early in the 20th century. Shortly after the inaugural Tasmanian Government Tourist and Information Bureau began operation in 1914, for example, its director, Evelyn Emmett, was also made an inaugural member of the Scenery Preservation Board (Walker 2005), which was established in 1915 to protect the "flora and tourism-value scenery" of the state's first parks (Crossley 2009, p. 3). By 1920 tourism had become a motivating concern of the Board (Quarmby 2006), and in 1929 Emmett began promoting the tourism advantages of bushwalking (Emmett n.d.). Indeed, for a time the Hobart Walking Club's *Tasmanian Tramp* magazine received financial assistance from the Tourism Bureau "in recognition...of the assistance outdoor recreational groups provided in promoting the interests of the Tourism Bureau" (Quarmby 2006, p. 126).

Despite its attraction as a tourism destination, however, Tasmania struggled economically. To this day, its population remains on average poor and undereducated by Australian standards, despite a thriving arts sector and notable achievements in the physical sciences. Traditionally it has relied on agriculture and extractive industries such as mining and forestry for export income. In the mid-20th century extensive dam construction created cheap hydro-electric power that attracted heavy industries, and a policy of what came to be known as hydro-industrialisation eventually led to fierce environmental conflict. In the early 1970s proposals by the state government's Hydro Electric Commission (HEC) to inundate a beautiful and unique body of water in the remote and mountainous south-west of the island called Lake Pedder led to the formation of what is believed to be the first Green political party in the world. Environmental activism did not save Lake Pedder, but a decade later a much more sophisticated campaign by the Wilderness Society to protect the nearby Franklin River from damming, led by Bob Brown, brought widespread media attention to the vast wilderness through which it flowed.

In December 1980, as concern about a Tasmanian government agency's proposals to dam the Franklin was mounting, Tasmania's Department of Tourism produced a marketing strategy for the following five years. Although the department at this time was not concerned so much with making tourism pay a return to the community as with simply helping it become self-sustaining (Department of Tourism 1980), it tied its recommendations in the report to existing objectives that qualified support for protection and preservation of the natural environment upon which the industry depended by linking it to government policy:

> OBJECTIVES: (Extracted from Tasmanian Tourism Strategy Plan)... 4. To develop a tourism industry that is compatible with the Tasmanian socio-economic life-style, and with the Government policy in relation to the protection and preservation of the State's natural and man-made heritage. (Department of Tourism 1980, Appendix C, parenthetical text part of original document)

As Lester (2007, p. 29) notes in her study of media and environmental conflict in Tasmania, "Words like 'wilderness' and 'nature', alongside others like 'progress' and 'development', produce meanings and understandings that shape fundamental decision-making and actions". The above extract sets many of the discursive parameters of the government's future tourism–environment politics by relating protection to non-specific state government judgements and policies that would soon facilitate the framing of wilderness as a tourism commodity.

In the Australian summer of 1982-83, during a blockade of early work associated with the construction of the dam intended to inundate the Franklin, Brown and 1271 others were arrested for their activism (Lester and Hutchins 2009). Also in 1982, the Franklin and huge tracts of surrounding national park were inscribed on the World Heritage List. In 1983 the High Court of Australia ruled that the Australian government had the power to prevent the Tasmanian government from damming the Franklin. The judgement invoked a normative cosmopolitan discourse that explicitly framed "vital habitats" of "regional eco-systems" in terms of global and institutionalised "intense concern about the conservation of the world's resources" and "support for the concept of the 'Common Heritage of Mankind'" (Murphy 1983 in Palmer and Robb 2004, p. 30).[1]

Within months of the High Court judgement, the Tasmanian government commissioned a study into the tourism potential of the south-west that, among other things, was directed to find ways to expose tourists to the state's wilderness (Evers Consulting 1984, Appendix 2, p. 1). The government moved so quickly because it was keen to take advantage of the attention that news reporting of the Franklin River campaign had delivered:

> Wilderness does represent an opportunity to increase visitation, extend duration of stay and head more towards genuine destination tourism. It does so because of the publicity which has surrounded it over the past decade and because, as we have said, that which is available – and potentially accessible – is genuinely unique. The spectacular gorges, rapids, rainforest, high country, beaches, rivers and so on are of immense potential appeal to tourists.
>
> (Evers Consulting 2004, p. 53)

The *South West Tasmania Tourism Study: Main Report* (1984) (the Evers report) was prepared by Evers Consulting, which was led by Nick Evers, a former Head of the Tasmanian Premier's Department (1975–82) who would later become Tasmania's Minister for Tourism (1988–89). In a section headed "Wilderness", the Evers report acknowledged the advance collateral publicity for tourism in Tasmania's south-west that had been generated by media reports of the Franklin dam campaign but also the vulnerability of wilderness, which, in accordance with the discourse of tourism as business, was itself now referred to as a "product":

> The challenge here is the extremely delicate one of seeking to devise strategies that will expand the market without destroying or diminishing the quality of the very product which will attract visitors. Not all of that which is available is – or could, or should – be readily accessible and some of that which is accessible is extremely vulnerable.
>
> (Evers Consulting 2004, p. 53)

Echoing the terminology of the 1980 tourism report referred to earlier by writing of their need to consider "the two principal elements of the product – the natural and the man-made" (Evers Consulting 1984, p. 52), the Evers report's authors demonstrated their awareness of the social constructedness of wilderness:

> For purposes of editorial convenience, the natural element will be described here as the "wilderness" experience, notwithstanding the fact that "wilderness" is essentially a state of mind and means different things to different people (e.g. many people already describe the opportunity to see wilderness as a highlight of their visit to Tasmania when, in fact, what they have seen would bear no relationship to wilderness as defined by Kirkpatrick and others).
>
> (Evers Consulting 1984, p. 52, parenthetical text
> part of original document)

In 1985 the government called for tenders for a private operator to construct and run commercial huts on the Overland Track (Crossley 2009, p. 35) – an existing 65 kilometre public walking trail through the centre of the Cradle Mountain–Lake St Clair National Park in the Tasmanian Wilderness World Heritage Area.

The tender was won by Sydney architect Ken Latona and Sydney town planner Joan Masterman. The two had already worked together on reports into the siting and design of buildings in fragile environments in mainland Australia, and Latona described his initial response to Tasmania's landscape in reverential terms (Latona 1994). However, by prefacing his discussion of his venture into Tasmanian tourism with the observation that the landscape had already been much modified, and that such modification had been unsympathetic to the natural environment, he positioned himself as educator and mentor rather than a developer (Latona 1994, p. 32).

The establishment of the Cradle Huts ecotourism operation was a profound change in the use of national parks and the source of deep conflict in the Tasmanian community: "Critics recalled national parks' democratic origins and argued that the prospect of huts located on public land being locked against other walkers was 'disgraceful'" (Quarmby 2006, p. 280). In Latona's commentary on his reasoning, however, the discourse of Tasmanian tourism as the business of accessible wilderness was expressed in the philosophically cathartic and commercially penetrating language of reverse equity:

> When the chance came unexpectedly in 1985 to immerse myself in a place still largely untouched, I was nervous. As part of Tasmania's World Heritage Area, how could anybody "design" for this place… Fortunately the terms "sustainability" and "eco-tourism" had not been popularised or commercialised (so I was not able to hide behind the terms) and I was only able to justify my decision to proceed on the basis that these four small walkers huts would provide "equity of access" for people without the skills, endurance or confidence to experience by immersion the immenseness and importance of this place.
>
> (Latona 1994, p. 32)

From accessible wilderness to accessible nature

Although the state tourism office already had a visiting journalist program (VJP) at this time, its international component had until recently been largely dependent on the Australian Tourist Commission (ATC). In 1993, however, a new public relations practitioner with journalism experience in the United States, Delia Nicholls, was recruited to introduce a more strategic approach. No longer would the international component of the tourism department's VJP simply respond to requests for hosted visits initiated by the ATC or journalists themselves. Henceforth, in combination with on-ground marketing and public relations representatives in key overseas markets, the VJP would actively pursue international personalities and trend-setting travel journalists who could provide coverage in the kind of high-circulation, high-end publications whose readers would respond to what would become known as Tasmania's tourism brand attributes, the most significant of which were its natural attractions. Such influential writers would be unlikely to come to Tasmania of their own accord but would have to be wooed, sometimes over a number of years (Nicholls, D. 2009, pers. comm., 9 March). It was a strategy that weighed the risks of trying simultaneously to meet the needs of the journalist, the public relations practitioner and the tourism industry against the benefits of a positive story (Nicholls, D. 2009, pers. comm., 9 March).

By 1994, Tasmania was considered well-credentialed enough as an ecotourism destination to host the World Congress on Adventure Travel and Ecotourism. The four-day congress, which was attended by 540 delegates, 9 per cent of whom were from the media (Busch 1994), was a critical discourse moment in Tasmanian tourism public relations – a period when specific events would challenge "'established' discursive positions" (Carvalho 2008, p. 166). In advance of the congress, the state tourism office prepared a document in which it stated that travel journalists "need[ed] to understand and represent our product correctly to different markets" (Tourism in Natural Areas Project Team 1993) and also recommended that the tourism office ensure "all images are acceptable to the government agency responsible for administering the locations" (Tourism in Natural Areas Project Team 1993, original emphasis). In an appendix, it reproduced a note from the Forestry Commission that included among five experiences it considered to be special to state forests "[o]pportunities to learn about issues relating to forests and their management, including contentious areas that people have heard about in the media" (Tourism in Natural Areas Project Team 1993, Appendix B). At the congress itself, "ecotourism" was strategically deployed in government discourse as both a right of commercial access to wilderness and a badge of honour for what was now the government business enterprise Forestry Tasmania (see Hodgman 1994 and Groom in *The Mercury* 1994e), which was promoting the recreational and adventure tourism opportunities available in its forest reserves. Early in the proceedings, Tasmania's Minister for Tourism, Sport and Recreation, Peter Hodgman, delivered a speech that exemplified this change (Hodgman 1994, p. 13–14). Accessible wilderness was still a catchcry – for example, "We have a duty and responsibility to manage these [wilderness] areas and make it accessible…" (Hodgman 1994, p. 13) – and framing I call "the ecotourism solution" was clear – for example, "It is through understanding and appreciation that these places will be preserved, which is the power of ecotourism" (Hodgman 1994, p. 13; see also reference to ecological modernisation below). However, nature rather than wilderness was increasingly prominent terminology, state forests were explicitly referenced as potential ecotourism venues and, notably, there was an overt government appeal to an imagined consumerist cosmopolitan community – that is, "We are part of a global community and tourism has no boundaries" (Hodgman 1994, p. 13).

New discourses emerge through a combination of existing discourses (Fairclough 2003, p. 127). Following the 1983 High Court decision to protect the Franklin River, the discourse of accessible wilderness had emerged as a combination of the discourses of accessible scenery, transformative wilderness and reverse egalitarianism. Now a discourse promoting tourism in state forests was joined to the discourse of accessible wilderness in a discourse of accessible nature. On the afternoon of the opening day of the congress, however, high-profile Tasmanian environmentalist Bob Brown delivered a paper that attacked Forestry Tasmania as having "now drawn the sheepskin of ecotourism around its shoulders" (Brown, B. 1994, p. 12). The theme of the congress was "Discovering the great outdoors: The road to our sustainable future". It is unclear whether Tasmania's tourism department had any input into the choice of theme, but shortly before the congress the government had announced that it was proceeding with the construction of a road through an area on the west coast (Brown, B. 1994; *Mercury* 1994b, 1994d) that Brown had christened the Tarkine in honour of its original Aboriginal inhabitants (Buchman 2008, p. 117). In his speech at the conference, Brown called for a halt to road construction, and the following day the Wilderness Society staged a protest outside the congress venue calling for ecotourism operators to join forces in campaigning against logging (*Mercury* 1994d). On the closing night of the congress, 300 delegates signed a petition to the Australian prime minister asking him to halt logging in Tasmania's high-conservation-value forests (*Mercury* 1994b).

In the introduction to the published collected speeches of the congress, written by Richard Busch, editor of the conference's US co-sponsor *National Geographic Traveler* magazine, Brown's speech was described as "one of the most stirring presentations of the entire congress" (Busch 1994, p. 1). Busch reported Brown's criticism of the Tasmanian government for permitting old-growth logging and attempting to justify "roads through pristine areas for the stated purpose of encouraging ecotourism" (Busch 1994, p. 1). The implication was that this travel journalist had rejected a government's attempts to use ecotourism to frame forestry and tourism as compatible (a frame I label "compatible sectors").

The accessible nature discourse in Tasmania's whole-of-government context included elements of cosmopolitan concern for the environment exclusive of concern about the state's forestry practices, which in turn were framed as environmentally sustainable and delivering community benefits in addition to revenue, such as managed reserves for recreation and adventure pursuits. Stamou and Paraskevopoulos (2006) write that nature-based tourism encompasses but is not confined to ecotourism, where ecotourism is consistent with what Maarten Hajer (1995) describes as ecological modernisation, because rather than protecting nature by banning activity it protects it by generating money that contributes to its management and builds local support for conservation projects. Brown's discourse, by contrast, was more closely aligned with what Dryzek describes as green rationalism, which accommodates activism and political conflict. In addition to Green party politics, green rationalism acknowledges that:

> [p]olitical pressure can be exerted at a distance upon the state. Here, social movements have at their disposal a number of instruments. They include the rhetorical ability to change the terms of policy debate; creation of fear of political instability; the production of ideas; and the embarrassment of governments.
>
> (Dryzek 1997, p. 189)

At the World Congress, Brown's discourse also included elements of what Dryzek describes as ecological romanticism in its passion, appeals to the emotions and attribution of agency to nature:

> Ecotourism, like being Green, like being in love with this planet Earth, is not an easy concept in this age of materialism. But it is a vital, ethical concept. Our task is to foster it, to protect it from those who would corrupt its meaning, and to enjoy it as a term which accords the Earth the respect which we human beings owe to it and to ourselves.
>
> (Brown 1994, p. 12)

For Brown, "genuine ecotourism" led the way towards humans regulating them-selves to ensure the landscape was not "progressively distressed or destroyed by tourism" (Brown, B. 1994, p. 12). Thus, he was opposed to some commercial tourism ventures that sought access to protected areas. Whereas the government tended to commodify cosmopolitan concern, Brown's ecotourism discourse politicised it.

In local news the representation of events at the congress was different from that of *National Geographic Traveler*'s Busch. Although *The Mercury* included reports of the protest and the petition, it balanced the former on the same page with a separate short interview with Forestry Tasmania's managing director headlined "Forestry Tasmania 'ally of green tourism'" (*Mercury* 1994c). A month after the congress, *The Mercury* praised the Tasmanian organisers of the event but its text delegitimised the congress and, by extension, cosmopolitical concern for the state's unprotected environment by republishing criticisms of the congress's internationally based management that the newspaper said had already appeared in a front-page article in Australia's tourism industry magazine *Travel Trade*, which had described it as "the shadowy Coloradobased [sic.] Adventure Travel Society" (*The Mercury* 1994a).

From wild to mild

Featured among the field trips offered to delegates at the World Congress on Adventure Travel and Ecotourism was a second enterprise by Latona and Masterman (Australian Tourist Commission, Department of Tourism, Sport and Recreation Tasmania & the Adventure Travel Society Inc.1994, p. 2) incorpo-rating a walk through a national park – one that was more accessible than Cradle Mountain–Lake St Clair. The Freycinet Peninsula, on the island's east coast, boasted tranquil, often-sunny weather, far-less-rugged topography than the Overland Track, fascinating Aboriginal and French-seafaring history, and one of the most postcard-perfect beaches in the world, Wineglass Bay. Just outside the park, the pair had built Friendly Beaches Lodge, and Masterman would ultimately choose this lodge and walk as the tourism product she would retain and continue operating when her business partnership with Latona ended a few years later.

Tourism Tasmania's international public relations practitioner at the time, Nicholls, had no doubt that Latona and Masterman's determination to create and maintain ecotourism experiences she felt respected the environment and promoted sustainable tourism practice was genuine, impressive and valuable. On her appointment to Tourism Tasmania, she had recognised the attraction of natural experiences that could so expertly pamper international travel journalists body, soul and conscience. It was the beginning of an informal public relations partnership between a government agency and tourism entrepreneurs that would create an enduring international profile for Tasmania as a sustainable tourist destination:

> I think Tasmania wouldn't have an ecotourism industry – and still doesn't really have that much of a legitimate set of tourism products that are eco-friendly – without Ken Latona and Joan Masterman. They were the people who really set us on that track, apart from the national parks. In 1994, Ken and Joan had already been in business maybe six or eight years by the time we had that ecotourism conference where I think this state really, really recognised that it needed to go down that ecotourism marketing angle, but without Ken and Joan's product we wouldn't have had any credibility in that market because they were the only two who had really done the hard yards. They had really… And he was very generous with the [Visiting Journalist] Program. He always gave us free media visits. He gave free for staff to give them an understanding of his product, he gave freely to the journalists, he never, ever quibbled about that. He took helicopters sometimes without charging us; he was incredibly generous – the most generous of any of them.
> (Nicholls 2009, pers. comm., 9 March)

The struggle among interest groups for ownership of the meaning and stories of wilderness, the complexities associated with the deployment of the word in marketing, public relations, news and travel journalism, the discursive strategies of a government determined to present forestry and ecotourism as compatible, and the spread of ecotourism from the windy, rainy western mountains to the sunny, sandy eastern beaches had seen "wilderness" increasingly give way to "nature" in Tasmanian public relations discourse. Yet even as this transition proceeded, wilderness would continue to appear in Tasmanian government tourism marketing, retaining its power to promote by suffusing the island's tourism and state-of-origin branding with marketable clean, green cachet.

Nature as brand

In the month of the World Congress on Adventure Travel and Ecotourism, the Tasmanian tourism office commissioned the "largest ever qualitative consumer research" among interstate Australians (Tasmanian Department of Tourism, Sport and Recreation 1995, p. 8). According to the office, this research established the island's "unique and breathtaking natural beauty set within a clean, green environment" and its "diversity of landscapes offering nature-based experience (including wildlife) which are within easy reach" to be its strongest competitive advantages (Tasmanian Department of Tourism, Sport and Recreation 1995, p. 8). Then, in 1995, the tourism office launched its new positioning – the logo of a stylised Tasmanian tiger emerging through grass at the edge of a stream and the slogan "TASMANIA Discover your natural state" (Tasmanian Department of Tourism, Sport and Recreation 1995, p. 8). Reviewing this two years later, Tourism Tasmania comfortably accommodated wilderness within its discourse of accessible nature:

> Tasmania was re-defined as a destination for an intelligent audience that sought hands-on, physically active vacation experiences. A holiday for thinkers and doers promising the unexpected in a natural environment.
>
> Ian Kidd's design depicting the thylacine [(Tasmanian tiger)] in a wilderness environment is a symbol of this experience, expressing discovery, surprise, intrigue, the unexpected, tranquillity and natural.
>
> (Tourism Tasmania 1997, p. 12)

Such an analysis ignored the fact that the Tasmanian tiger is extinct. Instead, the animal was invoked as evidence of the quality of Tasmania's wilderness – a wilderness so remote that it might still harbour creatures not verifiably observed for more than 60 years. The logo was soon adopted by the entire Tasmanian public sector, yet for all its visual and emotional appeal, the balance it struck between the promotion of access and the promise of purity was as precarious as it was commercially tantalising.

Also in 1997, Tourism Tasmania recommended an extension of its branding under the banner of Brand Tasmania in one of its own publications and included the state's forest industries in the purview:

> In more global terms, Tasmania's unique point-of-difference stems from the same set of attributes which underpin our tourism industry. Our position in the Southern Ocean which is the basis of our unique natural features also provides us with a largely unpolluted and disease free environment and the basis for our developing and increasingly globally competitive agriculture, aquaculture and forest based industries.
>
> (Tourism Tasmania 1997, p. 18)

Asserting the brand essence "Tasmania is natural" (Department of Premier and Cabinet 2006), the Tasmanian government in the early 2000s promoted accessible nature, embraced the forestry industry and sought to distinguish the state's exports and services in global markets as the products of a "clean environment", "clean air", "clean soil", "clean communities", "clean oceans", "pure waters" and "clean, green solutions" (Department of Premier and Cabinet 2006). As Hansen explains, "Invoking nature/the natural in advertising and other public discourse is a key rhetorical device of ideology in the sense that referencing something as 'of nature' or as 'natural' serves to hide what are essentially partisan arguments and interest and to invest them with moral or universal authority and legitimacy" (2010, pp. 156–157). In a summary of the evolution of Tasmania's brand published in 2006, the government paid tribute to a strictly delineated "succession of conservation debates, starting with the decision to flood Lake Pedder and stopping the damming of the Franklin River" for putting "Tasmania and its environment firmly on the international stage" (Department of Premier and Cabinet 2006). In the years since the government had embraced the state's wilderness, World Heritage listing and the natural advantages of remote islandness had enveloped the destination in a marketable aura of purity. Thus, despite the discursive shift to accessible nature documented in this chapter, wilderness would continue to feature in Tourism Tasmania's marketing and public relations throughout the first decade of the 2000s.

Conclusion

Prior to the 1983 High Court decision to protect the Franklin River, Tasmanian tourism was largely in the business of choosing places for visitors to gaze upon. Early in the century, tourism was a motivating concern of the Scenery Preservation Board, whose proposals for reserves "were submitted to government departments such as Mines, Forestry and later the Hydro-Electric Commission for approval" (Castles 2006). But Tasmania's Wilderness World Heritage Area was a very different matter. Its inscription on the World Heritage List in 1982 not only created the conditions by which the country's High Court could prevent new hydroelectric development within its boundaries; it also fundamentally changed the relationship between Tasmanian tourism and nature. The term "nature" can encompass both "scenery" and "wilderness", but it is impossible to disentangle the Wilderness World Heritage Area's use-value to tourism from UNESCO's evaluation of the region as remote (see Lester 2007) and thereby largely removed from what Urry (2002) refers to as the collective tourist gaze.

There are two reasons that Tasmanian tourism was originally able to appropriate the term "wilderness" for a multitude of commercial purposes outside the WHA that many would argue have nothing to do with the concept. First, World Heritage listing gave these claims a convoluted marketing credibility (see Ryan and Silvanto 2009 for an interesting discussion of the World Heritage List as an exercise in place-branding). If concrete evidence of this is needed, it can be found in an express recommendation by the Tasmanian government and the tourism industry that the Australian Tourist Commission's images of Australia "need to be enhanced to not only reflect the 'sun, surf and outback' but also the nation's other natural qualities and difference, including world heritage" (Tasmanian Government, Tourism Tasmania and Tourism Council Australia (Tasmanian Branch) n.d., p. 24). Secondly, the environment movement's Franklin dam blockade gifted the tourism industry a reserve of advance publicity that it built upon over subsequent years. By contrast, Forestry Tasmania had nothing to gain from the concept of wilderness except, perhaps, the ability to dilute criticism by claiming that sufficient wilderness – or the only true wilderness – was already protected (Lester 2007). Paradoxically perhaps, the government's shift from accessible wilderness to accessible nature left marginally more discursive space for the re-emergence of notions of wilderness as remote, untrammelled, mythic, normatively charged and worthy of cosmopolitan concern. The importance of wilderness to tourism marketing meant that many international travel journalists visiting the state would encounter a version of it in at least one of its many stages of commodification, engage with it and perhaps mediate its strengths and vulnerabilities (McGaurr, Tranter and Lester 2014). And just as the government had been able to leverage off the publicity the environment movement had garnered for wilderness in the 1980s, so the environment movement in the first decade of the 2000s would find ways to gain access to the media for its own messages by taking advantage of recognition for wilderness maintained internationally to a considerable degree by Tourism Tasmania's marketing and the response of travel journalists.

Note

1   In Australia's federal system, the Commonwealth government can override state government decisions in some instances. Where a dispute arises, it is resolved by the High Court of Australia.

References

Australian Tourist Commission, Department of Tourism, Sport and Recreation Tasmania & the Adventure Travel Society Inc. 1994, *Guide to Field Trips Tasmania: "Ecotourism in Practice": 1994 World Congress on Adventure Travel and Ecotourism*.

Brown, Bob 1994, "Ecotourism or wreckotourism?", in *Proceedings of the 1994 World Congress on Adventure Travel and Ecotourism*, The Adventure Travel Society Inc., Englewood, pp. 11–12.

Buchman, Greg 2008, *Tasmania's Wilderness Battles: A History*, Allen & Unwin, Crows Nest.

Busch, Richard 1994, "Introduction to collected speeches, presentations, and reports that came before the 1994 World Congress on Adventure Travel and Ecotourism held in Hobart, Tasmania November 7–10", in *Proceedings of the 1994 World Congress on Adventure Travel and Ecotourism*, The Adventure Travel Society Inc., Englewood, pp. 1–2.

Carvalho, Anabela 2008, "Media(ted) discourses and society: Rethinking the framework of critical discourse analysis", *Journalism Studies*, vol. 9, no. 2, pp. 161–177.

Castles, Gerard 2006, "Scenery preservation board", in Alison Alexander (ed.), *Companion to Tasmanian History*, viewed 11 September 2012, www.utas.edu.au/library/companion_to_tasmanian_history/S/Scenery.htm

Crossley, Louise 2009, *Paradoxes of Protection: Evolution of the Tasmanian Parks and Wildlife Service and National Parks and Reserved Lands System*, Australian Greens, viewed 18 January 2010, http://christine-milne.greensmps.org.au/content/paradoxes-protection-managing-tasmanias-parks

Department of Premier and Cabinet 2006, *Tasmanian Brand Guide*, Government of Tasmania, Hobart.

Department of Tourism 1980, *Tourism Marketing Strategy for Tasmania 1980–1985*, Government of Tasmania, Hobart.

Dryzek, John S 1997, *The Politics of the Earth: Environmental Discourses*, Oxford University Press, Oxford.

Emmett, Evelyn Temple n.d., "History of Tasmania's Tourist Bureau", unpublished memoir.

Evers Consulting Services Pty Ltd. 1984, *South West Tasmania Tourism Study: Main Report*, Evers Consulting Services Pty Ltd.

Fairclough, Norman 2003, *Analysing Discourse: Textual Analysis for Social Research*, Routledge, London.

Hajer, Maarten 1995, *The Politics of Environmental Discourse: Ecological Modernization and the Policy Process*, Clarendon Press, Oxford.

Hansen, Anders 2010, *Environment, Media and Communication*, Routledge, London.

Hodgman, Peter 1994, "Welcome to Tasmania", in *Proceedings of the 1994 World Congress on Adventure Travel and Ecotourism*, The Adventure Travel Society Inc., Englewood, pp. 13–14.

Latona, Ken 1994, "Cradle Huts and Freycinet Experience", in *Proceedings of the Sustainable Design and Ecotourism Seminar*, Department of Tourism, Sport and Recreation Tasmania, Hobart, pp. 32–33.

Lester, Libby 2007, *Giving Ground: Media and Environmental Conflict in Tasmania*, Quintus, Hobart.

Lester, Libby & Hutchins, Brett 2009, "Power games: Environmental protest, news media and the internet", *Media, Culture & Society*, vol. 31, no. 4, pp. 579–595.

McGaurr, Lyn, Tranter, Bruce & Lester, Libby 2014, "Wilderness and the Politics of Place Branding", *Environmental Communication: A Journal of Nature and Culture*, doi: 10.1080/17524032.2014.919947.

Mercury, The 1994a, "Hollow echoes from eco event in Hobart", 4 December, p. 9.

Mercury, The 1994b, "Ecotourism summit ends with anti-logging petition", 12 November, p. 7.

Mercury, The 1994c, "Forestry Tasmania 'ally of green tourism'", 11 November, p. 7.

Mercury, The 1994d, "Warning of fight ahead to protect environment", 11 November, p. 7.

Mercury, The 1994e, "Groom plea to unlock wild areas", 8 November, p. 10.

Palmer, Alice & Robb, Cairo AR (eds) 2004, *International Environmental Law Reports Volume 4: International Environmental Law in National Courts*, University of Cambridge Press, Cambridge.

Pearson, Stephanie 2014, "Surviving Tasmania", *Outside*, 20 January, viewed 29 August 2014, www.outsideonline.com/adventure-travel/australia-pacific/australia/The-Devil-Made-Me-Do-It-Travel-Tasmania.html

Quarmby, Debbie 2006, "The politics of parks: The history of Tasmania's national parks 1885–2005", unpublished doctoral thesis, viewed 27 November 2009, http://research repository.murdoch.edu.au/470/

Ryan, Jason & Silvanto, Sari 2009, "The World Heritage List: The making and management of a brand", *Place Branding and Public Diplomacy*, vol. 5, no. 4, pp. 290–300.

Stamou, Anastasia G & Paraskevopoulos, Stephanos 2006, "Representing protected areas: A critical discourse analysis of tourism destination building in a Greek travel magazine", *International Journal of Tourism Research*, vol. 8, pp. 431–449.

Tasmanian Department of Tourism, Sport and Recreation 1995, *Strategies for Growth*, Tasmanian State Government, Hobart.

Tasmanian Government, Tourism Tasmania & Tourism Council Australia (Tasmanian Branch) n.d., *Tourism 21: A Partnership for Tourism Success. Strategic Business Plan for*

Tourism 1997–2000, Tasmanian Government and Tourism Council Australia (Tasmanian Branch), Hobart.

Tourism Tasmania 1997, *Brand Tasmania: Marketing Tasmania as a Unique Holiday Destination*, Tourism Tasmania, Hobart.

Tourism in Natural Areas Project Team 1993, "Ecotourism and adventure travel marketing in Tasmania: 'Images & media formats'", Tourism Tasmania, Hobart.

Walker, Marian 2005, "Tourism", in Elison Alexander (ed.), *The Companion to Tasmanian History*, Centre For Tasmanian Historical Studies, University of Tasmania, Hobart, pp. 364–365.

5   The authority

In this chapter I argue that when governments are engaged in environmental conflict, place-branding can be instrumentalised as publicly funded tourism offices try simultaneously to promote the brand and shield it from media scrutiny. However, I also reveal factors that can contribute to an alternative outcome. I begin the chapter by exploring ways in which Tasmania's Visiting Journalist Program (VJP) in the early 2000s can be theorised as an attempt to secure control over the flow of information. I then analyse a broader marketing response that relies for its effectiveness on blurred editorial boundaries between advertising and journalism. Following this, I consider networks and structures that can contribute to the absence of controversy in travel journalism that does not rely on financial support from tourism offices or commercial tourism operators.

Regulating the flow of information

During the first decade of the 2000s, travel coverage of Tasmania in prestigious publications was listed among the "highlights" in Tourism Tasmania's annual reports. The tourism office was comfortable with using public funds to attract travel journalists to the island. Tourism Tasmania stated publicly that the aim of its VJP was to secure positive coverage for the state (Tourism Tasmania 2009), and the following comment from its senior public relations practitioner in 2009 expresses a belief that the maintenance of journalistic integrity is compatible with prior agreement about what objectives will be met by the published article:

> Obviously it's not our place to impinge on journalistic integrity and them pursuing a story, but particularly when we're funding a trip I think that we have to have mutual objectives about what we're trying to do. And I think for most of the journalists that we deal with they completely understand and respect that they're here as the guests of Tasmania and the Tasmanian government and the Tasmanian taxpayer money, then the agreed objectives of the story are what needs to be the focus.
>
> (Dowty 2009, pers. comm., 3 June)

Although most of the six public relations practitioners I interviewed who had direct experience in Tourism Tasmania's VJP appeared uncomfortable discussing forestry matters, in other respects their confidence in the ability of hosted visits to procure positive stories suggests that, to their knowledge, negative comment in travel journalism was genuinely rare.

International travel journalists who participated in the VJP were far more likely than hosted domestic travel journalists to be guided by a Tourism Tasmania representative throughout their itinerary. Comprehensive, crowded itineraries and attentive VJP guides were represented by public relations practitioners as helping ensure travel journalists had experiences of which the destination could be proud, as the following quote attests:

> One of the comments always is that there's too much in each day. The thing with the international journalists is that they're not here for very long but they want to see so much, and it's quite often they think that Tasmania's small so it's hard to explain to them that you actually can't fit all of that in three days. So they don't have a lot of spare time. No. Because often if they're an international journalist their guide's with them, and then their guide takes them out for dinner and because they're not familiar with the place, and if you think about it, if you're in a foreign city that you don't know and you head out for tea somewhere, you could end up anywhere. And, you know, while we've got them here you want to expose them to the good, the best food and wine, or the restaurants that best suit their target audience, so you either make bookings for them to do that and send them to those places either independently or with a guide.
>
> (2009, pers. comm., 16 March)

For many international travel journalists, this kind of attention made the job of researching the destination simple and enjoyable, and Tourism Tasmania's VJP was regularly praised by those it hosted or assisted. Comments by the *Observer's* Jamie Doward describe the kind of hospitality hosted international travel journalist could receive:

> It was absolutely superb. We were lucky enough to have a woman [in England] who was working for an agency for the Tasmanian tourist board who escorted us there and took care of things, made sure that we flew into Melbourne and stayed overnight before flying on to Tasmania, which broke the journey up a bit. And everything was very, very well planned. The Tasmanian tourist board, as soon as we got there, had a fantastic itinerary and made sure that we really did see the whole of Tasmania – fantastic bits of Hobart and then the really remote bits as well, and got a really good taste of the island, because we sampled everything. I think, in the six days we crammed in more than I would expect to cram into a couple of weeks... This woman was unusual because normally when I do a travel trip I'm on my own or with a girlfriend or something but this one was unusual in that I was part of a press crew and those

can be a bit tedious. But it was fantastic, as I say, because they'd put so much thought into making sure we weren't just hanging around, we were always moving around the island seeing the full sights and its full beauty… [O]nce we got to Tasmania the Tasmanian tourist board guy was on hand and took over as well, and he had fantastic local knowledge, obviously, having grown up on the island himself and, you know, was always with us to take us around.

(Doward 2009, pers. comm., 26 August)

In the case of travel journalists who had an interest in what one public relations practitioner described as "issues" rather than "experiences" (2009, pers. comm., 16 March), however, the VJP was cautious. In describing their response to such situations, some public relations practitioners found it more difficult than their senior counterpart quoted earlier to reconcile institutional expectations of positive coverage with their own understanding of journalistic integrity. Ambivalence or professional anxiety about travel journalist interest in forestry matters were evident in the talk of a number of interviewed public relations practitioners who had worked in the tourism VJP (see below).

If the publicity value of the publication or the individual writer was high enough for the VJP to host a journalist interested in issues as well as tourism experiences, crowded itineraries could make it difficult for him or her to find time to pursue other avenues of inquiry. This was the experience of British freelance journalist Paul Miles after he alerted the VJP to his interest in a pulp mill proposed for the state's premier wine tourism region prior to visiting the state to research stories for *The Financial Times* and *Condé Nast Traveller* late in 2007:

I think that because the tourism people were possibly anxious about what I might see or do I think they pretty much kept me as busy as possible…

(Miles 2009, pers. comm., 9 March)

Controlling access to sources and frames

Authorities' efforts to manage the access of the media to sources in times of conflict are part of their attempts to control meanings in the public sphere (see Wolfsfeld 1997). In December 2007 national news magazine the *Bulletin* published accusations by prominent Tasmanian novelist and commentator Richard Flanagan that Tourism Tasmania was intimidating staff into refusing to put travel journalists in touch with him (Fleming 2007). For more than three years, battles between Flanagan and the Tasmanian government over forestry practices had been played out in the local, national and international news media. In March 2004, in the lead-up to an Australian election in which the forestry dispute would become an issue of intense media interest, the NGO People for the Ethical Treatment of Animals called on Britons to boycott holidays to Tasmania in protest against its logging practices. The campaign was supported by British Liberal Democrat spokesman for the environment Norman Baker, who introduced a parliamentary motion in favour of the boycott and persuaded dozens of his Westminster colleagues to sign a petition calling on Tasmania to stop old-growth logging. Foreign correspondents and local journalists wrote about the proposed boycott for the British press (Fickling 2004; Woolf 2004), and the *Guardian* published opinion pieces by Flanagan and Greg Barns, a political commentator living in Tasmania. Barns opposed the boycott on the basis that it was a distraction from pressing Tasmanian issues of high unemployment, low education levels and a raft of other social problems (Barns 2004). By contrast, in his piece entitled "Paradise lost – with napalm", Flanagan framed the issue as one of cosmopolitical concern:

> [I]n an Australian election year, with the forests emerging as a major issue, [it] form[s] part of a chorus of international condemnation that shows Australians that the forests are not just a natural resource but are globally significant wild lands.

> (Flanagan 2004a)

But Flanagan also articulated a more detailed thesis: "in the lineaments of the struggle in a distant island, it is possible to see a larger battle, the same battle the world over – that between truth and power" (Flanagan 2004a). The forestry conflict, he said, had created a "subtle fear" that "stifled dissent" and was "conducive to the abuse of power. To question or to comment is to invite the possibility of ostracism and unemployment" (Flanagan 2004a). In July the same year, following the death of a former premier who had also been a tourism minister extremely popular with the tourism industry, Flanagan criticised the man's forestry legacy in an article in a large interstate broadsheet (Flanagan 2004b). Two months after that he published a travel article in the *New York Times* that included three paragraphs on the logging of Tasmania's native forests (Flanagan 2004c).

In December that year, the private logging company Gunns – at the time Forestry Tasmania's biggest customer – sued the Wilderness Society, five of its members and others for millions of dollars in an attempt to halt activism, instigating a protracted legal battle that would make headlines for many years; and in February 2005 Gunns publicly announced its plans to build a pulp mill in the state's premier wine-tourism region, the Tamar Valley, provoking opposition from environmentalists but also wine makers, food producers and restaurateurs, some of whom had long-standing relationships with Tourism Tasmania's VJP (Denholm 2007; Alps, D 2009, pers. comm., 19 March; see Chapter 6). In an article Flanagan published about Gunns in May 2007 entitled "Out of control: The tragedy of Tasmania's forests" (2007a), a version of which was published in June that year in Britain's *Telegraph Magazine* under the title "Paradise razed" (2007b), he further developed a frame I call "warlike conflagration", which had appeared in a more limited version in 2004 in his *Guardian* commentary and *New York Times* travel piece, and also appeared in texts by the environment movement. This frame generally refers to the use of napalm to burn the forest floor after logging, and in his 2007 articles Flanagan invoked three catastrophic wars in his descriptions of continued clear-fell logging of old-growth forests in the Styx Valley (see following section): memories of devastation and human misery following the use of napalm in the Vietnam War (2007a, 2007b); "a Great War battlefield" (2007a, 2007b, p. 25), referring to World War I; and the destruction of Hiroshima and Nagasaki at the end of World War II, called to mind by references to "mushroom clouds" (2007a) or "atomic-bomb-like mushroom clouds" (2007b, p. 25). References or allusions to specific wars were not always present in this framing,[1] but whereas the government business enterprise Forestry Tasmania tended to rely on scientific argument in framing forest management in the state as sensitive and sustainable, "warlike conflagration" always represented it as environmentally brutal.

Flanagan, his articles and/or the environment movement were sources of information for some overseas travel journalists, and the "warlike conflagration" frame appears in a number of the travel journalism texts discussed in later chapters. This suggests that any attempts Tourism Tasmania made to deny Flanagan's contact details to those travel journalists actively requesting it for the purposes of reporting on the forestry issue would have been largely ineffective in limiting the circulation of this frame in their published texts because they would probably already have encountered it.

It is difficult confidently to account for the extent to which the controversy that surrounded forestry matters in Tasmania did or did not influence the interview talk of travel journalists who chose not to refer to the state's environmental controversy in their published texts. This, in turn, makes it hard to judge the extent to which crowded itineraries and intensive management of travel journalists' itineraries succeeded in shielding them from frames such as those circulated by Flanagan. News journalist Doward's travel article about Tasmania appeared in the *Observer* in April 2004, less than a month after an article about the proposed boycott of travel to the state appeared in his paper's sister publication the *Guardian* (Fickling 2004) and just a few days before Flanagan's *Guardian* comment was published, but he said he did not recall the forestry issue when speaking to me in 2009. Doward had raised the subject of Flanagan himself by volunteering the information that he had read one of his novels, but when I followed up on this he had nothing more to say about him. As a staff news journalist he only occasionally wrote travel journalism and when commenting generally on his decisions about content he attributed them to the needs of his audience. However, his explanation of his decision not to refer in his text to another matter of cosmopolitan concern – a contagious facial tumour afflicting the endemic Tasmanian devil – reveals his understanding of "what you're supposed to be focusing on" as a journalist writing for the *Observer*'s travel section – particularly in terms of a difference between news and travel journalism:

> I could see how if I started going down that line my news editor might start— I mean the travel editor might start getting a bit baffled as to why I'm supposed to be writing a travel article when I've gone on a sort of eco rant and, you know, I'm there to do a job which is to try and explain to people why they should or should not go to Tasmania, not to do a forensic number on

various diseases facing Tasmanian wildlife…You're trying to tell people why they might want to go there or indeed in some travel pieces I've written why they don't want to go there, and to share that experience. And the problem is you get so diverted by riffing on all sorts of side issues it can get just sort-of dull for the reader and you lose your perspective of what you're supposed to be focusing on.

(Doward 2009, pers. comm., 26 August)

Such comments suggest, firstly, that some travel journalists do not consider environmental concerns to be tourism concerns even when nature is part of a destination's place-branding and, secondly, that workplace acculturation of staff journalists plays a part in their journalistic decision-making. It is noteworthy, however, that in addition to praising its tourism products and natural environment Doward's published article (Doward 2004) began with a discussion of the environmental threat of introduced foxes and provided quite a news-like critique of the state's tourism industry, indicating that there was in fact some scope for journalistic agency at the *Observer*.

Regulating staff

From 1997 to 2000 and throughout the decade of the case study the Tasmanian government and the tourism industry were signatories to a strategic business plan called *Tourism 21*, which was periodically updated. In 2004, as in 1997, a whole-of-government approach remained a cornerstone of the agreement:

> Brand management will occur hand-in-hand with positioning strategies, aiming to preserve tourism core appeals through policy and alignment across whole-of-government and relevant industries.
> (Tasmanian Government and Tourism Council Tasmania 2004, p. 13)

The extent to which "positioning strategies" might be capable of preserving the core appeals of nature, cultural heritage and wine and food is debatable, but in 2006 the government clarified its approach to place-branding in a document intended to explain and promote the practice to the community, explicitly noting a need to align stakeholders who may be in conflict in its effort to draw lessons from brand management in enterprises:

> The challenge for governments in managing image is about developing strategies that achieve the same commitment and sense of purpose in their policy making and communication as brand managers achieve in enterprises. This requires strong alignment of message across a variety of stakeholder representatives, even some that may at times be in competition or in conflict with one another.
> (Department of Premier and Cabinet 2006, n.p.)

The cusp of the new century heralded a significant brand extension for Forestry Tasmania, which, in the space of a single financial year, adopted a tourism strategy, gained national tourism accreditation, joined the state's peak tourism industry body and confirmed its intention to expand into large-scale commercial tourism (Forestry Tasmania 2000). Its first major attraction, the Tahune Forest AirWalk near Geeveston south-west of state capital Hobart, began operation on 1 July 2001. Just seven months earlier, however, the organisation had announced its intention to log large sections of the Styx Valley in the next three years (Buchman 2008), the consequences of which would be played out in protests and media coverage both nationally and internationally (see, for example, previous section). Important aspects of this activism would seek to persuade potential visitors that Tasmania's forestry practices were incompatible with a tourism brand founded on wilderness and nature.

Despite a whole-of-government approach to branding, some Tourism Tasmania staff found it difficult to reconcile tourism and logging. Public relations practitioners and guides interviewed for this case study were passionate advocates for the state: they had to be in order to do their job. It also seems reasonable to extrapolate from the extent of their professed attachment to the island that it was personally as well as professionally important to them for visiting travel journalists to feel a strong connection with the destination. They generally understood the watchdog role of journalism well enough to know that environmental conflict had news value. Sometimes, however, it was impossible for them to shield journalists from evidence of forestry, as this anecdote from the VJP's senior public relations practitioner responsible for international travel journalists for much of the 1990s and the early years of the following decade demonstrates:

> It's— well, you've got to have blinkers on in public relations if you think that you're going to just market tourism in Tasmania as an eco-destination and not have people start to ask questions when they start to see things that aren't reflecting that marketing position. And that's what our dilemma has always been. We can't present ourselves as an ecotourism or a green destination and have clear-fell logging along the road. I often had that experience. I remember flying a *National Geographic Traveler* journalist in a helicopter and she only had two days here and she was doing a recci to see the story ideas and we took off in the helicopter from Cambridge and headed north over towards Cradle Mountain and straight over the Styx where they were logging. And she said, "What's that?" and I told her it was— I didn't— I just in a matter-of-fact straightforward way [said] that this was logging – forestry logging – and she said, "Oh, well, we've got a lot of that in Washington State" and didn't say any more, but it was a pretty devastating sight.
>
> (Nicholls 2009, pers. comm., 9 March)

While an account of forestry that Tourism Tasmania considered neutral could be provided by guides if travel journalists persisted in asking about forestry matters (Dowty, R 2009, pers. comm., 3 June; Nicholls, D 2009, pers. comm., 9 March), overt or perceived pressure not to give a personal opinion critical of Tasmania's logging practices or the pulp mill to curious travel journalists appears to have caused anxiety among some staff associated with the VJP. Among those I interviewed who had guided or conducted public relations for Tourism Tasmania's VJP, there were mixed responses to requests from travel journalists to give an opinion about forestry. These ranged from refusing to give anything but a neutral account to speaking off the record as a Tasmanian citizen to commenting as a scientist.

Environmental activism or public opposition to logging or the pulp mill prior to an association with Tourism Tasmania was not necessarily an impediment to being recruited by the organisation. Di Hollister had been a vocal opponent of the first controversial road through the Tarkine to be described by the government as a tourist drive and a Green member of the Tasmanian parliament before guiding for Tourism Tasmania's VJP. High-profile Launceston restaurateur and occasional expert wine and food guide for the VJP Kim Seagram was appointed to the Tourism Tasmania board despite having been quoted in an article in a national newspaper (Denholm 2007) in which wine and food tourism operators voiced their opposition to the Tamar Valley pulp mill proposal. And prior to her appointment as international public relations practitioner, Gabi Mocatta had published a travel article (Mocatta 2004) researched with a small amount of support from the VJP that had been critical of forestry policies related to the Tarkine (Mocatta, G 2009, pers. comm., 7 September). All three had exceptional credentials and possessed the kind of passion for place considered invaluable in Tourism Tasmania public relations.

As the decade progressed, Hollister was one Tourism Tasmania guide who would find herself increasingly given what she described in 2009 as "very difficult jobs where I know that people are coming and they will probably write a story on what's happening in the forests or what's happening with the Tarkine road or whatever, but you can't hide this, you can't shield it" (Hollister, D 2009, pers. comm., 24 March). Whereas former government scientist Nick Mooney, who had sometimes been called upon by Tourism Tasmania to act as a specialist guide for travel journalists, said he never declined an interview but had little faith in travel journalism's capacity to accurately portray complex environmental issues (Mooney, N 2009, pers. comm., 15 June), Hollister spoke in cosmopolitan language that suggested she believed the genre could contribute to the public sphere:

We really have to be aware that there are people from other parts of the world who are influential writers and reviewers and commentators who are aware that while this is a most amazing area, and amazing piece of land, and amazing heart-shaped piece of land at the end of the earth which can offer probably the greatest diversity of landscape that you'll find in such a small piece of land in the Southern Hemisphere, that— that there are issues, that there are controversial issues that are still happening here and controversial practices… departments and governments must be aware that questions are being asked by people who come.

(Hollister 2009, pers. comm., 24 March)

It might be useful for me to elaborate here on a distinction I make in this book between two frames of environmental cosmopolitan concern my Tasmanian research revealed. "*Place-branded* cosmopolitan concern" celebrated ecotourism for its sustainable practices and educative function but ignored any challenges to the brand of the destination being reviewed. "*Brand-sensitive* cosmopolitan concern", by contrast, promoted the place-branded tourism attribute that the environment movement considered to be threatened and encouraged travel in order to experience and appreciate its global value, but represented it as contested and advocated greater protection. In Tasmania's case, what the government regarded as attacking the brand was, according to those who deployed "brand-sensitive cosmopolitan concern", defending the brand from damage that it would suffer if the contested logging practices continued. Far from discouraging tourism, this discursive strategy promoted tourism by praising the place-branded environment, which simultaneously increased the textual impact of descriptions of environmental degradation. Operating within the discourse of accessible nature, "brand-sensitive cosmopolitan concern" can be teamed with a variety of perspectives on how much commercial tourism development should be permitted in protected areas. However, it is less commodified, more cosmopolitical than many of the other accessible-nature frames. One of its most important attributes is that it partially reconciled competing loyalties for some actors in the tourism sector with challenger sympathies (see chapters 6 and 7). Unlike occasional calls by some activists for distant publics to boycott tourism in an attempt to bring about policy change in a destination (in addition to the instance cited above, see Takach 2014 for a discussion of the "Rethink Alberta" campaign), "brand-sensitive cosmopolitan concern" generally represents concern for the place-branded environment as being in the place's long-term best interests as a tourist destination. This analysis supports Lury's thesis that although brands generally function to regulate staff (see Arvidsson 2006; Lury 2004), at moments of tension "the open-endedness of the brand can contribute to an indeterminate politics or a politics of indeterminacy" (Lury, 2004, p. 141).

There is no simple conclusion to be drawn from the views and experiences of public relations practitioners and guides with experience of working for or with the VJP. In Wolfsfeld's political contest model, elites attempting to accumulate and maintain maximum bargaining power in their dealings with the media are keenly aware of the need to control the flow of information within and from their organisation (Wolfsfeld 1997, p. 27). The manner in which Tourism Tasmania's guides were encouraged to chaperone hosted journalists in the first decade of the 2000s was in some respects similar to that of "minders" in the post-Vietnam model (Lewis et al. 2006, see Chapter 3) of military media management. Accordingly, unless travel journalists participating in the VJP were able to make their own arrangements outside the constraints of their VJP itineraries, the level of freedom and assistance afforded to any wishing to include environmental conflict in their texts and the openness with which questions about that conflict would be addressed often depended on the attitude of the guides they were assigned and the public relations practitioners overseeing their visits. In Wolfsfeld's model it is also the case that "dissensus" among elites can reduce authorities' control over the political environment (Wolfsfeld 1997). Where public relations practitioners' and guides' personal attitudes about forestry matters were at odds with government policy, the extent to which they were prepared to voice their own views and assist journalists wishing to investigate environmental conflict was further influenced by their views on the role of public servants.

Duelling frames

Even when kept to the tightest schedule, resourceful hosted travel journalists can use investigative news techniques to gather evidence about environmental conflicts during their funded trips, either for publication in the resulting travel journalism article (Fair, J 2009, pers comm., 17 March; Miles, P 2009, pers. comm., 9 March; Greenwald, J 2009, pers. comm., 6 March) or on a return visit for publication in a separate article (Greenwald, J 2009, pers. comm., 6 March; Walterlin, U 2009, pers. comm., 26 June). When this happens, tourism VJPs can simply choose not to host the journalist for future visits, as sometimes happens (Nicholls, D 2009, pers. comm., 9 March), but this leaves the negative image unchallenged. An alternative approach is for tourism offices to "partner" with newspapers and magazines to produce supplements promoting the destination, sometimes with copy written by established travel journalists. This is the course of action Tourism Tasmania took some years after the publication of a critical article by BBC *Wildlife Magazine*'s James Fair in 2000. In this section I compare and contrast the production and text of Fair's 2000 travel journalism with that of a 2005 supplement he also wrote.

By the turn of the century, both the Wilderness Society (Wilderness Society 2011) and Forestry Tasmania (Forestry Tasmania in Tourism in Natural Areas Project Team 1993, Appendix B) had come to recognise the value of engaging in tourism for public relations purposes. In 1999 the Wilderness Society launched its campaign for the Styx forests 90 kilometres west of Hobart by decorating a 77-metre high *Eucalyptus regnans* in the valley to create what the movement described as "the tallest Christmas tree in the world" (Wilderness Society 2011). Around the same time, it in effect became an ecotourism operator itself when it started encouraging visitors to go to the valley to see the trees it was campaigning to save (Wilderness Society 2011; see also Chapter 7). The Styx Valley and the site of Forestry Tasmania's first large-scale commercial tourism operation the Tahune Forest AirWalk were both day-trips from Hobart, but when the AirWalk opened in 2001 it would benefit from marketing via Forestry Tasmania and Tourism Tasmania on a scale far beyond the financial resources of the Wilderness Society. In 2000, however, when BBC *Wildlife Magazine*'s James Fair was invited to join a group tour by Tourism Tasmania's VJP, he contacted the Wilderness Society before travelling and was briefed about its concerns for the Styx (Fair, J 2009, pers comm., 17 March). Fair then decided he would visit the Styx while in Tasmania – a side-trip he organised himself but which relied on the assistance of Mooney, the government wildlife biologist who had been an expert guide on his VJP tour. In addition to being a wildlife expert, Mooney was someone public relations practitioners considered a Tasmanian "character" (see later in this chapter), and this made him a popular choice as a guide for journalists early in the case study. Nevertheless, Fair's appreciation that such a side-trip was not something Tourism Tasmania would have wished to support reveals a degree of reflexivity about the promotional role of travel journalism and Mooney's willingness to assist him. As he commented in 2009, "It wasn't part of my itinerary, which isn't surprising in many ways" (Fair, J 2009, pers comm., 17 March).

Among British journalists on Fair's hosted visit was the *Observer*'s Euan Ferguson (Hollister, D 2009, pers. comm., 24 March; Fair, J 2009, pers. comm., 15 April), whose extensive, glowing article containing a section on the Bay of Fires Walk (Ferguson 2000, see Chapter 6) made the cover of his newspaper's "Escape" travel section with the tagline "Is this the most perfect place on God's earth? Euan Ferguson thinks so". At the *Observer*, freebies would often be allocated to well-regarded staff writers willing to spend some of their own holidays researching travel stories (Doward, J 2009, pers. comm., 26 August) and the following comment from the newspaper's Doward about his own practice links enthusiasm with the task of selling the destination to readers:

> [Y]ou're trying to make someone share your enthusiasm and the spirit of the trip…so you try and share some of that sense of excitement and fervour with the readers, and plus you get a bit carried away in the writing and it becomes a bit too effusive and you miss out on a lot of points. But hopefully some of your enthusiasm may rub off on the readers and they might investigate Tasmania for themselves, having read a few paragraphs of your article.
> (Doward 2009, pers. comm., 26 August)

The Tasmanian tourism industry considered the VJP "very valuable" (Hanna, D. 2009, pers. comm., 26 June) in gaining coverage of its products and the destination in travel media, but Ferguson's article revealed that the VJP could, on occasion, also deliver the government itself significant direct exposure for its framing of tourism and forestry as compatible with each other, and of forestry as compatible with Tasmania's "natural" branding. In his text, Ferguson praised the island's scenic attractions seen from the air but also touched on forestry matters, simultaneously publicising the impressive age of the state's "old, old forests", describing its logging of these forests as "the careful sustainable stuff, for the whole eco thing is huge down here", promoting forestry roads near Cradle Mountain as providing access for tourists, and endorsing the state's wine and food (Ferguson 2000, p. 3). Such exposure in a newspaper like the *Observer* (the *Guardian*'s Sunday sister paper, with hundreds of thousands of readers) was an outstanding return on government investment in Tourism Tasmania's VJP, but as Fair's quite different representation of forestry practices demonstrates, there were no guarantees of positive coverage even when travel journalists were wined and dined. In his piece for *BBC Wildlife Magazine*, Fair employed the same storyline of a plane flight over forests followed by a drive along logging roads to frame the roads in the Styx Valley as disruptive to nesting eagles, the state's forestry practices as "the kiss of death for biodiversity", its logging industry as "rampant", and the government as culpable. Fair used his own first-hand experience of the forest to frame Tasmania's natural branding as flawed and employed the voice of a credentialed local – the scientist Mooney – to give credibility to his claims, writing, "As we leave, Mooney gestures incredulously at the devastation. 'In 20 years' time, people will be appalled by this sort of destruction,' he says. 'Just like whaling today'" (Fair 2000, p. 84).

Fair's 2000 feature about Tasmania was the earliest example in my case study samples that incorporated "brand-sensitive cosmopolitan concern", and in following chapters I provide many additional examples. However, my aim in the rest of this chapter is to explore ways in which authorities can respond when such framing emerges in travel journalism or other forms of media. Below I demonstrate how partnerships between media organisations and government or quasi-public tourism offices can reset the way environmental conflict is framed in travel media to make it more politically benign.

Fair was proud of his 2000 feature critical of logging in the Styx, and viewed it as evidence of his magazine's editorial independence and good journalism:

> I'd been in touch with the Wilderness Society, so I went out there [to Tasmania] and I happened to meet someone from, well he was from the Parks and Wildlife Service. You know. You know, I'd always ask people about those sorts of issues. We were talking about it and basically as a result of the conversation he said, Well, I'll take you out there if you want – if you've got a day spare. And I thought, well, that would be an interesting thing to do…he was going up there anyway, I think. He was going to investigate a wedge-tailed eagle's nest for some reason, I can't remember why. And he said, "Well, come along if you want," and I just thought, well that would be something I hadn't seen on this trip. Obviously a tourist board is keener to take you away from places like that. I think as any good self-respecting journalist would do, you just do a bit of research and it doesn't take long before, when you do it in Tasmania, things like the Franklin River come up, or Tasmania and environment, or Tasmania and wildlife.
>
> (Fair 2009, pers. comm., 17 March)

As someone who was also an occasional guide for commercial wildlife operators, Mooney appreciated the challenges they faced in making their businesses profitable and sustainable, but he believed they had the potential to contribute to a strong, rational case for conservation by giving a monetary value to wildlife (Mooney, N 2009, pers. comm., 15 June). This frame, which I call "the ecotourism solution", can achieve contrasting discursive outcomes, depending on whether it is paired with "compatible sectors" or "brand-sensitive cosmopolitan concern". In the following interview extract, Mooney combines "brand-sensitive cosmopolitan concern" and "the ecotourism solution" to contest the government's frame of "compatible sectors", all within the discourse of accessible nature. In the last few sentences of the quote he rejects any suggestion that forestry and tourism are compatible by using his own support for good ecotourism access to natural places as an argument *against* the forestry industry. Tasmania's place-branding message is challenged by Mooney's argument that forestry and ecotourism are competitors not only for natural resources but for scarce *accessible* natural resources:

> I used to go down every summer to the Antarctic guiding on the Russian ships, and [in Tasmania I worked a lot for] Tonia Cochrane…and the Cheesemans [Ecological Group]. These are visiting specialist wildlife groups that come here from the States… And that's just to keep an eye on the industry and what people's expectations are and all the rest of it. And those people I'll take to where I want to see the animals. But often those places are obliterated now by forestry. So we can't go to a lot of the places that were incredibly convenient. 'Cause, if you think about it, you're actually— the government will give you a story that there are kazillions of trees in reserves, whatever, but they're simply not accessible. So really you end up as a tourism operator competing with log trucks for the same trees, because you both need an economy of access, mileage, good roads, all this stuff. So there is a head-on collision of values there, which in conservation terms there might be a trade-off with lots of protected areas elsewhere but it's not much good for people who want to just be there and enjoy it. The accessibility is a real issue.
>
> (Mooney 2009, pers. comm., 15 June)

With its "passion for wildlife" (BBC Media Centre 2011b), *BBC Wildlife Magazine* was an ideal forum for the mediation of "brand-sensitive cosmopolitan concern". Indeed, after relating Mooney's narrative of the homeless eagles, Fair carefully resuscitated Tasmania's natural branding with glowing praise for a marine wildlife tourism product that had only recently begun operation but would ultimately win many accolades from international travel magazines and make donations to environmental programs including the government's Parks and Wildlife Service. Importantly, however, connection-building and meaning-making that proved textually decisive had taken place on the ground in Tasmania because Fair shared Mooney's interest in the good health of the ecotourism industry and faith in "the ecotourism solution", as evident in the following interview extract from Fair:

> I do subscribe to the idea that in order to protect an environment or eco-system, countries and habitat or whatever, one of the best ways you can do that is send people there who want to see wildlife – that gives people an incentive for protecting the environment.
>
> (Fair 2009, pers. comm., 17 March)

Five years after Fair's initial hosted visit to Tasmania, Tourism Tasmania hosted him again, to research and write a 24-page supplement for distribution in his magazine (Fair, J 2009, pers comm., 17 March). Until late 2011 *BBC Wildlife Magazine* was published by BBC Worldwide (BBC Media Centre 2011a; BBC Press Office 2011), a subsidiary of the government-owned British Broadcasting

Corporation required "to maximise the value of the BBC's assets for the benefit of the licence fee payer by creating, acquiring, developing and exploiting media content and brands around the world" (BBC Worldwide n.d.). As such, *BBC Wildlife Magazine* accepted advertising, and this meant Fair's editorial position in 2005 was less clear cut than it had been in 2000:

> When I went in 2000, as is the deal with any travel piece of that nature, you take the trip and they have no right to see the copy before it's published or anything like that. Although they didn't say after at all, "I wish you hadn't written anything about the Styx Valley", or anything like that. Whereas in 2005 there was a slightly less sort-of— It wasn't quite as straightforward a relationship in that sense because we were being paid to produce a supplement by the tourist board.
>
> (Fair 2009, pers. comm., 17 March)

In 2000, Fair had not felt overt editorial pressure from Tourism Tasmania to avoid forestry issues, commenting that "they weren't going to take me to the Styx Valley but they certainly weren't unhappy that I went" (Fair, J 2009, pers comm., 17 March). As evidence that the organisation had been pleased with the article he produced as a result, he cited its desire for him to write the text for the magazine supplement (Fair, J 2009, pers comm., 17 March). In view of Tourism Tasmania's expectation of positive coverage from hosted travel journalists, however, harnessing the promotional reach and reputation of *BBC Wildlife Magazine* via a supplement ensured a more predictable outcome than funding Fair for a second visit to write travel journalism that the tourism office would not see before it was published:

> I certainly talked to people about [environmental issues]. And I did a box. I mean it was more than a box, it was a substantial box in the supplement looking at the issues to do with the damming of the Franklin River and the knock-on environmental movement that sprung from that. And we looked at how that is replicated today in the campaign against logging and stuff like that. Now that was one area where...I can't remember exactly what it was but there were a couple of things they weren't happy about me writing, the Tasmanian tourist board. It wasn't particularly censorious but it was a little bit censorious...We drew attention to the political and environmental – call it what you like – battles of the past 20, 30 years. We did— you know, they weren't going to try and stop us from mentioning that. And we had a little sort-of battle over it, I seem to remember.
>
> (Fair 2009, pers. comm., 17 March)

The box to which Fair referred above was entitled "The dam busters". While reporting that "conservationists say that some old-growth forests are still being logged" and "arguments over logging can and do carry on well into the night", it was otherwise dismissive of Tasmania's contemporary environmental conflicts. It stated that "[p]rotection of the environment is taken seriously by politicians in Tasmania", noted recently expanded areas of protection in the Styx Valley and the Tarkine, and quoted government figures for the total landmass and areas of native forest already protected, which it referred to as "environmental safeguards that few other countries in the world can match" (Fair 2005, p. 18).

Fair's comment in the supplement box that protection had recently been extended to parts of the Styx Valley and the Tarkine was accurate. The agreement, which provided a level of protection below that of national park, had included significant assistance to the Tasmanian forestry industry, and its authors had framed this in terms of its employment and tourism benefits, in keeping with Tasmanian government framing of a symbiosis between forestry and tourism:

> The Agreement recognises that timber and tourism can co-exist to create a secure future for country towns. Tasmania aims to be the supplier of choice to the world – a place recognised for quality forest products with world-class environmental credentials.
> (Australian Government & Tasmanian Government 2005)

Nevertheless, there was continuing environmental controversy in the state surrounding the activities and actions of Forestry Tasmania's biggest client, Gunns Ltd., and ongoing international activism in relation to the Styx Valley (see above and Chapter 7). To attribute information that old-growth forests were still being logged to conservationists rather than also to a government source gave the impression that it was a matter of interpretation at the time.

The remainder of the boxed text concerned itself with the Franklin dam campaign (see Chapter 4). However, in 2005 that subject was in no way controversial. Far from considering the Franklin campaign something that should be forgotten, Tourism Tasmania actively promoted cruises on the Gordon River that made this long-ago dispute an important part of their interpretation. As such, the inclusion in the supplement of this piece of history cannot be regarded as evidence of any lack of censorship by Tourism Tasmania. Fair did, however, slightly reframe Tourism Tasmania's usual discourse in this regard by writing that the Franklin campaign had "set a precedent for future environmental battles" (Fair 2005, p. 18).

Supplements in newspapers and magazines were one of Tourism Tasmania's favoured tactics for circulating its branding message of Tasmania as "natural", as further evidenced by a subsequent supplement in London's *Daily Telegraph* (Telegraph Create et al. 2008) subtitled "Your 16-page guide to one of the most unspoilt islands on Earth", which included articles from a number of writers who had previously participated in the VJP, including Fair. Thus, the VJP can be seen as an effective mechanism for drawing travel journalists into broader networks of promotion. For Tourism Tasmania, the BBC *Wildlife Magazine* supplement added value to Tasmania's branding by association with the brand of a magazine it described in its annual-report summary of the campaign as "one of the world's most credible wildlife publications" (Tourism Tasmania 2006, p. 20). Yet both the July 2000 travel journalism article and the October 2005 Tasmania supplement were entitled "Explorer's Guides"; and although the latter was a 24-page supplement whereas the former was part of the magazine proper, the supplement was prominently branded as BBC *Wildlife Magazine*. BBC *Wildlife Magazine* distributed 50,000 copies of the supplement to readers of its October 2005 edition and supported this with online content (Tourism Tasmania 2006, p. 20). An additional 3000 copies were downloaded from the website of travel agent Austravel. In its annual report Tourism Tasmania described the supplement as brand-aligned and "Tasmania's major campaign for the United Kingdom market in 2005–2006", reporting that Austravel's "land sales grew by 150 per cent over the campaign period" (Tourism Tasmania 2006, p. 20). Such a concerted and comprehensive marketing campaign can have left little trace of the concern for Tasmania's forests BBC *Wildlife Magazine* had published in 2000. And whatever its tourism marketing purpose, from a public sphere perspective it circulated claims and frames that countered those of actors opposed to Tasmania's forestry practices that had gained access to the British news media in 2004.

Networks and professional judgement

Although on occasion the VJP proved to be a source of travel journalists and other writers who would later contribute to marketing products, its primary aim was, of course, to gain positive coverage in travel journalism, because this could be obtained at far less expense than the cost of a supplement. Hutchins and Lester note that the interests of media outlets and their workers are "more closely aligned with dominant powers existing within the space of flows...than they are [with] grassroots social movements concerned with the preservation and/or conversation of place" (2006, p. 437). This often fortified Tasmania's place brand against dissensus within government tourism organisations and the tourism industry, whether or not visiting travel journalists accepted financial assistance.

> In all areas of news, reporters are required to negotiate and interpret the agendas and messages of the individuals and groups that they deal with... Those advocating or acceding to the interests of capital are more likely to be located within the privileged formation of the space of flows. In this environment, media managers, public relations consultants, spin doctors, stage-managed events and image manipulation are an accepted reality – "part of the game" – of engagement with the media.
>
> (Hutchins and Lester 2006, p. 446)

It is a paradox perhaps indicative of the brand's capacity for a degree of autonomy and agency (see Lury 2004) that the productivity of brand resistance from within was sometimes irresistible to those charged with filtering out incompatible expressions (see Arvidsson 2006). When the *San Francisco Chronicle*'s travel editor at the time, John Flinn, expressed an interest in Tasmanian tigers and devils prior to a visit to the state in 2004 funded by his newspaper, Tourism Tasmania again enlisted the assistance of senior government wildlife biologist Mooney (see above) as an expert guide. For many years, Mooney had been charged by the government with attempting to verify supposed sightings of the extinct thylacine (Tasmanian tiger) and had gained a marketable fillip from his reputation as a tiger hunter (e.g. Flinn 2005b). He was also a Tasmanian devil expert. In the following comment, former senior Tourism Tasmania public relations practitioner Nicholls acknowledges Mooney's outspokenness but also his public relations appeal:

> He [Mooney] has got an opinion, had an opinion. And he often got into trouble I think…for being – not overly opinionated, but for having an opinion at all. But he's a character, and I thought that would be the perfect person for John to travel with because he could tell him the science, he knew it all, he was funny, he was interesting, and I felt having talked to John that he would like Nick, and Nick was very happy to drive him up there. He said, "I'll just drive him up there and take him out to Joe's," and that's what he did.
>
> (Nicholls 2009, pers. comm., 9 March)

As travel editor of the *San Francisco Chronicle*, Flinn was himself influential but he also had friends among the elite of popular travel writing and publishing (Flinn, J 2009, pers. comm., 2 March). Despite earlier efforts by Nicholls to entice the *Chronicle* to send a travel journalist to Tasmania (Nicholls, D 2009, pers. comm., 9 March), Flinn's visit had finally been prompted by the personal recommendation of guide-book company Lonely Planet's co-founder Maureen Wheeler, a board member of Tourism Tasmania from February 2000 until February 2006 (Flinn, J 2009, pers. comm., 2 March).

The late Geoff "Joe" King mentioned by Nicholls in the above quote operated a night-time wildlife tour that often featured Tasmanian devils feeding in the wild and Mooney had been instrumental in his decision to take up that occupation. In their separate interviews, Nicholls and Flinn indicated that they had developed a strong professional respect for each other (Flinn, J 2009, pers. comm., 2 March; Nicholls, D 2009, pers. comm., 9 March) and Nicholls was comfortable with Mooney being Flinn's guide.

Having decided to visit Tasmania, Flinn's overriding concern was to serve his readers' interests as expertly as possible (Flinn, J 2009, pers. comm., 2 March). San Francisco has a large and affluent gay population, and Flinn was aware these readers might have heard that Tasmania had once had Draconian anti-homosexual laws. As well as writing about the Tasmanian devil he wanted to use his article to alert his gay readers to the fact that Tasmania's anti-gay laws had now changed. This change had come about following nine years of campaigning that had mobilised and deployed cosmopolitan concern locally, nationally and internationally. At the time of Flinn's visit, the person who had led that campaign, Rodney Croome, was working closely with Tourism Tasmania in a project to improve Tasmania's reputation within gay and lesbian circles. Croome sometimes guided journalists with an interest in gay matters and Nicholls arranged for him to meet Flinn and show him around Hobart (Croome, R 2009, pers. comm., 2 April; Flinn, J 2009, pers. comm., 2 March; Nicholls, D 2009, pers. comm., 9 March). While strongly supportive of the environment movement and grateful for what he had been able to learn from the Franklin dam campaign for his own activism, in his promotion of the state since the legislative changes Croome focused on presenting a positive story of a gay-friendly Tasmania without reference to forestry debates (Croome, R 2009, pers. comm., 2 April). Flinn was also guided during his visit by Ken Latona (re Latona, see chapters 4 and 6), who took the journalist part way along the Overland Track in Cradle Mountain–Lake St Clair National Park to one of his commercial huts, where Flinn enjoyed a hot shower and a gourmet meal. In his text, Flinn implicitly acknowledged concerns with luxury ecotourism by positioning himself as a convert: "There was a time in my headstrong youth when I looked down on this sort of backcountry decadence. I'm happy to report that with the passing of years I've gotten over it" (Flinn 2005a). Latona, King, Mooney and Croome were among those who featured prominently in Flinn's article "A Devil of a Time in Tasmania" (Flinn 2005a), while Mooney was the star of a second article, "Desperately Hoping to Catch a Tasmanian Tiger by the Tail" (Flinn 2005b). Although Flinn and Mooney discussed forestry issues on their lengthy drive to King's remote property (Flinn, J 2009, pers. comm., 2 March), and although Flinn was travelling at the expense of his paper, he did not refer to Tasmania's forestry dispute in his articles (Flinn 2005a, 2005b). Nor did he mention King's concerns about off-road vehicles riding along the foreshore of his property. Asked why he did not report the forestry dispute, he answered that it was not "an imminent, huge problem that would have affected an area that a tourist might care about" but also that he felt it was "a little bit out of bounds" (Flinn, J 2009, pers. comm., 2 March).

As the discourse of a travel editor who was also a former news journalist, Flinn's comments were in keeping with a firm distinction he felt needed to be made between news journalism and travel journalism. This distinction, in his opinion, was so pronounced that it made him uncomfortable with the term "travel *journalist*", which he felt implied considerable journalistic rigour – the "searching of, and dealing more in terms of hard-edged controversy and things like that and also just doing more investigation" (Flinn, J 2009, pers. comm., 2 March). Yet although he preferred to refer to himself as a travel *writer*, Flinn did not always avoid controversy in his texts. In a 2007 article he referred to in our discussion, for example, he wrote about a wildlife tourism venture that enabled tourists to swim with endangered manatees in Florida. Although he privileged the operator's framing of his product as helping to increase public support for the animals' continued protection, he did not shy away from giving the views and contact details of environmentalists' opposed to the practice (Flinn, J 2009, pers. comm., 2 March). Thus, in the case of Flinn's Tasmania articles, we may give some weight to the expectations and deep structural embedding of his tourism networks implied by the phrase "a little bit out of bounds" in influencing his opinion that, despite Tasmania's "natural" branding, unprotected forests were not of interest to potential travellers and, consequently, neither was the state's forest conflict. Flinn's readiness to observe that some readers "familiar with the situation" had written to say he should have talked about it (2009, pers. comm., 2 March) highlights his own reflexivity about the subjectivity of travel journalism but is also of interest as evidence that there is an appetite for political comment in travel journalism among some readers.

Some years after Flinn's visit to Tasmania, freelance travel journalist Sharon Otterman was commissioned to write a travel article about Tasmania for *The New York Times* (Otterman 2007), which also did not allow its writers to accept hosted travel. As part of her research, she spoke to Violent Femmes bass guitarist Brian Ritchie, who had moved to Tasmania from New York and at the time of their conversation was establishing himself as someone who would become an important part of Hobart's cultural life. In his interview with me, Ritchie explained that he would not take a public position on Tasmania's forestry conflict because it would diminish his ability to be an "effective cultural force" (Ritchie, B. pers comm., 20 March). Ritchie also demonstrated an appreciation of branding, referring to a government-supported music and arts festival he later curated as "a branding tool for the state" (Ritchie, B pers. comm., 20 March). Like Flinn, Otterman had a strong news journalism background but, again like Flinn, this did not lead her to incorporate environmental conflict in her piece even though she was aware of disputes (Otterman, S 2009, pers. comm., 20 June). Her decision to focus on artistic culture in her article and interview Brian Ritchie rather than, for example, novelist Richard Flanagan, reflected the power of endorsement from a celebrity who was also a former New Yorker, her assessment that culture was the emerging essence of Hobart and her wish to distinguish her piece from others about Tasmania that had already appeared in the *Times* "Travel" section, many of which, such as Flanagan's piece published in 2004, had dwelt on the island's natural environment or outdoor adventure.

Here then, as in the Flinn example, we see cultural and political cosmopolitanism diverging rather than converging in source struggles for publicity via travel journalism. In such circumstances, the happy face of cultural cosmopolitanism can gain ground even when there is coverage of environmental conflict in the local news media, the travel journalist concerned has a news journalism background and the journalist is travelling without financial assistance from the VJP.

In the *Times*, Otterman's representation of Hobart as a "Foodie" and "Culture" destination was further enhanced by its categorisation as such when it appeared at number 40 in the newspaper's "44 places to go in 2009" (Sherwood and Williams 2009). Soon after this list was published, Tasmania's tourism minister distributed a media release entitled "New York Times Promotes Tasmania as Top Destination" (O'Byrne 2009). The information was subsequently reported in Tasmania's capital city daily newspaper, *The Mercury* (2009). This action harks back to the uses of place-branding not just to promote a place externally but also in attempts to manage public opinion internally and shape identity by providing evidence that a particular government has been able to lead a place to a strong reputation, thereby bolstering support for place-branded frames. In the case of news coverage of the minister's communication, the media were fulfilling the role ascribed to them by Hutchins as "mediators and interpreters of global networks of power and information" (Hutchins 2004, p. 588) but also as mediators of the brand at the interface between the space of places and the space of flows (see Chapter 3).

"44 places to go in 2009" did not include Tasmania in its "Eco" category, despite the heavy nature focus of six of the eight articles published by the *Times* in the first decade of the 2000s that were listed by publication date in its online Tasmania travel guide in that year. Otterman's 2007 feature remained at the top of this list until late 2014 (*New York Times* 2014), giving her representation of Tasmania primacy for a full seven years. Of course, the appearance of so many nature-based articles in this list meant her framing of the island as harmonious did not go unchallenged. A lengthy feature by Darcy Frey listed second until 2013 contrasted the friendliness of Tasmanians with the reality of contemporary environmental conflict, while Richard Flanagan's 2004 article, listed seventh until 2013, included criticisms of Tasmania's forestry practices mediated through the "warlike conflagration" frame. However, the likelihood that readers would look beyond the first feature in the list is is debatable. As Matthew Hindman explains, "despite – or rather because of – the enormity of the content available online, citizens seem to cluster strongly around the top few information sources in a given category" (2009, p. 18, see Chapter 8).

Conclusion

When authorities' control over the political environment lessens, travel journalists may become aware, or more aware, of contradictions between the place's identity and the image that place-branding projects. In such instances, structures and strategies that traditionally privilege elite definitions in travel journalism can function to shield the journalist's audience from evidence of contradictions and conflict the government believes might compromise its branding. The brand is thus simultaneously more vulnerable and more politically instrumental. In this chapter I explored the ways in which elite public relations practice, blurred editorial boundaries, elite networks, and struggles for publicity among sources can reduce the likelihood that challenger frames from non-elite sources or dissenting voices from within government will be mediated by travel journalists during times of environmental conflict. Examples presented suggest that elite sources enjoy considerable definitional advantage within individual media organisations as a result of the close proximity of travel journalism to tourism. Professional networks within and between travel media and the tourism sector can also stifle noise at the brand's interface. In Tasmania's case, a senior travel journalist with considerable autonomy and tourism industry networks built up over a long career who was travelling without financial assistance from Tourism Tasmania chose not to report environmental conflict he had discussed with one of his sources, while a less experienced travel journalist chose to differentiate her article from those that had come before by focussing on the arts culture of the destination. Ottoman's article gave a celebratory but urban and harmonious representation of the island's identity. However, if her piece had been read in combination with other articles available through the *Times*' "Travel Guides: Tasmania", a more complex Tasmanian identity would have emerged, shaped by wilderness and environmental conflict as well as boutique urban chic and an arts-infused optimism.

Among some institutional actors a frame of "brand-sensitive cosmopolitan concern" was evident that combined a passionate attachment to Tasmania as a place of global environmental significance with support for tourism and concern about logging practices they believed were a threat to the brand. In this chapter I have identified ways that elite definitional advantage could be maintained or regained when the brand was challenged. In the following chapter I explore ways in which journalistic agency and the media's own branding sometimes combined to facilitate the circulation of "brand-sensitive cosmopolitan concern".

Note

1   For example, the word "napalm" did not appear in Flanagan's 2004 *New York Times* article. I can only speculate as to the reason: it may have been in deference to American sensitivities regarding the Vietnam War or perhaps was a result of the gentle prose style and pace of the article.

References

Arvidsson, Adam 2006, *Brands: Meaning and Value in Media Culture*, Routledge, Abingdon.

Australian Government & Tasmanian Government 2005, "A way forward for Tasmania's forests: The Tasmanian community forest agreement", Department of Agriculture, Fisheries and Forestry, last reviewed 21 October 2009, viewed 29 December 2011, www.daff.gov.au/forestry/national/info/a_way_forward_for_tasmanias_forests

Barns, Greg 2004, "Can't see the wood for the trees", *The Guardian*, 6 April, viewed 31 December 2011, www.guardian.co.uk/world/2004/apr/06/australia

BBC Media Centre 2011a, "BBC Worldwide to complete disposal of BBC magazine titles", 20 October, updated 28 October, viewed 29 December 2011,www.bbc.co.uk/media centre/worldwide/201011magazines.html

BBC Media Centre 2011b, "BBC Wildlife Magazine unveils new look with major redesign", 1 September, updated 18 October, viewed 10 November 2012, www.bbc.co.uk/ mediacentre/worldwide/010911wildlife_redesign.html

BBC Press Office 2011, "BBC Worldwide and Exponent Private Equity agree BBC magazines transaction", 16 August, viewed 29 December 2011, www.bbc.co.uk/ pressoffice/bbcworldwide/worldwidestories/pressreleases/2011/08_august/bbc_magazines. shtml

BBC Worldwide n.d., "About us", viewed 29 December 2011, www.bbcworldwide. com/about-us.aspx

Buchman, Greg 2008, *Tasmania's Wilderness Battles: A History*, Allen & Unwin, Crows Nest.

Denholm, Matthew 2007, "Pulp friction", *The Weekend Australian Magazine*, 12–13 May, pp. 14+.

Department of Premier and Cabinet, Tasmania 2006, *Tasmanian Brand Guide*, Government of Tasmania, Hobart.

Doward, Jamie 2004, "Devils and the deep, blue sea", *The Observer*, 18 April, "Escape" p. 10.

Ferguson, Euan 2000, "Devilishly beautiful", *The Observer*, 30 April, "Escape" pp. 2–3, 10.

Fickling, David 2004, "Tasmanian boycott urged over threat to forests", *The Guardian*, 22 March, viewed 31 December 2011, www.guardian.co.uk/world/2004/mar/22/animal-welfare.environment

Fair, James 2005, "Tasmania: A BBC Wildlife Magazine explorer's guide", supplement in *BBC Wildlife Magazine*, October.

Fair, James 2000, "Explorer's guide", *BBC Wildlife Magazine*, July, pp. 84–85.

Flanagan, Richard 2007a, "Out of control: The tragedy of Tasmania's forests", *The Monthly*, May no. 23, viewed 8 June 2009, www.themonthly.com.au/node/512

Flanagan, Richard 2007b, "Paradise razed", *The Telegraph Magazine*, 28 June, pp. 25+.

Flanagan, Richard 2004a, "Paradise lost – with napalm", *The Guardian*, 21 April, viewed 31 December 2011, www.guardian.co.uk/world/2004/apr/21/australia.environment

Flanagan, Richard 2004b, "The selling-out of Tasmania", *The Age*, 22 July, p. 13.

Flanagan, Richard 2004c, "Tasmania", *The New York Times*, 12 September, viewed 1 November 2012, http://travel.nytimes.com/2004/09/12/travel/sophisticated/12ST-TASMANIA.html

Flinn, John 2005a, "A devil of a time in Tasmania", *The San Francisco Chronicle*, 23 January, viewed 7 January 2012, http://articles.sfgate.com/2005-01-23/travel/17357830_1_nick-mooney-tasmanian-wallabies

Flinn, John 2005b, "Desperately hoping to catch a Tasmanian tiger by the tail", *San Francisco Chronicle*, 23 January, viewed 7 January 2012, http://articles.sfgate.com/2005-01-23/travel/17357926_1_tasmanian-tiger-creature-abominable-snowman

Fleming, Katherine 2007, "Gunning for Flanagan", *The Bulletin with Newsweek*, 27 November, p. 12.

Forestry Tasmania 2000, *Annual Report 1999–2000*, Forestry Tasmania, Hobart.

Hindman, Matthew 2009, *The Myth of Digital Democracy*, Princeton University Press, Princeton.

Hutchins, Brett 2004, "Castells, regional news media and the information age", *Continuum*, vol. 18, no. 4, pp. 577–590.

Hutchins, Brett & Lester, Libby 2006, "Environmental protest and tap-dancing with the media in the information age", *Media, Culture & Society*, vol. 28, no. 3, pp. 433–51.

Lewis, Justin, Brookes, Rod, Mosdell, Nick & Threadgold, Terry 2006, *Shoot First and Ask Questions Later: Media Coverage of the 2003 Iraq War*, Peter Lang, New York.

Lury, Celia 2004, *Brands: The Logos of the Global Economy*, Routledge, Abingdon

Mercury, The 2009, "Tassie's big tick from the Big Apple", 19 January, p. 3.

Mocatta, Gabi 2004, "The Tarkine: What future a precious wilderness in north-west Tasmania?", *Australian Geographic*, July–September, pp. 36–53.

New York Times, The (NYT) 2014, "Travel guides: Tasmania", viewed 17 October 2014, www.nytimes.com/travel/guides/australia-and-pacific/australia/tasmania/overview.html

O'Byrne, Michelle 2009, "New York Times promotes Tasmania as top destination", media release, Tasmanian Minister for Tourism, 18 January.

Otterman, Sharon 2007, "Tasmanian goes boutique, nice and slow", *The New York Times*, 29 July, viewed 9 January 2011, http://travel.nytimes.com/2007/07/29/travel/29next.html

Sherwood, Seth & Williams, Gisela 2009, "The 44 places to go in 2009", *The New York Times*, viewed 21 January 2012, www.nytimes.com/interactive/2009/01/11/travel/20090111_DESTINATIONS.html?partner=permalink&exprod=permalink

Takach, Geo 2014, "Visualizing Alberta: Duelling documentaries and bituminous sands", in Robert Boschman & Mario Tronto (eds), *Found in Alberta: Environmental Themes for the Anthropocene*, Wilfrid Laurier University Press, Waterloo, pp. 85–103.

Tasmanian Government & Tourism Council Tasmania 2004, *Tourism 21: A New Ten-year Vision: 2004–2014*, Hobart.

Telegraph Create, Tourism Tasmania, Tailor Made Travel & Qantas 2008, "*The Daily Telegraph*: Tasmania: Your 16-page guide to one of the most unspoilt islands on Earth", supplement in *Daily Telegraph*, 12 April.

Tourism Tasmania 2009, "Visit us: Visiting Journalist Program", viewed 5 September 2009, http//travelmedia.tourismtasmania.com.au/visit/vjp.html

Tourism Tasmania 2006, *2005–06 Annual Report*, Tourism Tasmania, Hobart.

Wilderness Society 2011, *Styx Valley of the Giants: Self-drive and Walking Guide*, Wilderness Society, January, viewed 7 June 2012, www.wilderness.org.au/images/Styx_selfdrive jan2011.pdf

Wolfsfeld, Gadi 1997, *Media and Political Conflict: News from the Middle East*, Cambridge UP, Cambridge.

Woolf, Marie 2004, "Tasmania hits back at 'Mother England' after MPs call for boycott over forest destruction", *The Independent*, 5 April, viewed 23 March 2015 http://parlinfo. aph.gov.au/parlInfo/download/media/pressrel/AI5C6/upload_binary/ai5c65.pdf;fileType =application%2Fpdf#search=%22marie%20woolf%202004%22

6   The travel media

Two forms of branding cooperate and sometimes compete in the relationship between tourist destinations and travel journalists: place-branding, which has been my primary focus thus far, and the publication's branding, which I will attend to in this chapter. Although the travel media are, in some important respects, part of the tourism industry and have a vested interest in the positive mediation of destinations and tourism products, for the genre of travel journalism to be of practical use to corporeal travellers its descriptions and advice must be reliable. One way for individuals to test a publication's reliability is to take the trips they read about, but this overlooks the role played by travel journalism in helping people choose between destinations. The number of travel journalism articles that can be consumed by a publication's readers far exceeds the number of destinations visited. In travel media, as in tourism, readers and potential readers use brands to assess the value they can expect to derive from a product both for practical purposes and for the construction of their own identity. Travel sections in broadsheet and tabloid newspapers are generally subsumed under the brand of the parent publication, but travel magazines must forge their own reputations. Glossy high-end travel publications often include claims of specialist knowledge and integrity when positioning their products in the market. *Lonely Planet Traveller* guarantees "trusted, independent travel advice that has been gathered without fear or favour" (2014, p. 4); *Conde Nast Traveller* pledges "Truth in Travel…honest, first-hand opinion and must-have information…the unbiased inside track, with integrity and attitude" (2014, p. 12); *National Geographic Traveler* assures us that "nobody knows this world better", promises to report on "destinations of distinction and character" and says it supports "efforts to keep them that way – believing that to enhance an authentic sense of place will benefit both travelers and the locations they visit" (2014, cover and p. 4); and *Travel + Leisure* insists it is "the world's most influential travel brand", offering "insider access to destinations around the globe" (2015) from writers who "travel incognito wherever possible" and "generally do not accept free travel or take press trips" (2014, p. 18).

There are strong structural incentives for travel media institutions to be on good terms with government tourism organisations even if their staff and freelance journalists do not accept hosted travel. Nevertheless, in the relationship between the media and antagonists in political conflicts, "[p]ower is a question of relative dependence: who needs whom more at the time of the transaction" (Wolfsfeld 1997, p. 14). A travel publication's brand may benefit from editorial content containing "constructive" criticism of a destination's policies if from a media-branding perspective it can be seen as contributing to a high standard of service to readers and being in the long-term best interests of the destination itself. This may be the case even when, as in most instances, criticism is *generally* absent from the publication's editorial content, or absent from other editorial content about the same destination. The following comments from freelance United States travel journalist Stephen Metcalf are worth quoting at length for their nuanced explication of how the complexities of the travel media business model can accommodate a degree of this kind of journalistic agency by travel journalists secure in their habitus:

> Before anyone gives me an explicit command about how serious or unserious they want a specific piece to be, or how much they want me to play up the deliciousness of the food and underplay the complexity of the local politics – you know, before anyone says anything explicit – we are all working within a set of tacit assumptions. I mean, I'm at this point, I think it has to be said, something of a professional. And as a professional I understand that I'm writing for a specific outlet. And I understand that that outlet is – that their business model – is advertising driven. It's certainly newsstand sales [that] make up a proportion of it, so it's – quite a lot of it – is advertising-driven, and their advertisers are travel companies and airlines… I am writing within a certain set of very, very established expectations, and those expectations are so well established they barely even need to be articulated. So, interestingly, I've never, ever had the open conversation with an editor of either a book review or a travel outlet in which they've said, "Look, you can't piss off our advertisers," but I think that's only because we all know that, and we all start from that assumption, and I understood that I was writing what was essentially a travel piece. Now the interesting thing is [that] within that understanding there's some room to play. And one of the reasons there's some room to play is that…people do want to read journalism and they want the journalism to be very distinct from the advertising. And they understand when something is an ad, i.e. something is designed entirely to sell them a product by the maker of the product. And they understand that journalism is something about an individual sensibility going to a faraway place and encountering it with a fair degree of honesty and sensitivity… I do think that people don't want the same thing when they read journalism as they want when they look at an advertisement. And people who produce magazines understand this.
>
> (Metcalf 2009, pers. comm., 26 June)

In this chapter I argue that a frame of "brand-sensitive cosmopolitan concern" (see Chapter 5) is tolerated by some travel magazines because it contributes to these publications' branding as tourism's watchdog without undermining the industry on which they depend. In the following section I focus primarily on Stephen Metcalf's

2008 Tasmanian wine and food story for *Travel + Leisure* researched and published during a fierce debate over a pulp mill proposed for a wine and food tourism region. In the subsequent section I consider the brand benefits to travel publications of Ken Latona's nature, food and wine ecotourism venture Bay of Fires Walk. Together these examples also demonstrate that extending the brand benefits of nature to other products such as wine and food can be a risky enterprise for brand managers in destinations where environmental conflict is rife.

This chapter overlaps in some respects with Chapter 7 and together the two contextualise and interpret travel journalism that challenged Tasmania's place-branding.

Circulating concerns through brand extensions

As early as 1998–99 Tourism Tasmania had reported that it was using marketing campaigns to ensure "our unique natural environment, flora and fauna are supplemented by the authentic built heritage, fresh foods, quality cool climate wines and the friendliness of Tasmanian people" (Tourism Tasmania 1999, p. 17). In that and subsequent years the state tourism office devoted considerable resources to supporting wine and food tourism by, for example, developing a wine and food strategy, producing wine and food brochures, establishing a wine and food touring route through the state's best-known wine producing region, the Tamar Valley, and, in a single year, hosting 27 international journalists to have a "food and wine experience" (Tourism Tasmania 2003, p. 33). Nevertheless, when Tasmania's largest company, the woodchip exporter Gunns Ltd, announced in February 2005 that it intended to build an AUD 1.9 billion pulp mill in the same valley as the wine touring route, it soon gained government endorsement. By the time United States travel journalist Stephen Metcalf visited the island in 2006 to research a food and wine tourism article for the US edition of *Travel + Leisure*, opposition to the pulp mill had made it one of the state's most serious environmental conflicts. The environment movement was opposed to the type of pulp mill proposed on many grounds, including the pollution it would cause and an expectation that it would increase and prolong the harvesting of native forest timber, regardless of its location. By contrast, not all of those in the wine and food tourism industry opposed to such a mill being located in the Tamar Valley would necessarily have been opposed had it been located elsewhere. As it was, opposition by winemakers and food growers in the valley and nearby Launceston made the dispute directly relevant to the subject of Metcalf's article.

Travel + Leisure funded Metcalf's trip, though he did receive some logistical assistance from Tourism Tasmania (Alps, D 2009, pers. comm., 19 March; Metcalf, S 2009, pers. comm., 26 June; Seagram, K 2009, pers. comm., 15 September). In the course of his research, he came in contact with a range of winemakers, food growers and restaurateurs who, on balance, left him with the impression that the pulp mill proposal was a cause of great anxiety and a threat to the reputation of Tasmania as a clean and green producer (Metcalf, S 2009, pers. comm., 26 June).

Among those concerned about the location of such a mill in the Tamar Valley whom he met but did not quote was Launceston restaurateur Kim Seagram (Seagram, K 2009, pers. comm., 15 September). This was prior to Seagram's appointment to Tourism Tasmania's board but during her long association with the organisation as a representative of the wine industry and an occasional expert guide for visiting journalists with an interest in wine and food.

Among those Metcalf interviewed and did quote was Tamar Valley restaurateur Daniel Alps, whose restaurant was situated in a high-profile vineyard. Alps had contributed to the food and wine components of Latona's tourism operations (see Chapter 4 and later in the current chapter for discussion of these tours) and, like him, had come to value "wilderness" both as part of the experience and for its promotional value:

> I've worked with Cradle Mountain Huts and Bay of Fires up until this year… [W]e were getting organic products into a national park and the walking. Doesn't get any better than that when you're thinking about the experience but it took a while to get that into my head, and into Ken's, and so that was [the] fascinating thing. The people who are doing the walk are the people who are active people who really are there to appreciate the wilderness. They also love good wine and they also know about good food. So to deliver those three together is an overwhelmingly good experience.
>
> (Alps 2009, pers. comm., 19 March)

Disappointed that Tourism Tasmania was not supporting the people in the wine and food tourism industry in their efforts to stop the pulp mill being built in the Tamar Valley, Alps believed it was reasonable and valuable for those stakeholders to express their concerns to travel journalists – that is, to use the Visiting Journalist Program (VJP) as a vehicle for publicising their own political views on what they considered to be a threat to their businesses:

> [T]he thing is, we're talking about it more now. Tasmania I think has gone through this huge transformation in the last six years where everyone was feeling so threatened as a stakeholder in our state as things were going on that we had no control over. So what did we all do? We all started spilling out all our emotions to every journalist that came, to try and get our message out there, that this is not good; we need to change this. It helps us if someone wants to listen and write it down. Because we know we're doing a good job – you can see we're doing a good job, you can taste it – but we need to let people know that we're dissatisfied with the way that it's all going. Because part of the thing with the VJP and government – and if we're talking about the quieter politics of it, you know, we subsidise VJP to a degree as well, we help pay for their lunches to help promote us – which is, well, why not get a little bit of bang for your dollar, because the tourism department weren't coming forth in supporting us in any way, shape or form.
>
> (Alps 2009, pers. comm., 19 March)

Alps, who had entertained innumerable food and wine travel journalists, attributed the way they would ask deeply personal questions about what it was like to live and work in the valley to the fact that they felt an affinity with him because they were part of an "artisanal industry" (Alps, D 2009, pers. comm., 19 March) crafting words just as he crafted food or his neighbours crafted wine: "it's that sort of [artisanal] industry versus big industry that doesn't give a rat's arse about anything apart from the bottom line, and there's a real struggle" (Alps, D 2009, pers. comm., 19 March). Alps' views in this respect appear to relate to the craft of writing rather than the travel media industry. But he knew the promotional value in the genre of a good brand-aligned story of accessible nature and clean, green produce, in words but also in action:

> ...we don't go to markets; the suppliers come to our door. And [travel journalists] love hearing that. They only love hearing that when you start telling and when they start seeing people rock up on an hourly basis. And they can see the venison come in the door and they can see all the veggies and all that sort of stuff, showing them that, and actually see the produce that they bring, which they don't see every day, like black radishes, for example, whatever, that provokes an emotion in them that they didn't think that they were going to be exposed to... [Y]ou look at Tasmania as a small island, it's clean and it's green, it's got a good brand. For the Tasmanians, we forget that it's 40 per cent national park but we definitely leverage off that as a marketing tool. And only part of our national parks are actually used – there are some other fabulous ones that no one ever hears of.
>
> (Alps 2009, pers comm., 19 March)

This was the frame that during the pulp mill debate Alps and others remastered as "brand-sensitive cosmopolitan concern" by adding references to the pulp-mill conflict. In Metcalf's article, Alps' close-to-source philosophy and practice were described in some detail, setting the stage for his concerns about the pulp mill aired later in the piece.

Alps attributed what was, in his experience, travel journalists' desire to gain quite a deep understanding of what it was like to live and work in Tasmania to personal interest but also to their need to "sell" the destination. This combination of motivations can be theorised as evidence of degrees of cultural cosmopolitanism instrumentalised as consumerist cosmopolitanism:

> They also want to know a lot more than what's going on: "What's it like to live here? What challenges do you suffer? How far do you live from home?" They all ask do I live here, do I live in town? They ask me a lot of personal questions – a hell of a lot of personal questions – which means that they're very generally interested because there must be some sort of fantasy going on in their head wondering, "Well, could I live here?" And that— as humorous as it is, that is part of what they need to get into to try and sell a place, to a degree. So all journalists are very keen to find out their own bent on what

part of the area that would affect them if they were living here do they want to get in touch with.

(Alps 2009, pers. comm., 19 March)

Importantly, Alps, like many Tasmanian restaurateurs and winemakers, did not rely solely on visitors for his income, having a strong local clientele who travelled to his restaurant from nearby Launceston. His work gave him a significant degree of independence from Tourism Tasmania and close ties with his local and regional community. The following short quote encapsulates not only the strength of his conviction that as a genuine stakeholder in the brand he was entitled to voice his opinions to journalists but also his awareness of the risk involved in speaking out. His opening statements recast the affective discourse deployed in local media by those with a long family history in the forestry industry by arguing that his, too, was a family business in which he had invested most of his life:

> I'm a business man and I'm protecting my own family. I'm doing what I believe and I've done – you know, I've been a chef – since I was 14. It's not as though I keep picking up different things and running with them; there's a consistency there as well which has to be noted to do that. So I had absolutely no problem with it whatsoever. In fact I was happy with myself for doing it and I actually think it's benefited the restaurant. I actually— I lay awake at night with a few sleepless nights thinking whether it was the right thing to do, but I think it's benefited the restaurant. I think there's a lot of people who come to us and talk to us. They don't agree with it, they come to the restaurant.

(Alps 2009, pers. comm., 19 March)

That both Seagram and Alps had been mainstays of the wine and food component of Tourism Tasmania's VJP for many years was an indication of their influence in the wine and food tourism industry. The negative publicity of any criticisms of the pulp mill Alps might make to travel journalists was a significant challenge for the state's branding. Metcalf introduced Tasmania's forestry conflict through a textual tussle with his sources similar to one evident in an article in *National Geographic Adventure* by United States travel journalist Adam Sachs (2006) in his defence of Latona's commercial developments in national parks (see the following section). After quoting a source who criticised the commodification of "artisanal purity", Metcalf defended it as "utterly necessary" as an alternative to extractive industries (Metcalf 2008). Thus Metcalf, like Sachs but with a somewhat different discursive outcome, stayed true to his primary tourism-operator sources while simultaneously dismissing concerns that commodification was tainting their products' authenticity. Metcalf then described forestry practices using the "warlike conflagration" frame (see Chapter 5) second hand but concluding with his own experience of seeing plantations grown in place of native forests: "I saw the legacy of logging with my own eyes: in the middle of a dense tangle of primeval forest, blue gum trees stand in rows, like obedient schoolchildren" (Metcalf 2008). Later he makes the concerns of some locals for the Tasmania brand explicit: "its many critics claim the mill would pump sulphurous effluent into Bass Strait, to the severe detriment of marine life, not to mention Tasmania's new clean-and-green image" (Metcalf 2008).

In their analysis of news coverage of a pulp mill dispute in Argentina, Silvio Waisbord and Enrique Peruzzotti found that lay people became primary definers, not as victims of environmental catastrophe but as voices of potential side-effects (see Beck 1992), because the news organisations in that country were not "bound by professional expectations and norms to defer to 'scientific knowledge'" in news and risk definition (Waisbord and Peruzzotti 2009, p. 703). Something similar may pertain in cosmopolitical travel journalism. In Metcalf's article, "cultural rationality" (Cox 2010, p. 199) prevailed in the definition of pulp-mill risk despite arguments against such fears presented by Tasmania's foremost winemaker, Andrew Pirie. Recognised as the pioneer of the island's contemporary viticultural success, Pirie had taken a job with a winery located in the valley and owned by the company planning to build the pulp mill. In the following extract Metcalf explains his belief that, as a journalist, he needed to meet with Pirie and hear his side of the story to better understand Tasmania's contemporary dilemma:

> I met him I think fairly late in my trip and to that point I'd spoken to a number of people who were in the food and wine business and they all said the same thing, which is that they were shocked – they were shocked that he would agree to do this. They saw this in fairly black-and-white terms – that the food movement was new, exciting, fragile and a direction for Tasmania to go in going forward, and that to reindustrialise the island or to emphasise its industrial nature was to have threatened that, and that their chance to do something unique was really endangered by Gunns, and specifically by Gunns, and specifically by that pulp plant... And what can you do as a journalist?[1]
>
> (Metcalf 2009, pers. comm., 26 June)

In his interview (pers. comm., 26 June) Metcalf explained that part of his interest in Tasmania's pulp mill dispute had been sparked by his experience of an environmental dispute in his home region – reasoning also advanced by journalists Jenkins and Tourtellot in subsequent chapters. Although Metcalf did not describe Tasmania's environment directly as globally significant, his own concern for it as an international traveller gave this impression, as do other observations in his text, such as his comment that its air, soil and waters are "some of the least contaminated on the planet" (Metcalf 2008). Seagram's comments on Metcalf's opinions suggest she viewed them as important brand feedback:

> I think it starts raising awareness. And for somebody like Stephen to be concerned at the impact, obviously it's a really special place. So, you know, you've got two sides of the coin. And hopefully we can actually raise awareness within our own community. And this is what I've learnt from Economic Development strategies and a number of different things – to say, "Listen,

we've got to really start mapping out our future as to where we're going to put our energies and monies and time, so that we're all pushing our barrow in the same direction."

(Seagram 2009, pers. comm., 15 September)

In his text, Metcalf described tourism and extractive industries as competitors – a direct challenge to government attempts to use place-branding to achieve "strong alignment of message" across stakeholders who might be "in competition or conflict" (Department of Premier and Cabinet 2006, p. 11). But the extent to which Metcalf remained within the unstated boundaries of travel journalism established by his publisher is evident in the comments of one of his other important sources, local wine critic Graeme Phillips, who acknowledged the legitimacy of reporting on the pulp mill dispute but described the published article as in other respects a "puff piece" (Phillips, G 2009, pers. comm., 26 August) – a term also used ironically to describe travel articles including his own by Metcalf (2009, pers. comm., 26 June). As Phillips explained Metcalf's style and, by implication, that of travel journalism generally: "everything's good. Almost. Food and wine's great. East coast is fabulous. No other place on Earth like it" (Phillips, G 2009, pers. comm., 26 August). Metcalf was generous to the operators and identities themselves – even Pirie – reserving his cosmopolitan concern for nontourism threats to tourism. Near the end of his article, Metcalf's appeal to his readers to appreciate that their lives are somehow connected with the lives of distant others took the form of a reference to Alice Waters, a prominent US restaurateur and noted campaigner for organic produce, followed by an explicit reminder that Tasmania is not only like "no place on earth" in its abundance but also like "every place on earth" in its vulnerability to "the forces of exploitation" (Metcalf 2008).

Importantly, although Metcalf's article was available online long after its print publication, so too were entirely positive *Travel + Leisure* articles about Tasmania by David Hochman (2001) and Bonnie Tsui (2004). Interestingly, however, Metcalf's article, like Tsui's, was used on the magazine's website as an opportunity for providing links to promotional material by Tasmanian tourism operators in sidebars, suggesting that a degree of political comment in travel journalism does not necessarily reduce its value as a tourism marketing tool.

In Tasmania, *The Mercury* did not mention Metcalf's 2008 article in *Travel + Leisure*, despite in 2007 having itself extensively reported concerns about the mill by many in the tourism industry, including fears expressed by Alps (Alps in Duncan 2007) and nationally recognised food and wine columnist Leo Schofield (Schofield 2007) that it could damage the state's brand and strong reputation among travel journalists. Rather, during the remainder of the year in which Metcalf's feature on Tasmania appeared, *The Mercury* published seven separate news articles celebrating *Travel + Leisure* accolades for the state as a whole or one of its tourism products. One of these articles (*Mercury* 2008) included quotes from the Minister for Tourism, while another (McKay 2008) incorporated quotes from the CEOs of Tourism Tasmania and Tourism Industry Council Tasmania.

The brand value of brands

Sometime after my interview with Alps, he left the valley, as he had threatened to do in Metcalf's article, and established a gourmet store in Launceston. In view of his association with Cradle Huts and Bay of Fires Walk, this seems an appropriate point at which to consider the sample of articles about the Bay of Fires I mentioned in Chapter 1.

As discussed in Chapter 4, in the 1980s and 1990s Ken Latona and his then business partner Joan Masterman were trail blazers in demonstrating the tourism advantages of luxurious ecotourism, but their success soon went far beyond their own products, imbuing the marketing of the entire state with an aura of environmental responsibility and aesthetic sophistication. In the first decade of the 2000s the public relations value of the Latona and Masterman walks through national parks and the pampering they offered walkers in the form of food, wine, accommodation and interpretation lay in their appeal to prestigious, high-circulation travel media (Nicholls, D 2009, pers. comm., 9 March; McGinity, M 2009, pers. comm., 23 October). From a place-branding perspective, these tourism products made it easy and pleasurable for travel journalists to represent Tasmania's natural environment in feature-length glossy narratives of personal discovery and rejuvenation.

Latona's third Tasmanian tourism venture – a four-day guided soft-adventure walk south through Mount William National Park to a luxury lodge at the secluded northern end of the Bay of Fires in the island's north-east – began operation in 1999. Some years before, he had parted company with Masterman. He had kept Cradle Huts in the World Heritage Cradle Mountain – Lake St Clair National Park. Masterman had retained the Friendly Beaches Lodge and Freycinet Experience Walk on the Freycinet Peninsula, which was also on the east coast but well south of the Bay of Fires. In the years that followed, Latona developed an even stronger relationship with Tourism Tasmania, joining its board in 2003.

The geographical Bay of Fires extends for nearly 30 kilometres along Tasmania's mild north-east coast. The bay's northern extreme falls within Mount William National Park. In turn, most of Mount William National Park is further north than the bay. Traditionally, locals have applied the name Bay of Fires to the bay's southern end, which is a conventional beachside vacation destination popular with Tasmanian families and characterised by holiday houses, water sports, horse-riding and opportunities for the use of off-road recreational vehicles. Bay of Fires *Walk*, by contrast, is an exclusive multi-day tourism product including an overnight trek through Mount William National Park led by fit young guides who tell Tasmanian stories, cook Tasmanian food and serve Tasmanian wine along the way. The walk starts well north of the bay, heads south along secluded beaches and ends just outside the park at the private lodge, which is largely hidden in bush. Grant Hunt, who in 2009 was the chief executive of the company that bought the operation from Latona in 2007, readily acknowledged that most of the walk was through parts of the park that were north of the bay and paid tribute to the contribution of the name to the success of his business, observing that "Ken Latona did his historic research and named the walk the Bay of Fires Walk, which has got a lovely romantic, emotional notion to it" (Hunt, G 2009, pers. comm., 7 October).

The derivation of the name is attributed to British explorer Tobias Furneaux, who saw Aboriginal fires lining this coast when he sailed beside it in 1773. In the context of the walk, the name Bay of Fires is intended to signify a deep connection with place and cultural heritage. As such, Latona's original appropriation of the name was an example of traditional promotional uses of affect to create name awareness and brand attachment – a strategy that had proved successful for conservationists in Tasmania when applied to physical features of the landscape during the Franklin dam campaign (Lester 2007). In 2009 new operator Hunt was also attuned to the other crucial marketing and public relations attribute of this walk – the fact that it is through a national park, even if that park is not named after the bay at the walk's conclusion.

The establishment of Cradle Huts in the Wilderness World Heritage Area (see Chapter 4) in 1987 had initially exposed Latona and Masterman to opposition from Tasmanians who disapproved of tourism developments in protected areas. Later, however, their walks could surf any waves of publicity the conservation movement was able to generate for Tasmania's landscape, which the movement branded as a global asset. The beach walks in Freycinet and Mount William national parks had the added advantage of being able to exploit Tasmania's reputation for wilderness while packaging themselves as hidden treasure to be found not in forests but on the sweeping white-sand beaches of an idyllic island, thereby also capitalising on Tourism Australia's marketing of Australia as a place of sea and sand.

In its first five years of operation (2000 to 2004 inclusive) – the period before plans to build a pulp mill in the Tamar Valley were announced (see previous section) – the Bay of Fires Walk featured in travel journalism published in a wide range of high-profile, high-circulation British and United States newspapers and magazines, including, in Britain, the *Telegraph* (Chipperfield 2000), the *Observer* (Ferguson 2000), the *Independent* (Street-porter 2004; Wheeler 2002) and *BBC Wildlife Magazine* (Fair 2000), and, in the United States, the *New York Times Magazine* (Spindler 2001), *Travel + Leisure* (Hochman 2001) and *Outside* (Perrottet 2002). This was a very impressive list of publications, and the authors were equally noteworthy and experienced. Tony Perrottet was an expatriate Australian travel journalist living in New York who, early in his career, had filed news stories of military conflict from South America, while Mark Chipperfield, David Hochman, Euan Ferguson and the late Amy Spindler had strong journalism backgrounds. Janet Street-Porter and Tony Wheeler – who was born in England and educated at the London Business School but lived in Australia – were minor celebrities in Britain: Street-Porter was a broadcaster, while Wheeler was the influential co-founder of the guide-book company Lonely Planet, whose other co-founder was his wife, Maureen Wheeler, who had joined the board of Tourism Tasmania in February 2000. The tourism operation's ability to elicit so much coverage from high-end international publications was strong evidence of its branding power, in the interests of both Latona's business and Tasmania. However, it was also far removed from the daily experience of most of the island's residents, as one public relations practitioner with Tourism Tasmania and Brand Tasmania experience acknowledged:

> You do the Bay of Fires Walk, you're not going to see any local material, you're not going to meet anyone in fact. You're only going to meet the other 10 people on the trip. So it's quite a different view of a place. You do Bay of Fires Walk, there's no local towns, it's a remote beach, it's fully controlled, there's 10 people on the walk and you get to a lovely thing at the end and then out you fly.
>
> (McGinity 2009, pers. comm., 23 October)

As a socially constructed and detached, geographically secure, demographically exclusive, culturally staged tourism product, Bay of Fires Walk was an ideal marketing tool. As such, it soon became a symbol of Tasmania's branded naturalness. Whereas wilderness during the Franklin dam campaign had symbolised a place that was "desired, invaluable, in urgent need of protection" (Lester 2010, p. 138), through tourism marketing and repeated elaboration in travel journalism the Bay of Fires Walk in the first decade of the 2000s came to signify a desirable, valuable place protected by accessibility. This was reflected in all the features mentioned above, which incorporated varying degrees of environmental cosmopolitan concern commodified in the promotion of Bay of Fires Walk and Tasmania's natural environment, which itself was described by Latona in one article as "a good marketable commodity now" (Latona in Spindler 2001). Travel journalists responded to the Bay of Fires Walk's staged authenticity (MacCannell 1999, see Chapter 2) by publicising the sustainable practices of the tourism operator and, by implication, the destination, and sometimes thereby promoting environmentally sustainable practices in day-to-day life and the care and protection of the natural environment more generally. They praised the destination as a place worth visiting and valuing and did not challenge the island's place-branding. As such, their framing was "place-branded cosmopolitan concern" – that form of environmental consumerist cosmopolitanism representing the market as capable of driving progressive social change.

A star of articles about the Bay of Fires Walk second only to the beaches, and sometimes not even to those, was the Bay of Fires Lodge – one of architect Latona's "living, breathing things that could (by design) be felled as easily as the Tasmanian gum trees of which they are built" (Spindler 2001). Here, hand pumping water for a morning shower was not an inconvenience but a privilege that warranted mention in nearly every article; low-fat meals were not only healthy but put less pressure on the drainage system (Spindler 2001); and there was "wisdom to be gleaned" from using the "surprisingly elegant" composting toilets (Hochman 2001). Journalists in the sample sometimes noted Latona's debt to Australian architect Glenn Murcutt, whose philosophy of constructing buildings that would "touch the earth lightly" (Spindler 2001; see Dovey 2000) had inspired Latona's work, or they referred to the sense he gave that the style of the lodge epitomised a relationship with the nomadism of tribal Aboriginal culture (Hochman 2001). None of the journalists in the full Bay of Fires sample of 11 articles took the Murcutt/Latona discourse as a cue to engage with contemporary Tasmanian Aboriginality. Rather, a number mediated the Bay of Fires' cultural heritage by employing a tourism frame I describe as "distanced brutality", a term that refers to the possibility of mediating historical cruelty or environmental destruction but, crucially, with a strong element of regret. This frame was employed by Tourism Tasmania (for example, Croome 2005; Department of Tourism, Parks, Heritage and the Arts 2005) and travel journalists generally (for example, Chipperfield 2000, 2002; Curwen 2010; Flinn 2005a, 2005b; Gill 2007; Perrottet 2002; Spindler 2001) in relation to various combinations of the following: the brutal treatment of convicts in colonial times; environmental degradation such as the destruction of hillside forests and heavy-metal pollution of waterways surrounding the west coast mining town of Queenstown in the 19th and 20th centuries; the extinction by disease and at the hands of bounty hunters of the Tasmanian tiger in the 1930s; highly discriminatory anti-homosexuality laws that were not repealed until 1997; and the post-contact devastation of Tasmania's Aboriginal population. As effective and brand-aligned destination promotion, the "distanced brutality" frame paired temporal distance with contemporary remorse by consigning such brutality to the past, either with assurances of a more sensitive present and future (see, for example, references to the extinction of the Tasmanian tiger in Department of Tourism, Parks, Heritage and the Arts 2005) or by conveying a sense of regret or disapproval about the past that served as a foil to heighten the positive effect of other parts of the text. As such, it was not so much cosmopolitan concern as the thematic commodification of cultural heritage – a juxtaposition of regrettable past and "natural" present that could still support place-branding. The following paragraph by Spindler is an example of the way this juxtaposition of regrettable past and "natural" present can still support place branding:

> The native full-blooded Aborigines were exterminated, the Tasmanian tiger extinguished, convicts tortured. And yet nature seems determined not to give in completely to man's inhumanity to other living things. Despite it all, the place is still astonishing. Tasmania is said to have the cleanest air and water in the world...
>
> (Spindler 2001)

Another travel journalist whose article was included in this sample, Chipperfield (2000), adopted the "distanced brutality" frame by introducing the Bay of Fires Walk with a very detailed account of Aboriginal history in the area. Like others in the sample, he later also used the tribes' nomadic lifestyle as a metaphor for the many satisfactions of Tasmanian ecotourism:

> Little wonder that the more enlightened early European visitors to Van Diemen's Land (Tasmania's former Dutch name) believed the island's

inhabitants to be the most exulted of the planet's noble savages, a people living in complete harmony with their environment and themselves.

(Chipperfield 2000)

Yet even Chipperfield – an expatriate Briton living in Australia and publishing in London's *Telegraph* newspaper – made no mention of contemporary Tasmanian Aboriginal communities. The lack of living Aboriginal voices was a persistent feature of travel journalism about the state during the first decade of the 2000s that was directly related by the tourism industry to a perceived lack of contemporary Aboriginal tourism products (Hanna, D 2009, pers. comm., 26 June). Aboriginal groups had been pursing land claims in the Bay of Fires for decades, but without a tourism presence their modern communities were largely invisible in international travel journalism.

By definition, the "distanced brutality" frame could not be applied to the ongoing logging of old-growth forests, and of eight articles about the Bay of Fires in high-profile British and United States publications between 2000 and 2004 that I analysed only one drew attention to forestry disputes (Fair 2000, see Chapter 5). The remaining three articles in the sample were published after Gunns' plans for the pulp mill in the Tamar Valley wine tourism region were announced (Curwen 2010; Gill 2007; Sachs 2006) and all included reference to Tasmania's forestry disputes. AA Gill of the London *Times* and freelance journalist Adam Sachs writing for *National Geographic Adventure* were food reviewers as well as travel journalists, while the third journalist – the *Washington Post*'s Thomas Curwen – had once been a finalist for the Pulitzer Prize. All three articles covered other parts of the island in addition to the bay.

Sachs' (2006) published discourse on Tasmania's environmental conflict was partially aligned with that of conservationists, acknowledging that "beyond the confines of the wilderness area" there was "a struggle for preservation" (2006, p. 64). In the manner of many of the other articles about Latona's ventures, it framed ecotourism as the solution to environmental insensitivity. However, by skillfully combining publicity for Latona's tourism products and forgiveness for Tourism Tasmania's exaggerated marketing of the state as pristine and pure with criticism of government-sanctioned logging practices, his discourse used its "ecotourism solution" framing to defuse the political charge of "brand-sensitive cosmopolitan concern" (see Chapter 5). Sachs, who also did Latona's Cradle Huts walk, noted that visitors were likely to be exposed to anti-forestry bumper stickers outside the national park but cast "posh hikers" such as himself as the saviours of Tasmania's fragile environment.

Gill (2007) explored Tasmania's identity from a British perspective, in keeping with his philosophy that travel journalists write for their readers at home, not those they visit (Gill 2005). Although he came to the state with Austravel (Gill 2007) and was hosted by the Tourism Tasmania VJP (Dowty, R 2009, pers. comm., 3 June; King, G 2009, pers. comm., 7 June; Mocatta, G 2009, pers. comm., 7 September), his published text incorporated claims of "back-scratching corruption" associated with forestry. Conceding little ground to the government's desire for wholly celebratory coverage, he represented the island as a complex place-based community of gritty contrasts. Using logs chain-sawed into "portraits" of World War 1 soldiers as a metaphor, he concluded his article by representing Tasmanians as "these hard, naive people, shy and silent and capable, growing out of the stumps of their trees" (Gill 2007). Yet even at the hands of such a notoriously harsh reviewer and commentator, following his visit to Latona's lodge (Dowty, R 2009, pers. comm., 3 June), the Bay of Fires remained "as perfect a beach as you will find anywhere in the world" (Gill 2007). And in view of the publicity value of Gill's celebrity, the expense of a lavish hosted trip and the calculated risk it had taken in inviting him to pass judgement, Tourism Tasmania's response to the article was relief rather than disappointment:

> If you read AA Gill widely, that was a very positive article. That was a very positive article for AA Gill. He has to be a bit controversial because that's him. But I have seen him annihilate a destination, just wreck their reputation with tearing them to shreds.
>
> (Dowty 2009, pers. comm., 3 June)

Gill has recorded his thoughts on his own part in the production of travel journalism in the book *AA Gill is Away*, where he describes journalists as performing on "an invisible stage" and himself as read by "more people than will pick up a Booker Prize-nominated novel in a year" (2005, p. 3). However, in spite of acknowledging the power this gives him – "That's not a comparison of quality but a statement of impact" (Gill 2005, p. 3) – he downplays the authority of his opinions as no more valuable than anyone else's. Nevertheless, for a number of years Tourism Tasmania used his words to attract other travel journalists, posting an extract of pure praise on a media website it operated throughout the first decade of the 2000s but no longer maintains (Tourism Tasmania n.d.). Following the article's publication, a link to it also appeared on the *TasmanianTimes* website, described as Tasmania's independent online "forum for discussion and dissent", where an extract drew comment from politically engaged Tasmanians (*Tasmanian Times* 2007). In addition, blog discussion followed the *Timesonline* edition of Gill's report, and here Bruce Englefield – a British expatriate running a wildlife park on Tasmania's east coast – praised tourism as the mainstay of the Tasmanian economy and invited British readers to visit his "Garden of Eden" but also joined Gill in criticising clearing of the state's native forests (Englefield 2007). Moreover, a "Letter to the Editor" from a locally well-known Tasmanian novelist who was visiting Britain at the time Gill's article was published also appeared in *The Mercury*, reproducing and supporting his accusations of corruption and urging the premier to take note (Rose 2007). Thus Gill's celebrity enabled his criticisms to penetrate local media flows to a small degree, in competition with authority efforts to deploy only those portions of his text that appeared to support the brand.

Curwen's feature (2010) reflected something of the intensity of the pulp mill debate by referring to conversations about it between his fellow travellers while he was on the Cradle Huts walk on the Overland Track, prior to his participation in the Bay of Fires Walk. His feature recorded the beauty and fragility of local ecosystems but also the island's economic and social challenges, quoting a traveller who had been born on the island as saying that "Tasmania cannot become merely an environmental museum" (Curwen 2010). Curwen made no overt comment on Tasmania's environmental conflict himself but his references to debates about the pulp mill in combination with his praise of the island's environment hinted at "brand-sensitive cosmopolitan concern". However, his effusive celebration of Cradle Huts and Bay of Fires walk contextualised with concern for the environment *and* the local economy ensured the dominant frames in his feature were "place-branded cosmopolitan concern" and "the ecotourism solution".

Curwen (2010) also noted a recent claim in a list of eight "Threatened wonders" published by British travel magazine *Wanderlust* (2010) that the Bay of Fires was in danger of being overrun by tourists because Lonely Planet (Mocatta 2008) had named it one of its top destinations for 2009. Shortly after the Lonely Planet accolade had appeared in late 2008, the Tasmanian government had begun talking about creating a Bay of Fires National Park at the southern end to protect what the Minister for Tourism described as "the best wilderness in the world". But far from being wilderness, the southern end was a popular domestic tourism destination and highly contested. A three-way tussle over who owned and should be allowed to manage this land had soon erupted between tourism operators, the Aboriginal community and environmentalists. The results internationally of such disagreement included two news articles in the British press in August 2009 that challenged the tourism narratives that had been so carefully cultivated by Latona and Tourism Tasmania over a decade (Marks 2009; *Telegraph* 2009; see also Chapters 4). Particularly challenging in terms of the travel journalism narrative of the Bay of Fires Walk, which represents the Bay of Fires as a place of transformative environmental harmony, had been a focus in this international news journalism on the conflict between environmentalists and the Aboriginal community. *Wanderlust*'s secondary frame in its "Threatened wonders" list had been "the ecotourism solution". To this end it had urged travellers to avoid the Bay of Fires controversy by eschewing the crowded southern end of the bay and heading instead for the Bay of Fires *Walk* at the northern end. Thus, it had made visible to its readers the existence and claims of contemporary Indigenous Tasmanians but it had also demonstrated a shared and persistent travel-media ignorance of longstanding Aboriginal claims to Mount William National Park to the north. And although Curwen (2010) responded to *Wanderlust*'s concerns about the possibility of a deluge of tourists, he did not mention its reference to Aboriginal land claims.

Conclusion

International travel journalism is prohibitively expensive for all but the biggest publications that refuse hosted travel, while tourism operators and tourism offices in destinations are unlikely to be prepared to pay the expenses of international journalists whose newspapers or magazines do not have high circulations, particularly if the destination is geographically distant from the publication's market.

This means competition among destinations for access to those travel journalists writing for elite readers who can afford overseas travel is fierce, and tourism offices will make representations to travel editors of prestigious publications on behalf of their destinations even when those publications do not accept hosted travel (Nicholls, D 2009, pers. comm., 9 March). In place-branding terms, elite readers are also more likely to have consumer or business interests that may incline them to be curious about a destination's exports or economic opportunities. They may even have political influence.

This chapter has demonstrated that prestigious travel publications whose own brands promise authoritative and reliable editorial will sometimes publish articles containing political comment and hold destinations to account for what their journalists perceive to be breeches of brand promises.

Criticisms of forestry or reports of conflict in travel journalism about Tasmania, when they occurred, were usually a relatively small part of otherwise highly motivational representations of the environment. Metcalf's "brand-sensitive cosmopolitan concern" teamed it with the "warlike conflagration" frame and his own evidence for heightened impact. He did not overtly urge readers to take action but instead used his feature to represent environmental conflict as part of the human condition and local publics as members of imagined communities of global risks. And although his criticism was crowded out of local newspaper *The Mercury* by its preference for reporting the many accolades his publication bestowed on the state, his views nevertheless functioned as brand feedback to Seagram, who was a member of Tourism Tasmania's board by the time his article was published.

In the case of the Bay of Fires Walk, international travel magazines and newspaper travel sections were delivered an irresistible media-brand asset: luxurious and safe but environmentally sympathetic infrastructure and products in a beautiful, distant yet accessible landscape for their professional endorsement and recommendation. A national park protected this asset but the pulp mill threatened to damage it by bringing into question the reputation of the wine and food the island's place-branded environment had invested with symbolic purity and ecotourism entrepreneurs were serving to their guests. Thus, throughout the decade, and regardless of environmental disputes, Bay of Fires Walk, along with its birth sisters Cradle Huts and the Freycinet Experience Walk, was projected by the travel media as an indispensable symbol not only of Tasmania but of their own discernment and environmental responsibility. Even when "brand-sensitive cosmopolitan concern" was expressed for Tasmania's "natural" branding in travel journalism or conflict emerged at the southern end of the bay between Aboriginal, environmental and tourism interests (Wanderlust 2010), the Bay of Fires Walk at the "recommended" (Curwen 2010) end emerged from the texts unscathed.

Coda

The examples in this chapter suggest that travel journalism written in praise of businesses that derive significant kudos from "natural" branding, and contribute to that branding in return, can create powerful opportunities for environmental threats to be made visible. But as Alison Anderson (2014, p. 164) observes, "We inhabit a complex, communications environment with rapid, dynamic, over-lapping flows that reciprocally impact on one another in non-liner ways". Many of the travel features referred to in this chapter continue to be available online – among them Metcalf's 2008 feature mentioning Alice Waters in *Travel + Leisure* and Gill's 2007 feature in *The Sunday Times*. In 2014, however, Waters and Gill were among "80 international food and wine VIPs" invited by Tourism Australia to a gala event in Hobart (Tourism Australia 2014). The mere fact that such famous identities accepted invitations to the dinner at Hobart's new premium attraction, the Museum of Old and New Art (MONA), delivered Tasmanian tourism exceptional publicity regardless of whether or not they chose to write or talk to their home audiences about the event or the destination. And as discussed in Chapter 1, Gill's (2014) glowing, conflict-free review of one of Hobart's top restaurants published in *The Sunday Times* soon after his visit was, for Tasmania, the icing on the cake. Since his last trip to the island, a new state government had repealed a hard-won forest peace accord but the Tamar Valley pulp mill proposal had languished. In addition to a raft of compliments about Tasmania's food, produce, restaurateurs and other entre-preneurs, Gill described the state in *The Times* as having become "more humane" since his last visit, and credited it with being "very aware of its clean ecological credentials" (Gill 2014).

Note

1   Gunns sold Tamar Ridge winery in 2010.

References

Anderson, Alison 2014, *Media, Environment and the Network Society*, Palgrave Macmillan, London.

Chipperfield, Mark 2002, "Tasmania: Steaming through convict country", *The Telegraph*, 17 May, viewed 7 October 2011, www.telegraph.co.uk/travel/destinations/australiaand-pacific/australia/724276/Tasmania-Steaming-through-convict-country.html

Chipperfield, Mark 2000, "Australia: Walking with the ghosts of fire", *The Telegraph*, 25 March, viewed 7 October 2011, www.telegraph.co.uk/travel/destinations/australiaand-pacific/australia/other/722361/Australia-Walking-with-the-ghosts-of-fire.html

Condé Nast Traveller 2014, September, p. 12.

Cox, Robert 2013, *Environmental Communication and the Public Sphere*, 3rd edn, Sage, Los Angeles.

Croome, Rodney 2005, *Tasmania: Gay and Lesbian Visitors' Guide*, Blackheath: Gay Travel Guides and Tourism Tasmania.

Curwen, Thomas 2010, "Unpredictable, serendipitous Tasmania", *The Los Angeles Times*, 14 February, viewed 8 October 2011, www.latimes.com/travel/la-tr-tasmania14-2010feb14,0,2099318.story

Department of Premier and Cabinet, Tasmania 2006, *Tasmanian Brand Guide*, Government of Tasmania, Hobart.

Department of Tourism, Parks, Heritage and the Arts 2005, *Tasmanian Wildlife Tourism Strategy*, Government of Tasmania, Hobart.

Dovey, Kim 2000, "Myth and media: Constructing Aboriginal architecture", *Journal of Architectural Education*, vol 54, no. 1, pp. 2–6.

Duncan, Phillipa 2007, "Tourism rocket for bay: Anger at 'trite' mill comment", *The Mercury*, 17 July, p. 5+

Englefield, Bruce 2007, in "Have your say", following AA Gill (2007), "Tasmania: The end of the world", *The Sunday Times*, 8 April, viewed 5 may 2009, www.timesonline.co.uk/tol/travel/destinations/australia/article1595903.ece

Fair, James 2000, Explorer's guide", *BBC Wildlife Magazine*, July, pp. 84–85.

Flinn, John 2005a, "A devil of a time in Tasmania", *The San Francisco Chronicle*, 23 January, viewed 7 January 2012, http://articles.sfgate.com/2005-01-23/travel/17357830_1_nick-mooney-tasmanian-wallabies

Flinn, John 2005b, "Desperately hoping to catch a Tasmanian tiger by the tail", *The San Francisco Chronicle*, 23 January, viewed 7 January 2012, http://articles.sfgate.com/2005-01-23/travel/17357926_1_tasmanian-tiger-creature-abominable-snowman

Gill, AA 2014, "Table talk: AA Gill reviews Garagistes, Tasmania, *The Sunday Times*, 14 December, viewed 20 December 2014, www.thesundaytimes.co.uk/sto/Magazine/article1491624.ece

Gill, AA 2007 "The end of the world", *The Sunday Times*, 8 April, pp. 40–47.

Gill, AA 2005, *AA Gill is Away*, Simon & Schuster, New York.

Hochman, David 2001, "Tasmania's Bay of Fires Lodge", *Travel + Leisure*, June, viewed 7 October 20011, www.travelandleisure.com/articles/heating-up-down-under

Marks, Kathy 2009, "2009's hottest destination (and that's when all the trouble started), *The Independent*, 21 August, viewed 7 October 2011, www.independent.co.uk/news/world/australasia/2009s-hottest-destination-and-thats-when-the-trouble-started-1775235.html

MacCannell, Dean 1999, *The Tourist: A New Theory of the Leisure Class*, University of California Press, Berkeley.

McKay, Danielle 2008, "Tassie charms tourism world: Double tribute set to bring in dollars", *The Mercury*, 17 December, p. 20.

Mercury, The 2008, "Tassie is the Place to be", 12 July, p. 9.

National Geographic Traveler 2014, "Our mission", June/July, p.4.

Lonely Planet Traveller 2014, "Our promise to you", June, p. 4.

Metcalf, Stephen 2008, "Tasmania's gourmet paradise", *Travel + Leisure*, February, viewed 5 March 2011, www.travelandleisure.com/articles/tasmanias-gourmet-paradise.

Mocatta, Gabi 2008, "Bay of Fires, Tasmania, Australia", in *Lonely Planet's Best in Travel 2009: 850 Trends, Destinations, Journeys & Experiences for the Year Ahead*, Lonely Planet, Melbourne.

Perrottet, Tony 2002, "Devil's plaground: Southern gothic", *Outside*, November, viewed 7 October 2011, www.outsideonline.com/adventure-travel/australia-pacific/australia/Devil-s-Playground--Southern-Gothic.html

Travel + Leisure 2015, "Travel + Leisure mission statement", T + L Media Kit, viewed 27 January 2015, www.tlmediakit.com/

Travel + Leisure 2014, "The T + L code", December, p. 18

Rose, Heather 2007, "Mill sends sour message", letter to the editor, *The Mercury*, 14 April, p. 35.

Sachs, Adam 2006, "All that Taz", *National Geographic Adventure*, February, pp. 60–65, 90.

Schofield, Leo 2007, "Too precious to waste", *The Mercury*, 2 June, p. B03.

Spindler, Amy 2001, "On the edge", *The New York Times*, 1 April, viewed 1 November 2012, www.nytimes.com/2001/04/01/magazine/on-the-edge.html

Street-Porter, Janet 2004, "A walk on the wild side", *The Independent*, 21 August, viewed 7 October 2011, www.independent.co.uk/travel/ausandpacific/a-walk-on-the-wild-side-557309.html

Tasmanian Times 2007, "The end of the world", 19 April, viewed 31 December 2011, http://tasmaniantimes.com/index.php?/weblog/article/the-end-of-the-world

Telegraph, The 2009, "Lonely Planet sparks a row over its pick for 2009's 'hottest' destination", 21 August, viewed 7 October 2011, www.telegraph.co.uk/news/worldnews/australiaandthepacific/6065362/Lonely-Planet-sparks-a-row-over-its-pick-for-2009s-hottest-destination.html

Tourism Australia 2014, "Heston Blumenthal confirmed to attend Restaurant Australia gala dinner", Tourism Australia, 11 November, viewed 3 January 2015, www.tourism.australia.com/news/news-11043.aspx

Tourism Tasmania 2003, *Tourism Tasmania Annual Report 2002–2003*, Tourism Tasmania, Hobart

Tourism Tasmania 1999, *Tourism Tasmania Annual Report 1998-1999*, Tourism Tasmania, Hobart.

Tourism Tasmania n.d., "Well said: Recent praise", Tourism Tasmania Media Site, viewed 4 April 2009, www.travelmedia.tourismtasmania.com.au/inspired/wellsaid/index/html

Tsui, Bonnie 2004, "Tasmania bound", *Travel + Leisure*, November, viewed 3 December 2011, www.travelandleisure.com/articles/tasmania-bound

Waisbord, Silvio & Peruzzotti, Enrique 2009, "The environmental story that wasn't: Advocacy, journalism and the asambleísmo movement in Argentina", *Media, Culture & Society*, vol. 31, no. 5, pp. 691–709.

Wanderlust 2010, "Threatened wonders 2010", *Wanderlust*, February, viewed 8 October 2011, www.wanderlust.co.uk/magazine/articles/destinations/threatened-wonders-2010?page=all#

Wheeler, Tony 2002, "Tasmania: Walk this way for luxury", *The Independent*, viewed 7 October 2011, www.independent.co.uk/travel/ausandpacific/tasmania-walk-this-way-for-luxury-641014.html

Wolfsfeld, Gadi 1997, *Media and Political Conflict: News from the Middle East*, Cambridge UP, Cambridge.

7 The challengers

In Chapter 6, challenges to Tasmania's place-branding were mediated through travel journalism largely as a result of journalistic agency, media power, media branding and the close proximity of the environmental threat to travel journalism sources who did not rely exclusively on the tourism industry for their income. In the case of the last of these factors, the success of sources in gaining access to travel journalism demonstrated that brand extensions intended to bolster place-branding can, in times of conflict, help expose it to scrutiny. Place-branding proved incapable of "simultaneously mediat[ing] subjective qualities, tastes, and norms; and... objective financial worth" (Aronczyk and Powers 2010, p. 7) when the threat was perceived by travel journalism sources to have a direct impact on their incomes, leading these sources to risk deploying a damaged brand in travel journalism.

In this chapter I consider Tasmania's place-branding specifically as it encounters challenges to its credibility mounted by travel journalists ideologically and strategically committed to environmentalism. The chapter draws attention to strategies and tactics of environment movements, the scope for journalistic agency, and the role of rationality and affect – particularly the strategic effectiveness of deploying celebrity and the voices of passionate locals as part of "brand-sensitive cosmopolitan concern".

The View from the other side

Like BBC *Wildlife Magazine* in 2000 (see Chapter 5), the *New York Times* in 2004 (See Chapters 1 and 5), *National Geographic Traveler* in 2006 (see Chapter 9), and *Travel + Leisure* in 2008 (See Chapter 6), the United States' adventure magazine *Outside* was prepared to make space for "brand-sensitive cosmopolitan concern". On this occasion, journalistic agency and a form of challenger public relations countered the advantages the Visiting Journalist Program (VJP) gave the government's frames in the discourse of accessible nature by framing the journalist's own adventure in Tasmania as extreme access to contested forests. Mark Jenkins, who was a staff journalist for *Outside* at the time, travelled to Tasmania at the expense of his magazine and was able to activate a substantial anti-forestry network in his quest to access some of the island's most challenging wilderness. His objective in the Styx Valley was to do what Wilderness Society campaigner Geoff Law said to his knowledge "no human has actually done… cross end to end through one of the last contiguous stands of giant old-growth regnans" (Law in Jenkins 2005). Not only did Jenkins interview Law, who had been a key strategist in the Franklin dam blockade and subsequent forestry disputes, but he also quoted Richard Flanagan, who in addition to his literary and journalistic achievements is the first person to have kayaked "the 25-mile Class III-IV Styx River" (Jenkins 2005) – an impeccable credential for a Jenkins interviewee. Jenkins was himself a traveller known for his feats of physical endurance and as a result enjoyed considerable editorial freedom, which he put to the service of his environmental concerns. In the following quote he describes his editorial preoccupations, research methods and the freedom he was afforded by his publisher:

> I wrote a column called "The Hard Way" [for *Outside* magazine] for about eight years. And in that I did 75 journeys and 75 columns and none of them were someone else's idea. None of them were suggestions by travel companies or whatever. All of them were about issues or subjects that I care about. So, I don't know if I fit into your classic mould. Now I work for *National Geographic* magazine and the same applies. In fact, at *National Geographic* we are not allowed to take any junkets or get a free plane ticket or all those kind of things that are associated with travel journalism. We have a ban on that because it can influence how you write a story. I've never done that anyway, so for me it was an easy fit. So in terms of how information flows I see it as my obligation to write about the environmental issues of a place I go… I'm typically going someplace because I'm fascinated by the geography or the culture or particularly in the case of Tasmania I knew about the forestry issues there. I'd covered those same issues in the US, I'd read Richard Flanagan's couple of his books. I wrote him a note, said, you know, I'm thinking of coming down and writing a story about your area and he invited me and when I got down I thought, you know, the way to do this is actually to have some kind of experience of these grand trees and that's how Matt and I ended up deciding let's see if we can do a complete traverse of what little is left of the Styx, and that's what we did. And so, so often for me the – this is the way to put it – that the travel slash adventure for me is simply a narrative structure which I can use to talk about an issue.
>
> (Jenkins 2009, pers. comm., 20 March)

Jenkins was an ideal fit for *Outside*, which describes itself as "dedicated to covering the people, sports and activities, politics, art, literature, and hardware of the outdoors…[a]rmed with great writing that's always based on critical thinking and a sharp sense of humor" (*Outside* 2011). Thus, *Outside* proved a valuable forum for the "warlike conflagration" frame (see Chapter 5). The following description by Jenkins bears many of the hallmarks of the description provided by Metcalf in *Travel + Leisure* (2008, see Chapter 6), the difference being that Jenkins could claim first-hand experience of the aftermath of a burn:

What changed me more was the macabre graveyards of the clear-cuts. Peck drove us to the start of our bushwalk, through an apocalyptic scene: Charred logs lay like corpses across a battlefield; blackened stumps sat among funeral pyres of unremarkable trees.

(Jenkins 2005)

Jenkins described the vestiges of the Global Rescue Station – a camp surrounding a platform where activists, supported by the Wilderness Society and Greenpeace, had gained international media coverage by webcasting their five-month-long tree-sit 64 metres up in the Styx Forest canopy in the Australian summer of 2003–2004 (Lester and Hutchins 2009). In his published text, Jenkins quoted one of the activists, who spoke of ongoing work to make the station and surrounding forest a life-changing destination (Firth in Jenkins 2005). Like Metcalf (2008), Jenkins was also careful to include a complicating voice in his article – one directly related to the subject of his story. Just as Metcalf included the comments of a winemaker associated with a woodchipping company in his story about wine and food, Jenkins included some information from a Forestry Tasmania district manager, Steve Whiteley, in his story about the Styx. In his interview for my research, Whiteley recalled that "[i]t was a good story for an outdoor magazine about an adventure, and the more the characters and some of those things can be worked into that sort of article then presumably that's what the readers want so that's what the journalist writes" (Whiteley, S 2009, pers. comm., 4 August). Whiteley felt that Jenkins had been candid with him in describing the kind of article he was writing and what his part in it would be but did not consider the article an opportunity to provide anything but factual information. He described his positioning in the article as providing "input rather than balance" (Whiteley, S 2009, pers. comm., 4 August):

[T]here was an activist campaign running and there were a number of different things that were going on and from time to time FT or I were called upon to provide information. In this case it was fairly reactive, if you like, so there were a set of questions that the journalist wanted answered, there wasn't really an opportunity to portray any other perspective. So it was more an interrogation rather than a— certainly I didn't see it, and it wasn't, an equal opportunity to participate at the same level as many of the other participants were engaged.

(Whiteley 2009, pers. comm., 4 August)

As in Metcalf's article (2008, see Chapter 6), the inclusion of a voice opposed to the general tenor of the text did not result in a less critical framing of the state's forestry practices but it did enable Jenkins to argue that he had assessed the evidence offered by both sides in forming his own opinion:

I was reporting so it was my duty to try to speak to all sides of the issue and so it was my job to talk to— as a reporter I can't just talk to Geoff, I need to talk to everybody I can about different perspectives on what's happening in the

Styx. And so to do that I couldn't simply speak to Geoff Law at the Wilderness
Society, I felt like I needed to speak to Steve Whiteley, who was the district
manager for Forestry Tasmania. I felt like I needed to speak to all sides of it
and then come up with my own assessment.

(Jenkins 2009, pers. comm., 20 March)

Whiteley expressed no expectation of balance in what he described as opinion
pieces:

As long as articles don't purport to be balanced then people don't have to
write balanced articles. They can write opinion pieces with a particular
agenda. There's no question of that…They write opinion pieces to be interesting and sell magazines.

(Whiteley 2009, pers. comm., 4 August)

Whiteley cites as evidence of his view that the inclusion of facts from Forestry
Tasmania was tokenistic the article's retelling of what he described as "the
Tasmanian tiger bit…straight out of the Wilderness Society's campaign at that
stage" (Whiteley, S 2009, pers. comm., 4 August; for a contemporary example of
the Wilderness Society's narrative in relation to the Tasmanian tiger, see Wilderness Society 2010). Here, Whiteley is referring to Jenkins' transmission through
his text of challenges to Forestry Tasmania's "sustainable" branding – and, by
implication, Tasmania's "natural" branding – via the metaphor of the Tasmanian
tiger. Tasmania has an ambivalent relationship with the tiger: on the one hand it
uses a "distanced brutality" frame of historical brutality teamed with tourism and
contemporary regret (for an explanation of this frame, see Chapter 6) to manage
the brand contradiction of its extinction (see, for example, Department of
Tourism, Parks, Heritage and the Arts 2005); on the other hand, from 1995 the
image of a Tasmanian tiger "in a wilderness environment" (Tourism Tasmania
1997, p. 12) was one of the state's logos, intended to invoke the myth of the
animal's possible continued existence as a symbol of "discovery, surprise, intrigue,
the unexpected, tranquillity and natural [sic.]" (Tourism Tasmania 1997, p. 12,
see Chapter 4). Jenkins introduced the tiger in the first paragraph of his article but
did not inform his readers of its extinction until his final sentence. The animal was
portrayed as having become extinct at the hands of a government that allowed its
forest habitat to be destroyed and paid a bounty for its carcasses. By continuing to
log forests where tigers once lived the government was represented by Jenkins as
showing itself unwilling to learn from history and therefore of protecting the
environment in 2005, in direct contrast to the "distanced brutality" frame.

Forestry Tasmania represented its own tourism ventures as complementing
wilderness experiences by offering something more akin to adventure activities:
"Forestry Tas is looking for the 'Get out there' rather than the wilderness, [which] is
more 'Look from a distance' or 'Tread lightly'. So we're visibly interested in a point
of difference in what we're trying to do for that part of the market" (Whiteley, S
2009, pers. comm., 4 August). However, Whiteley did not see his role in the

interview with Jenkins as promoting those activities, despite *Outdoor*'s adventure branding. In his understanding that he was providing factual information, he confined himself to a rational, scientific discourse that could not compete in the subjective, affective genre of travel journalism with the emotion-laden discourse of Jenkins and his other interviewees (Whiteley, S 2009, pers. comm., 4 August).

Jenkins' article was unusual in that it was a travel journalism feature in which the cosmopolitical aspects of "brand-sensitive cosmopolitan concern" were textually prominent rather than a subsidiary theme. Whereas Forestry Tasmania regarded his story as part of the environment movement's campaign, Jenkins, who described himself as a "global correspondent", regarded himself as bringing cosmopolitan concern for the environment to the attention of his readers in America and particularly to those who might be dealing with similar issues:

> I have the same problem in my own state in Wyoming where you've got foresters who don't really get the fact that they're cutting down some of the last stands that will ever exist, because the climate's changing… [H]aving been to the Congo, the Amazon, all over Asia, all over Africa, all over Europe, all over South America, all over North America, I recognise that there are these tiny gems left, and they're very small and there are very few of them, and I kind-of believe in trying to protect every one of them because essentially we're just going to have little parks, that's all we'll have left, you know. The population of the planet's going to double, and all we're going to have are little tiny pieces of wilderness. They'll just be tiny. They'll be like Central Park. They're going to be almost nothing. But it's something that young people can still take a walk through and have a sense of what used to be on the planet. I think that's valuable.
>
> (Jenkins 2009, pers. comm., 20 March)

In talking about the article, author Jenkins and interviewee Whiteley both invoked their professional expertise in support of their practice – the news value of balance and his own cultural capital as a global correspondent in Jenkins' case, scientific expertise and a commitment to multidimensional land management in Whiteley's. Although Jenkins did not regard himself as a travel journalist, he believed in ecotourism and expected his article to encourage his readers to visit the state (Jenkins, M 2009, pers. comm., 20 March). Such strong support in such a long article (nearly 3,000 words) in a United States glossy adventure/travel magazine with a circulation in 2011 of 678,000 (*Outside* n.d.) was a public relations coup for Tasmania's environment movement. This was achieved in no small part by Flanagan's likely appeal as an adventurer as well as a novelist to *Outside*'s demographic. Moreover, many years after Jenkins moved to *National Geographic* magazine, he posted a version of the story under a new title to his *National Geographic* blog "Beyond the Edge" while it was still available on the *Outside* website and at the same time as another article mediating the island's environmental conflicts appeared in *Outside* (Pearson 2014, see Chapter 1) – an example of a very high degree of journalistic agency in the interests of challenger framing.

Tactical travel journalism

Sometimes the environment movement's tactics have an impact on travel journalism in a more indirect way than was demonstrated in the previous section. In these days of direct access to foreign publics via online media, some of Australia's largest environmental organisations have deployed networked technology strategically and tactically to attract the attention of journalists and gain access to mainstream print and broadcast news (Hutchins and Lester 2011; Lester and Hutchins 2009). In so doing, they have relied on elements of tactical media (Garcia and Lovink 1997; Lovink 2002, 2005; Meikle 2002) – "cheap 'do-it-yourself' media, made possible by the revolution in consumer electronics and expanded forms of distribution (from public access cable to the Internet)… exploited by groups and individuals who feel aggrieved by or excluded from the wider culture" (Garcia and Lovink 1997). In its purest form the term "tactical media" emphasises anonymity and rejects the institutionalisation that attends the evolution of many non-government organisations. However, when Geert Lovink coined the term in the 1990s, he made reference to tactical media practitioners working "both inside and outside the mainstream media" (Lovink in Meikle 2002, p. 120). This, together with his views that investigative journalism is "the basis of all 'tactical' output" but editorial desks are servile and censorious (Lovink 2002, p. 258), makes evidence of new-media tactics in the soft genre of travel journalism intriguing. In 2009 Lester and Hutchins elaborated and adjusted Lovink's concept of tactical media in their exploration of the broader strategic and tactical uses of new media in environmental conflict, and I draw on their approach here when focusing primarily on the actions of travel journalists.

The legacy of the Styx

In November 2002, the Wilderness Society, together with WWF and Planet Ark, bought billboard space in Sydney Airport and erected a billboard juxtaposing an image of Styx Valley forest due to be logged in 2003–04 with an image of forest that had been cleared and burnt. The billboard headline "Discover Tasmania before 2003" repurposed words that are part of the URL of Tourism Tasmania's holiday website www.discovertasmania.com.au. The airport advertising agency removed the billboard after one day, saying it had not been approved in advance by the airline Qantas. A report in *The Mercury* (Ribbon 2002) suggested the state's premier and minister responsible for Tourism Tasmania, Jim Bacon, had pressured Qantas to remove the billboard. Qantas denied this, but Bacon publicly attacked the environment groups who had erected it and claimed there was "no truth in the statement that Tasmania's forests are threatened in the way that the last of our forests are about to disappear" (Bacon in Ribbon 2002, p. 3). Two weeks later, an anti-forestry website www.discover-tasmania.com was posted anonymously, its URL differing from the official state tourism office site's URL by the addition of a single hyphen. When the website owner was exposed a week later, *The Mercury* newspaper identified him as a former Tasmanian tourism operator, Gordon Craven, who said he was acting alone and had set up the site primarily to protest against removal of the airport billboard and to highlight the cruelty of the forestry industry's use of 1080 poison to kill animals that browsed on its seedlings (Bailey 2002, p. 3). Tourism Tasmania's chief executive at the time was reported by *The Mercury* as labelling the website "a 'direct hit' on the state's reputation which threatened visitor numbers and could have a multi-million-dollar impact" (Giason in Bailey 2002, p. 3). In the same article, Craven was quoted as saying that he "set up the site to shame the Government and Forestry Tasmania who use tourism, and the tourist operators who just stand by and let it happen" (Craven in Bailey 2002, p. 3). In a related dispute about Craven's registration of the associated but slightly longer domain name www.discover-tasmania.com.au for a tourism website that linked through to his original site, the World Intellectual Property Organization (2003) ruled against Tourism Tasmania. In later years, one of the forestry conflicts publicised by Craven was the campaign against plans by major Forestry Tasmania customer Gunns Ltd to build the AUD1.9 billion pulp mill in the state's most significant wine tourism area, the Tamar Valley – a dispute that also captured the attention of British travel journalist Paul Miles.

Miles was an environmentally and socially conscious freelance journalist who listed the NGO Tourism Concern as one of his non-media clients (Miles n.d.). Prior to visiting Tasmania late in 2007, he had been aware of its forestry conflicts – so much so that until then he had avoided writing about the island (Miles, P 2009, pers. comm., 9 March). After learning of the pulp mill dispute, however, he decided to tour Tasmania as a hosted and guided guest of the Visiting Journalist Program (VJP), thereby acknowledging the appeal of travel journalism as a vehicle for raising concerns about environmental issues. In his words, "I thought it might be quite good if I could try and write about the pulp mill and the controversy around that as well as writing about the good things that are happening in the state" (Miles, P 2009, pers. comm., 9 March). The extent of the value tourist destinations place on coverage in prestigious, high-circulation publications – in this case the British edition of *Condé Nast Traveller* and London's *Financial Times* – is evident in Tourism Tasmania's decision to host Miles in spite of his admission that he intended to investigate the pulp mill dispute. Nevertheless, he felt his candour made the organisation's British public relations representative extremely nervous. This led to a struggle for editorial control enacted in a debate in which expectations of genres and genre attributes were both explicitly and implicitly contested. In Miles' account of the conversations, the public relations practitioner appears to be invoking the news journalism ideal of balance specifically in response to her concern that Miles might have been intending to operate as an investigative foreign correspondent in Tasmania rather than as a travel journalist:

> I was very up front with her about it, yeah. I told her I wanted to talk about those issues too. And as I said, she was anxious, but she agreed that it would be okay.
>
> (Miles 2009, pers. comm., 9 March)

She did try to persuade me that things weren't as bad as some NGOs make out and that maybe I had only heard one side of the story and I should investigate both of them and I should also see how good the forestry is and that it was well-managed and everything.

(Miles 2009, pers. comm., 9 March)

Although interviewed public relations practitioners with experience in Tourism Tasmania's VJP demonstrated an understanding of the difference between *news* journalism and marketing, their discourse and that of other members of the tourism sector was less likely to differentiate strongly between *travel* journalism and marketing. This may be attributable partly to their own experience of working with travel journalists who so often ignored controversy or criticism in their published texts. In some cases it was probably also partly due to confusion created by the work practices of travel journalists themselves, many of whom sometimes accepted copywriting assignments in addition to working as journalists. Within these understandings and expectations, however, there was considerable hetero-geneity among public relations practitioners with Tourism Tasmania experience. However, with some important exceptions, an institutional rationale was evident whereby it was argued that any travel journalists who did insist on including negative comment about the state's forestry practices should be prepared to balance this with views about logging from pro-forestry sources. As evident in the following quotes from two different public relations practitioners, by the time Miles visited the state, Tourism Tasmania had adopted a strategy to manage travel journalists with environmental concerns by arranging interviews for them with government-accredited sources with specialised knowledge. This was a more active intervention than had been the practice early in the decade, when, if pressed, the senior public relations practitioner would provide travel journalists with contact details of people on both sides of the debate but would not arrange interviews for them with either side (Nicholls, D., 2009, pers. comm.). Reference below to a conscious decision to change tack and adopt more traditional government media-referral practices later in the decade suggests that criticism in international travel journalism was becoming more problematic for Tourism Tasmania as the decade progressed. This was partly because the pulp mill proposal had seen environmental concerns increasingly voiced by wine and food tourism operators who might not otherwise have taken an active interest in forestry disputes:

PUBLIC RELATIONS PRACTITIONER 1: ...I think we've learnt from things that have happened in the past, and by that I mean that perhaps we haven't...steered people in the right direction to speak to the right people. And what we're doing now is we're doing a lot more interviews with people with experience. So we'll send someone to a professor at the university to talk about the devil tumours. We'll send someone to meet with someone to talk about forestry practices if that's what it takes. We'll send someone to talk about climate change and the effects on Tasmania. You know, we won't profess to being them, because...if people are going to quote things we want them to quote *them*. And then we'll depend on those specialists in the field to do that. We'll also send an appropriate guide that we feel will handle that situation. So we certainly won't say, "Oh we better not have them come because they might write something about it." We'll just say, "Okay, well how can we give them the best information?" (2009, pers. comm., 8 March)

PUBLIC RELATIONS PRACTITIONER 2: … if we were taking journalists out to dinner and those issues came up, you'd give them the facts. You know, just in discussions, you'd say, "Well, this is the stage it's at…" We wouldn't make any comment. If they then wanted to speak to somebody about it further we'd look at what we could do to help them out speaking to appropriate people.

RESEARCHER. And what are appropriate people?

PUBLIC RELATIONS PRACTITIONER 2: …We've had a few instances and the thing that we always tried to do was give a balanced view. So if they wanted to talk to someone from the Wilderness Society, which was quite common, that's fine, we would not arrange – I don't think we ever directly arranged it for them, but they were free to go and talk to them. At the same time we'd offer a forestry person.

(pers. comm., 16 March)

In most cases, the discourse of public relations practitioners with experience in Tourism Tasmania's VJP lacked a reflexive sense that their own arguments might equally be used to justify travel journalism criticism of logging on the basis that it balanced place-branding representations of the state as "natural" in the rest of the article. Meanwhile, as mentioned earlier, busy itineraries functioned as an attempt at media management, but one that had limited effect if journalists were determined to pursue the issue.

Having secured editorial agreement from *Conde Nast Traveller* to cover the pulp mill dispute, Miles organised an alternative guide unconnected with the VJP to show him the proposed pulp mill site in the one free day his Tourism Tasmania itinerary allowed him (Miles, P 2009, pers. comm., 9 March). The resulting article (2008b, p. 34), which referred in its lead to Tasmania's forests as threatened "wilderness", was written in the third-person style of news journalism, favoured the framing of those opposed to the mill, included restaurateur Daniel Alps (see also discussion of Alps in Chapter 6), and included the counterarguments of Gunns. Miles' feature for the *Financial Times* (2008a), by contrast, was in the first-person style of a traditional travel journalism narrative and covered much of his Tourism Tasmania itinerary. In the draft he submitted to the newspaper, he contrasted Tasmania's "pristine wilderness" with what he described as the state's "reputation for feckless forestry practices" (Miles, P 2009, pers. comm., 9 March). In the draft he also described the process of clear-felling and burning associated with old-growth logging and explained the possible effects of the pulp mill on the island's wine and food industries. Miles said the newspaper cut these parts of the story before publication, which Miles saw as demonstrating that power in commercial travel journalism publishing resides with the editors and publishers (Miles, P 2009, pers. comm., 9 March). Miles, however, engaged in a form of "hit-and-run" (Meikle 2002, p. 119) tactical media that briefly challenged such power. Beneath the URL of Tourism Tasmania's website for tourists noted after his article, he listed the URL of the tourism anti-forestry website www.discover-tasmania.com.au (Miles 2008a). As Miles recalled in 2009, "I listed that and they included it in the feature… [T]hat's as close as I've got really, in the FT. I think that was kind-of a little bit subversive actually. I think they just assumed it was a link to the Tourism [Tasmania] website" (Miles, P 2009, pers. comm., 9 March). Yet although Miles was able to challenge the newspaper's power briefly by including this URL, the structural forces that generally privilege the messages of elite sources in travel journalism were not altered by his gesture. Commenting almost a year after the article appeared, he remained despondent about the power imbalance in his relationship with editors (Miles, P 2009, pers. comm., 10 March).

Under the radar in the Tarkine

In February 2005, shortly after an Australian election in which Tasmania's forest disputes had featured prominently, the United States NGO Ethical Traveler mounted an online letter-writing campaign in association with the Wilderness Society (Ethical Traveler n.d.). The campaign asked members to urge the Australian Government to hold firm on all of its election promises in relation to the protection of Tasmania's old-growth forests. In reporting Ethical Traveler's actions, a related publication, *Earth Island Journal*, noted the importance of tourism to Tasmania's economy and observed that "the partner groups view their joint environmentalist–traveler campaign as a logical next step in protecting these extraordinary forests" (McColl 2005). *Earth Island Journal* ended by stating that Ethical Traveler's executive director, Jeff Greenwald, had given assurances that Ethical Traveler would "monitor" the situation to ensure the Australian government held to its promise (McColl 2005).

Jeff Greenwald is also a noted travel journalist and travel book author. In recounting a 2007 tour of Tasmania as a guest of Tourism Tasmania, he said he'd arrived with few preconceptions and had been only superficially aware of Ethical Traveler's 2005 campaign in conjunction with the Wilderness Society. While in Tasmania, however, he had also made contact with people to whom, as he explained, Tourism Tasmania would probably rather he had not spoken (Greenwald, J 2009, pers. comm., 6 March). The resulting article published in *Islands* magazine in 2008 duly praised a variety of tourist attractions and described the destination as a "global treasure" but also deployed the "warlike conflagration" frame. In addition, the article called on the Australian government to make "wise choices" for Tasmania's forests, but it did not mention Greenwald's association with Ethical Traveler.

Both Miles (2008b) in *Conde Nast Traveller* and Greenwald (2008) in *Islands* juxtaposed their criticisms of Tasmania's environmental practices with references to Tasmania's brand promise of "Australia's natural state" or "Your natural state" in what functioned textually as an ironic play on journalism's balance ethic. And like Metcalf (2008), Flanagan (2004) and Jenkins (2005), both these travel journalists' appealed for global sensitivity to Tasmania's forests through the voices of locals with an intense attachment to place. Greenwald went so far as to quote his Tourism Tasmania guide, Di Hollister, in reference to her concern for the Tasmanian devil. Neither Greenwald nor Miles noted in their articles that Hollister worked for Tourism Tasmania yet both paid tribute to her – Miles for her past life as a Greens Member of Parliament (Miles 2008a), Greenwald for her passion for her island (Greenwald 2008). Thus, tourism public relations were turned to the advantage of the authors' cosmopolitan concern through the voice of a passionate local. In addition, Greenwald expressed his personal active political cosmopolitanism by entreating Australia's government to intervene to protect Tasmania's rivers and forests:

> This is a critical time for all Tassie's residents...How Australia's new govern-
> ment manages the island's rivers and forests will affect every member of its
> ecosystem, from the earthworms to the devils to the kangaroos. To visit is to
> hope for wise choices, for Tasmania is a global treasure.
>
> (Greenwald 2008)

Greenwald expressed no sense of obligation to Tourism Tasmania for hosting him in 2007 (Greenwald, J 2009, pers. comm., 6 March). Rather, when discussing the kinds of articles he wrote, he spoke in terms of his publishers' expectations. *Islands*, he said, had wanted a traditional atmospheric travel narrative, whereas *Afar*, which funded a second trip to Tasmania inspired by the first, wanted something far more people-focussed (Greenwald, J 2009, pers. comm., 6 March). The extent to which Greenwald was prepared to write to direction is evident in the following interview extract, which refers to a dispute over proposals by Forestry Tasmania to pave a section of road through an area of rainforest in the Tarkine to create a "tourist loop":

> [O]ne of the reasons I was so keen to come back, was I really wanted to be able
> to focus my attention on the political conflict unfolding in western Tasmania.
> Now, though I was given that mandate by the magazine *Afar*, it was also made
> clear to me that it wasn't to be a good versus evil story. *Afar* magazine wanted
> to see the human side of the issue from both sides and as a result we spoke to
> people who were passionately committed to their point of view on both sides
> of the forestry argument and the Tarkine road argument. So, you know, there
> was no— though I may have my own prejudice in terms of what I'd like to see
> done to the area, the function of my story is not to editorialise but to just
> present how different people who grew up in the same part of Tasmania can
> have such different views about how to use the land and what the future of
> that forest should be.
>
> (Greenwald 2009, pers. comm., 6 March)

The Tarkine loop road proposal was opposed by local tourism organisation Cradle Coast Authority, peak tourism industry body Tourism Industry Council Tasmania and environmental group the Tarkine National Coalition (McGaurr, Tranter and Lester 2014). Scott Jordan of the Tarkine National Coalition was circumspect in his assessment of the value to his organisation's campaign of media coverage of controversy. He wanted to attract support from outside the state, but he also wanted to "bring the community on side" (Jordan, S 2009, pers. comm., 18 June). In his view, the generally conservative residents of north-west Tasmania would be alienated by reports of high levels of open conflict: "I think if we were to take a similar stance here to, say, the southern forests campaign [in and near the state capital, Hobart], while it might work for their aims down there, it would certainly alienate people in the north-west coast, and we would find that we would very quickly make the Tarkine a dirty word" (Jordan, S 2009, pers. comm., 18 June).

Although the Tarkine National Coalition did not target travel journalists in particular, Jordan believed travel journalism had the potential to engage readers who might know nothing about the Tarkine. Once engaged emotionally, he believed, these readers would be more likely to engage politically:

> I think it's incredibly valuable. The news journalism really engages people who are already engaged with the issue. And if they're already in love with the Tarkine then the news journalism will tell them what the threat is and that they need to get out and give, and that the issue's alive. The travel journalism really is what gets people to fall in love with the place. If it encourages people to come and visit it or just to look at pictures in a good article and see it as some place that's beautiful, then it opens doors for the news journalism to work. If you just got another article about another place that they're logging, there's no shortage of those, there's nothing really to inspire you to engage. But it's the travel journalism that convinces people that something is worth saving I think.
> (Jordan 2009, pers. comm., 18 June)

Despite objections by the Cradle Coast Authority and the Tourism Industry Council Tasmania, however, some tourism operators were very much in favour of the road. One prominent advocate said he had initially failed to realise the importance of the Tarkine and other natural attractions to tourism in the north-west but was now an enthusiastic supporter of associated tourism development. In his interview he referred to the positioning of the far north-west as "the edge of the world"; a scientific facility on the region's Cape Grim promoted by the Tasmanian tourism and agricultural industries as having recorded the cleanest air in the world; and the then-forthcoming UN Climate Change Conference in Copenhagen. In so doing, he framed environmental awareness as a tourism marketing tool in a manner similar to that of Tourism Tasmania, its public relations practitioners, the Cradle Coast Authority, the Tourism Industry Council Tasmania and other tourism operators interviewed for this case study (2009, pers. comm., 9 December).

Just as the value of international publicity had been sufficiently seductive to persuade Tourism Tasmania to host Miles in 2007 despite his stated interest in the pulp mill, it was attractive enough to elicit an unusual degree of cooperation with Greenwald from the Tarkine National Coalition in 2009, as Jordan explained:

> [W]e gave him some names of people that we perhaps under normal circumstances wouldn't have told the media to go off and get comment from these people. But his project was perhaps a bit different from what we'd normally do in media so we tried to assist him where we could…hopefully, if we generate some passion in people who are overseas reading that article [they might] then join the campaign in some way and contribute to letting our government know that this area does have international recognition and is worthy of protection.
>
> (Jordan 2009, pers. comm., 18 June)

Apart from its high-impact headline, "Bedeviled Island", published by *Afar* early in 2010, was less overt in its political subjectivity than Greenwald's *Islands* article had been. It gave space to views supportive of the proposed Tarkine road, reported claims that the road was a threat to what was then believed to be the last remaining wild population of Tasmanian devils free of facial tumour disease, and even covered Geoff King's protracted efforts to prevent the riders of off-road vehicles from damaging the foreshore of his property – a personal concern (see Chapter 5) that had rarely gained exposure in travel journalism despite his best efforts. It also mediated local contestation about the meaning of "wilderness".

In November 2010, *Afar* won the top award in the magazine category in one of the United States' most prestigious travel writing competitions, the Lowell Thomas Travel Journalism Awards, run by the Society of American Travel Writers, and "Bedeviled Island" won the top award in the category of environmental tourism article (Society of American Travel Writers n.d.). In this second Greenwald example, then, more traditional news journalism norms and practices were to the fore in relation to coverage of Tasmania's forestry debates.

Conclusion

Miles and Greenwald had a personal commitment to environmentalism and connections with groups whose campaigning for ethical tourism sometimes included environmental issues. In both cases, past uses of new media in environmental protests contributed to their ability to mount insider challenges to the definitional advantages enjoyed by elite tourism sources. Indeed, there was an element of Lovink-style tactical media in Miles' hit-and-run inclusion of one of Craven's URLs in his *Financial Times* article. By contrast, Ethical Traveler's online campaign in 2005 was openly networked. However, neither the *Financial Times* nor the *Islands* example represents a sustained assault on media power, as evidenced by Miles' continued lack of control over his published texts and Greenwald's willingness to meet *Afar*'s editorial requirements.

Where international travel journalists appeared able to exert some limited influence was at the margins of the island's brand. In the 2000s Tasmania's brand managers projected an increasingly diverse and culturally sophisticated image of the island by promoting heritage, wine and food experiences and providing government support to high-profile cultural events, but in late 2010 the most important component of Tasmania's brand was still overwhelmingly its natural environment (Tourism Tasmania 2011). Though initiated by Tourism Tasmania and pursued by Brand Tasmania, positioning of nature in the brand owed much to the environment movement's early success at public relations. Moreover, the existence of Tasmania's globally significant wilderness and the value of nature were constantly re-asserted through the very protests and other tactics the environment movement used to draw attention to Tasmania and its own causes, while Tourism Tasmania's branding efforts simultaneously built further awareness of Tasmania's place-branded environment on the global public stage – awareness the environment movement could continue to exploit. As early masters of branding in its own campaigning, the environment movement was itself ready to deploy similar tactics to those used by Tourism Tasmania to gain access to travel journalists, providing them with storylines, frames and guided tours either directly or by recommendation. And travel journalists with ties to tourism NGOs proved adept at turning Tourism Tasmania's VJP to their own advantage, while continuing to provide the destination with valuable endorsement among tourists and other travellers through the frame of "brand-sensitive cosmopolitan concern".

Although sources on both sides of the debate sometimes attempted to deploy their own facts and/or rational economic or scientific arguments, in articles written by travel journalists who had chosen to become "*advocates of the underdog*" rather than "*faithful servants to the authorities*" (Wolfsfeld 1997, p. 69, original emphasis), it was the affective discourse of character-driven stories and narratives of forest battlefields, old-growth graveyards, homeless eagles, doomed Tasmanian tigers and endangered devils that dominated, and carried the messages of the environment movement most decisively. Sources on both sides of the debate understood this, but inevitably cast as the villain in such stories, Forestry Tasmania was further hampered by explanatory appeals to science that were too complex to be developed in a travel journalism article. As in the case of Flinn's article discussed in Chapter 5, competition between sources was not confined to competition between challengers and elites. Importantly, travel journalists with an interest in challenging the brand were able to turn these source struggles to their own advantage, though usually only within the constraints of the genre's requirement for text that celebrated travel. However, Greenwald's 2010 article demonstrated that there was also another possibility – the inversion of the semi-honest broker in Wolfsfeld's model (Wolfsfeld 1997, p. 69) in the form of travel journalists whose sympathies were with the challengers but who allowed those opposed to the challengers "a significant amount of time and space to air their views" (Wolfsfeld 1997, p. 69).

For Jenkins and Greenwald, an ability to mediate criticisms of Tasmania's branding was significantly enhanced by assistance from the environment movement or activists in the form of production assets, exceptional behaviour or international status (see Wolfsfeld 1997). Both journalists also had high cultural capital, while Jenkins' article, like Metcalf's (2008), contributed directly to his publication's branding. But *Outside*, like so many other travel magazines discussed in this case study, had also once furnished Tasmania with an accolade its tourism office had disseminated through its marketing and on its corporate website throughout the decade (Tourism Tasmania 2009), and at the end of the case study Perrottet's (2002, see Chapter 6) brand-aligned article in the same magazine remained accessible online, just as Jenkins' did. Nevertheless, in 2014, when a version of Jenkins' article began its concurrent career under a different headline as a post on his *National Geographic* blog (see above), it periodically rose to the top of the results of a search of NationalGeographic.com for the term "Tasmania". This is an interesting outcome for a representation of the island's environmental conflicts first published in 2005 – one that raises questions about how travel journalism's impact on the cosmopolitan public sphere is related to what happens post-publication at the micro level of individual websites. Thus, in the next chapter I shift my focus from my Tasmanian case study investigating the production of travel journalism to a consideration of the way travel journalism published online by a single media organisation interacts with other genres visually and textually via the mechanism of the website search.

References

Aronczyk, Melissa & Powers, Devon 2010, "Blowing up the brand: 'New branded world' redux", in Melissa Aronczyk and Devon Powers (eds), *Blowing Up the Brand: Critical Perspectives on Promotional Culture*, Peter Lang, London, pp. 1–26.

Bailey, Sue 2002, "Architect of anti-forestry site hits out as identity revealed", *The Mercury*, 23 November, p. 3.

Department of Tourism, Parks, Heritage and the Arts 2005, *Tasmanian Wildlife Tourism Strategy*, Government of Tasmania, Hobart.

Ethical Traveler n.d., "Future remains uncertain for Tasmania's old-growth forests", viewed 29 December 2011, www.ethicaltraveler.org/act/future-remains-uncertain-for-tasmanias-old-growth-forests/

Garcia, David & Lovink, Geert, 1997, "The ABC of tactical media", viewed 27 January 2015, www.nettime.org/Lists-Archives/nettime-l-9705/msg00096.html

Greenwald, Jeff 2010, "Bedeviled island", *Afar*, March-April, pp. 64-73.

Greenwald, Jeff 2008, "Sympathy for the devil", *Islands Magazine*, 22 April, viewed 24 April 2015, www.islands.com/article/Sympathy-for-the-Devil

Hutchins, Brett & Lester, Libby 2011, "Politics, power and online protest in an age of environmental conflict", in Simon Cottle & Libby Lester (eds), *Transnational Protest and the Media*, Peter Lang, New York, pp. 159–171.

Jenkins, Mark 2014, "Navigations: Last stand in Tasmania", Beyond the Edge: A National Geographic Adventure blog, *National Geographic*, 19 February 2014, viewed 2 January 2015, http://adventureblog.nationalgeographic.com/2014/02/19/navigations-last-stand-in-tasmania/

Jenkins, Mark 2005, "Bush bashing", *Outside*, June, viewed 31 December 2011, www.outsideonline.com/adventure-travel/Bush-Bashing.html

Lester, Libby & Hutchins, Brett 2009, "Power games: Environmental protest, news media and the internet", *Media, Culture & Society*, vol. 31, no. 4, pp. 579–595.

Lovink, Geert 2005, "Tactical media, the second decade", viewed 15 March 2013, http://geertlovink.org/texts/tactical-media-the-second-decade

Lovink, Geert 2002, "Dark fibre: Tracking critical Internet culture", MIT Press, Cambridge, Massachusetts.

Meikle, Graham 2002, *Future Active: Media Activism and the Internet*, Pluto Press, Annandale.

Metcalf, Stephen 2008, "Tasmania's gourmet paradise", *Travel + Leisure*, February, viewed 5 March 2011, www.travelandleisure.com/articles/tasmanias-gourmet-paradise

McColl, Michael 2005, "Ethical Traveler: New hope for Australia's old-growth forests", *Earth Island Journal*, vol. 20, no. 1, viewed 12 November 2011, www.earthisland.org/journal/index.php/eij/article/ethical_traveler1/

McGaurr, Lyn, Tranter, Bruce & Lester, Libby 2014, "Wilderness and the politics of place branding", *Environmental Communication: A Journal of Nature and Culture*, doi: 10.1080/17524032.2014.919947.

Miles, Paul 2008a, "Remote possibilities", *The Financial Times*, 19–20 April, Life and Arts p. 11.

Miles, Paul 2008b, "Tasmania's forest under threat", *Condé Nast Traveller*, March, p. 34.

Miles, Paul n.d., *Paul Miles: Writer & photographer*, viewed 8 January 2012, www1.clikpic.com/paulmiles/

Outside 2011, "About Outside", 2 June, viewed 7 January 2012, www.outsideonline.com/about-outside/about-outside.html

Outside n.d., "Outside media kit", Maria Media Network LLC, viewed 19 September 2012, www.outsidemediakit.com

Pearson, Stephanie 2014, "Surviving Tasmania", *Outside*, 20 January, viewed 29 August 2014, www.outsideonline.com/adventure-travel/australia-pacific/australia/The-Devil-Made-Me-Do-It-Travel-Tasmania.html

Perrottet, Tony 2002, "Devil's playground: Southern gothic", *Outside*, November, viewed 7 October 2011, www.outsideonline.com/adventure-travel/australia-pacific/australia/Devil-s-Playground--Southern-Gothic.html

Ribbon, A 2002, "Airport ad gets the axe", *Mercury*, 3 November, p. 3.

Tourism Tasmania 2011, *Motivations Research*, Tourism Tasmania, Hobart.

Tourism Tasmania 1997, *Brand Tasmania: Marketing Tasmania as a Unique Holiday Destination*, Tourism Tasmania, Hobart.

Wilderness Society 2010, "Upper Florentine: Self-drive and walking guide", Wilderness Society, December, viewed 15 October 2012, www.wilderness.org.au/upper-florentine-self-drive-guide

Wolfsfeld, Gadi 1997, *Media and Political Conflict: News from the Middle East*, Cambridge UP, Cambridge.

World Intellectual Property Organization 2003, "World Intellectual Property Organization WIPO Arbitration and Mediation Center Administrative Panel Decision: The Crown in Right of the State of Tasmania trading as "Tourism Tasmania" v. Gordon James Craven Case No. DAU2003-0001", Australia Domain Name Decisions, Australian Legal Information Institute, University of Technology Sydney and University of New South Wales Faculties of Law, viewed 22 January 2012, www.austlii.edu.au/cgi-bin/sinodisp/au/cases/cth/AUDND/2003/2.html?stem=0&synonyms=0&query=Tourism%20Tasmania

PART III
In the media

8 The distractions and attractions of search

The websites of individual media organisations today are places of epic exploration and ceaseless surveillance. As we search these sites, information technology maps our paths, scrutinising our choices, identifying our favourite places, examining our experiences and evaluating our tastes. The aggregated information gathered feeds back to the actors and algorithms governing and constructing the virtual worlds we are helping to create, even as we traverse them. These processes are of interest in themselves but also for what they have in common with branding. Celia Lury (2004) and Adam Arvidsson (2006) harness the explanatory value of new media technology in their theorisation of brands, both scholars incorporating the concept of the loop. Here Arvidsson uses this approach to explain how brands function as a form of informational capital:

> As they move through the surveyed information environment, individuals dissolve into data clouds: life-style preferences indicated, particular web-surfing itineraries, purchasing patterns and so on. These can later be recomposed as data sets like life-style or customer profile that can feed directly into particular programming strategies…Brand management embodies this logic of ubiquitous surveillance and programing. The productivity of consumers unfolds in an informational environment where the brand acts as a kind of program, a platform for action, a loop that anticipates choices of action. At the same time consumer practice unfolds under more or less constant surveillance, where its autonomous productivity is translated into relevant forms of feedback.
>
> (Arvidsson 2006, pp. 129–130)

Thus, information technology is not only a metaphor for the way brands put the capacity of consumers to work in the interests of capital but also, in aggregate, an input into the processes of branding (Arvidsson 2006). Media organisations use both web analytics and data derived from monitoring social media in their own brand management and release some of these aggregated metrics to attract advertisers. Some media organisations may also share aggregated data derived from online marketing campaigns with campaign partners. In these ways, web and social media insights become part of an array of data that simultaneously contributes to place-branding and feeds back into the digital infrastructures from which those data were derived. This means, in effect, that when media organisations and government or quasi-public tourism offices come together in partnerships, digital surveillance and feedback can become oxygen for bubbles of brand-aligned content with the capacity to obscure, adjust or submerge non-aligned environmental frames.

The title of this chapter is a salute to Matthew Hindman (2009), who wrote of "the politics of search" in his 2009 book *The Myth of Digital Democracy*. Hindman describes the outcome of search engine operations as a new kind of gatekeeping, arguing that search engines "aggregate thousands of individual gatekeeping decisions made by others…shifting the bar of exclusivity from the *production* to the *filtering* of political information" (Hindman 2009, p. 13, original emphasis). As a result, "[m]ost online content receives no links, attracts no eyeballs, and has minimal political relevance" (Hindman 2009, p. 18). Hindman draws this conclusion from his analysis of the results of millions of web pages on six political topics.

Hindman was most interested in how links and searches channel people from one website to another, but searches operating *within* the websites of media organisations perform similar gatekeeping functions. Success in gaining access for environmental frames to websites that attract millions of unique visitors does not necessarily guarantee visibility. One difference in this regard between traditional and digital media is the indefinite shelf life of online content, which gives search engines considerable influence over what visitors discover. Visitors who search websites will usually be given opportunities to sort or narrow results, which can assist them greatly if they know what they are looking for. However, evidence tells us the majority will settle for the most simple search option. People generally enter only one or two terms per search and rarely look beyond the first page of results or use sophisticated techniques such as quotation marks, parentheses or Boolean operations like "and" or "or" (see Hindman 2009, p. 69). In this chapter, then, I ask whether brand-aligned travel copy in websites that aggregate copy from multiple mastheads and multiple genres can increase the visibility attained through site searches of harmonious representations of places experiencing environmental conflict. My case study is NationalGeographic.com and the interconnected environmental issues of the Athabasca bituminous sands and the proposed Enbridge Northern Gateway pipeline in Canada.

The National Geographic Society refers to itself as "inspiring people to care about the planet" (*National Geographic* 2014a) and labels its combined "print circulation, digital editions, apps, social media, websites and newsletters for the main edition as well as International, Worldwide and Traveler editions" its "brand universe" (*National Geographic* 2012). Its transnational mission is further reflected in its International Council of Advisors, which comprises "industry leaders and philanthropists representing 13 states, the District of Columbia, Azerbaijan, Canada, China, Egypt, Mexico, and South Africa" (*National Geographic* 2014b, p. 31). According to its media kit available online in December 2014, the website NationalGeographic.com attracts 23 million unique users a month, divided

–approximately 60:40 between site visitors from the United States and those from other parts of the world (*National Geographic* n.d.). The sections of the site it describes as its "Travel and Adventure pillar", which are intended to be "inspirational and aspirational", are aimed at "a well-traveled and well-heeled audience" (*National Geographic* n.d.), suggesting its reference to "The whole world online" (*National Geographic* n.d.) in its media kit refers to its ambitions for its content rather than, necessarily, a truly global readership, despite its website's impressive reach. NationalGeographic.com aggregates and makes available to non-subscribers selected copy from the Society's print magazines *National Geographic*, *National Geographic Traveler*, *National Geographic Kids* and (the discontinued) *National Geographic Adventure*, as well as dedicated web content such as news, photographs, videos and maps. Website copy is organised by both medium and subject in multiple drop-down menus including "Environment", "Travel", "Adventure", "Trips", "News" and "Maps". *National Geographic* describes itself as providing "visual leadership" and has a strong online emphasis on photography, including opportunities for audiences to upload their own photographs and enter photography competitions.

The Enbridge Northern Gateway pipeline, if constructed, would run between the Athabasca bituminous sands in Alberta and the town of Kitimat on a channel that leads through the Great Bear Rainforest to the ocean off the coast of British Columbia. The sands themselves are a source of much controversy in Canada and the United States because of the destruction of boreal forest and wildlife, and the production of high levels of carbon emissions and other pollutants created while mining and processing the bituminous material. In 2009 the sands were the subject of a long feature in *National Geographic* magazine called "The Canadian oil boom: Scraping bottom" (Kunzig 2009; see Remillard 2011), which expressed concern about environmental degradation. In 2011, another *National Geographic* magazine feature, called "Pipeline through paradise" (Barcott 2011a), canvassed attitudes towards the proposed pipeline and associated environmental risks in the Great Bear Rainforest. The twin pipes of the Northern Gateway would take imported gas condensate east and oil from the sands west. At the time of writing the Canadian government had approved the construction of the Northern Gateway provided it met certain conditions, but an opinion poll reported in April 2014 had found that only 38 per cent of people in British Columbia very much or somewhat supported the project, compared to 65 per cent of Albertans (Genier 2014). Tankers loading oil in Kitimat would have to travel back out along a channel through the Rainforest and then along the Rainforest coast, which opponents argue introduces the risk of oil spills. Prior to its partial protection, the Rainforest already had a long history of environmental disputation over logging. The part of the Rainforest that is protected received much of that protection in 2006. The Rainforest is also a tourism destination including ecotourism enterprises owned and operated by First Nations communities. It is the home of Kermode bears, evocatively known as spirit bears – a rare subspecies brought to international prominence in the 1990s as part of a campaign to ensure their survival that was intertwined with the efforts to protect their habitat from logging. These are not albinos but black bears carrying a recessive gene that causes them to be born white. They have been described as having "a sacred place in the hearts of the Kitasoo–Xai'xais people, who have shared their territory with the white bear for millennia" (Roscovich 2010).

Methods

On 8 October 2014 I conducted simple searches of NationalGeographic.com for four terms:

- British Columbia
- Great Bear Rainforest
- Alberta
- Athabasca

I typed each search term into the search bar on the home page. The first 10 results were presented as "All Results" on the first page returned by each search, where I was then given the option of filtering the results by "Photography" , "Videos", "Places", "Channel", "Magazine" and "News". There was no option to sort by date or relevance. Rather than filter the results, I confined myself to the 10 items before me, which were not listed by date, suggesting they had been sorted by relevance attributes determined by the search engine. I categorised results as "travel" regardless of medium if the pages they were linked to bore the masthead *National Geographic Traveler* or appeared in the "Travel" or "Trips" section of the site. This meant that although the content of photograph pages with the *National Geographic* masthead was often similar to the content of photograph pages with the *National Geographic Traveler* masthead (that is, very often the photographs were of natural features), they were rarely classified as travel in my analysis. Similarly, I only included *National Geographic Adventure* items of any kind in my travel category if they appeared in "Travel" or "Trips" sections of the website.

Results

Table 8.1 summarises the results categorised as "Travel". Had I included *National Geographic* "Photo competition" pages in these calculations as well as *National Geographic Traveler* "Photo competition" pages, the totals would have been higher, particularly for the Athabasca search, for which the first eight results were photo pages featuring visual images of attractive nature. The striking features in this table are the prominence of travel items and the lack of references in those items to environmental conflict. Below I compare the "travel" results for each search term with the content of the other categories in the results.

British Columbia

None of the British Columbia results were directly related to the proposed pipeline, but there was considerable variety. There were four travel pages, listed at

Table 8.1 Prominence of travel items in specific searches of NationalGeographic.com

Search term	Total	Placement	Reference to Enbridge pipeline or Athabasca bituminous sands or tankers as a problem	Environmental brand-sensitive cosmopolitan concern
British Columbia	4	1,5,6,8		
Great Bear Rainforest	4	1,5,7,9	1	1
Alberta	9	2,3,4,5,6, 7,8,9,10		
Athabasca	2	1,2		(1 indirect)

numbers 1, 5, 6 and 8, and two non-travel adventure results, listed at numbers 7 and 9. None of the travel results mentioned environmental concern or conflict. The adventure result listed at number 7 referred to Gwaii Haanas National Park Reserve and Haida Heritage Site as "the gem of the aboriginal visionaries who fought hard to protect it from the logging industry that has decimated so much of the North American northwest" (DeWitt 2010). Environmental news pages sponsored or in partnership with Shell (an interesting association but one more relevant to analyses of hard news) were listed at numbers 2, 3 and 10, and all considered environmental issues. A feature from the "Environment" section by wildlife photographer Paul Nicklen (2014, originally published in *National Geographic* magazine in 2006) at number 4 was overtly opposed to offshore oil drilling, and this was the only listing on the search-result page that featured a thumbnail image of non-urban nature.

Great Bear Rainforest

Results for the Rainforest were more strongly associated with environmental concern, partly because of the prominence afforded separate listings for text, images and a map from the 2011 *National Geographic* magazine story "Pipeline through paradise". Interestingly, the search-result headline for one of these items – "Great Bear Rainforest: Pictures, more from National…" – could have been mistaken for a celebratory photography page, although its subheading included the article's title, clarifying the subject. Four of the results of this search were travel pages, listed at numbers 1, 5, 7 and 9. Three of these referred to past environmental victories but only the one listed at number 5 mentioned unresolved environmental concern or conflict. Of surprise to me was the fact that this single overt example of "brand-sensitive cosmopolitan concern" (see Chapter 5) in a travel item referred directly to the Northern Gateway and was written by a reader in his caption for an image he had entered in the *National Geographic Traveler* "Photo competition 2014" (Reiff 2014).

The most immediately striking feature of the page listing the search returns for Great Bear Rainforest was the prominence afforded thumbnail images of spirit bears, which appeared in three results. Only one of these was a travel feature but it was the first listed item (Kennedy n.d.). Of the six thumbnails of nature in the Rainforest list, three accompanied travel results. Two of the other three nature thumbnails – images that were not associated with travel listings – were the second and third thumbnails of spirt bears. One accompanied a link to a video about a visit by photographer Paul Nicklen to the Rainforest, and the commentary to this video mentioned the pipeline conflict. Nicklen's visit to the forest had provided photographs for a *National Geographic* magazine cover story entitled "Spirit bear" (Barcott 2011a) written by the author of "Pipeline through paradise". (In regard to Nicklen's experiences in the Great Bear Rainforest in association with other environmental photographers opposed to the pipeline, see the documentary *SPOIL* (Jennings 2011).) The "Spirit bear" feature appeared in the results list at number 10, linked to the Beta version of the magazine issue in which it originally appeared, and in order to gain free access to the item it was necessary to register. This article did not mention the controversy, but "Pipeline through paradise", with its detailed discussion, appeared in the same Beta version of the issue.

Alberta

The Alberta and Athabasca returns were far more concentrated than those for British Columbia and the Rainforest. Apart from a single *National Geographic* photography page at the top of the list, which included three thumbnail images of nature, the Alberta returns were all from a text and video travel blog by *National Geographic*'s Digital Nomad Andrew Evans published more than a year before my search that all but ignored oil in any form. *National Geographic Traveler* and the provincial tourism office Travel Alberta were given equal credit at the end of a 30-minute compilation video embedded in the first Digital Nomad page linked from the search results, and both were also thanked for the entire Alberta trip in this blog post by Evans, which was the final in the Alberta blog series (Evans 2013a; Newman and Evans 2013). There was no indication of what kind of support Evans and cameraman Josh Newman had received from Travel Alberta.

Athabasca

The Athabasca returns were highly concentrated around photographs of the upper reaches of the Athabasca River in Jasper National Park – the location of the Athabasca Glacier, Athabasca Falls and Athabasca Pass. Only two of these first eight items were categorised as travel photos (numbers 1 and 2), but the caption to the first, written by the photographer to accompany this entry in the *National Geographic Traveler* "Photo competition 2013", described the Athabasca glacier as "fast-receding" (Krishnamurthy 2013). The other six photo results, one of which was linked to a page where photos could be purchased, were labelled *National Geographic* but their content and, therefore, their effect of pushing news items down the list of search results, was the same as the travel photos'.

The 2009 *National Geographic* article "The Canadian oil boom: Scraping bottom" (Kunzig 2009), with images by photographer Peter Essick, was ninth in the Athabasca returns, and this was the first indication that the Athabasca River becomes polluted when it runs through the oil mining and production area of the sands. Although an online version was available, the search result linked through to the full original print version on the Beta site mentioned above. When accessed following registration, one was greeted first by an image of threatened forest but immediately after by a forbidding image of mining photographed at sunset so that the site seemed to glisten in oily blackness. Chaseten Remillard (2011) analyses these as before and after images juxtaposing notions of nature as sublime and nature as resource. Images of human industrialisation of the landscape were, however, accompanied by other images, including some that depicted the economic and social gains locals could derive from the exploitation of the sands. Remillard describes the collection of images in total as representative of the ambiguity of contemporary environmental risk discourses:

> The images are paradoxically representative of long-standing discourses related to both development and preservation; illustrative of shocking environmental degradation; emblematic of refusals of individual responsibility; evidence for regulation, yet the embodiment of a sense of public distrust in the efficacy of regulation; a communication of local risk, and the situation of that risk at the periphery of human and physical geography.
>
> (Remillard 2011, p. 139)

The thumbnail image from the story that appeared in the search list was the photograph of the forest – an image that appeared benign until associated with the article's unsettling title, which was the headline for the search result.

The final item listed on the first page of search results was entitled "Satellite views of Canada's oil sands over time" (Handwerk 2011), and the three thumbnail images clearly showed the extent to which mining had expanded over three decades. The result linked to a page with a slide show of five images on five pages, some from "Scaping bottom", all with text and hyperlinks, all from the "News" section of the site and all sponsored by Shell. Many criticisms and concerns were canvassed in the first four pages. The fifth gave the economic arguments in favour of the mines.

The conflict context

When I conducted these searches again some months later, the results were not very different. Importantly, nine of the results for Alberta were still Digital Nomad blogs, and there were still three thumbnail images of spirit bears among the results for the Great Bear Rainforest, including the one in the same travel feature (Kennedy n.d.) that still topped the list. Of course, as time passes, these frozen moments of search history will bear less and less resemblance to current lists of search results for the same terms, but if considered in the context of environmental politics contemporaneous with the publication of some of the items listed, the content analysis I conducted yields interesting insights. To put the Alberta and

Rainforest results in their political context is to understand the discursive distraction achieved by the Digital Nomad blogs and the powerful symbolic work performed by spirit bears.

In July 2013, US comedians Andy Cobb and Mike Damanskis started crowd-sourcing funds to make a documentary about Alberta's oil industry. As part of their pitch, the comedians uploaded a trailer that parodied a marketing campaign by Travel Alberta called "remember to breathe" using images of environmental devastation (Cobb and Damanskis 2013). The corporation's CEO, Bruce Okabe, had recently been named one of the province's 50 most influential people partly on the basis of the original "remember to breathe" video posted on YouTube in 2011 (Alberta Venture staff 2014; Travel Alberta 2011). The three-minute promotion's images of mountains, lakes and downhill skiing, cut to a gentle, evocative soundtrack, had amassed much praise and millions of hits. Okabe told the *Calgary Herald* his organisation was simply protecting the province's tourism brand by calling for the parody to be removed (Okabe in Stephenson 2013).

Travel Alberta had filed its complaint against Cobb and Damanskis with YouTube on 14 August (Linnitt 2013). On 19 August, Andrew Evans had begun posting his Digital Nomad text and video blogs (Evans 2013b). His last real-time blog from Alberta was posted on 31 August, and on 3 September he uploaded the compilation video – *Digital Nomad Alberta* – that had been produced with the assistance of Travel Alberta (Evans 2013a; Newman and Evans 2013). The compilation video and other blogged videos and texts celebrated national parks, wildlife, Calgary, culture and communities but glossed over the oil industry with brief shots of a single oil pump attractively framed, a passing reference to "big energy" and a two-sentence geology lesson explaining how oil forms.

The same criticisms that could be made of *Digital Nomad Alberta* – that it visually misrepresented the scale of Alberta's oil industry – had been levelled at a slide show produced a few years earlier by the Alberta government, which had acknowledged the province's oil industry with just a single small image of an oil pump (see Takach 2013). In the months after *Digital Nomad Alberta* and the other blogs were uploaded, Evans' travel blogs continued to promote Alberta unencumbered by environmental concern. And although the Travel Alberta credit in the Newman and Evans compilation video was non-specific, cooperation between the tourism office and the media organisation was evident again in April 2014 when Evans, clearly identified as *National Geographic*'s Digital Nomad, was the presenter and interviewer in a two-minute video about bear viewing in Banff National Park posted to YouTube by Travel Alberta as part of its "remember to breathe" campaign (Travel Alberta 2014). Similarly to the way a copy-generating partnership between Tourism Tasmania and *BBC Wildlife Magazine* defused earlier "brand-sensitive cosmopolitan concern" in that publication (see Chapter 5), so travel blogs and a video benefiting from the support of Travel Alberta and *National Geographic Traveler* presented an alternative discourse to the one in *National Geographic* in 2009.

In the case of search results for the Great Bear Rainforest, travel items were fewer than for British Columbia and environmental concern was prominent overall, but the first item (Kennedy n.d.), a travel feature, did not refer to the pipeline. Instead, it harked back to the 2006 decision to protect part of the forest from logging, which suggests that the victory had been depoliticised by being incorporated into the province's branding, just as the Franklin dam blockade in Tasmania had become part of that state's tourism public relations (See McGaurr, Tranter and Lester 2014). The environmental conflict that achieved this protection for parts of the Great Bear Rainforest appears to be the origin of the spirit bear's contemporary trans-cultural symbolic power. Once part of the Mid-coast Timber Supply Area and originally known by that name, the Great Bear Rainforest was the location of fierce battles against logging and recreational hunting in the 1990s. At that time, the transnational Spirit Bear Youth Coalition was formed and a number of other environmental groups also adopted the rare spirit bear as their mascot. As environmentalists and some First Nations communities came together in opposition to logging, the name of the forest was changed to reflect its cultural value to local tribes and increase its media appeal. Again, there is some similarity here with the way that Tasmanian environmentalists in the 1990s renamed the Arthur–Pieman Conservation Area the Tarkine in honour of the area's original inhabitants when campaigning against a road through the region.

Much ecotourism in the Rainforest was closely aligned with conservation and aboriginal culture, and the spirit bear came to be commodified as a tourism attraction. When controversy erupted over the pipeline proposal, the spirit bear was redeployed by the environment movement as a visual symbol of nature's purity and vulnerability (see Postcard 2, WWF n.d. a; banner image, text and bottom image, WWF n.d. b), having already been elevated from regional to provincial tourism status. Among a number of examples of this elevation was the inclusion of a spirit bear in a video to accompany the branding of British Columbia as "Super, Natural" (Destination British Columbia 2014). The only bear in the three-minute promotion, it climbs out of the forest towards the camera with lumbering grace, introducing the words "all in the court of her majesty, Mother Nature" in a heavy-handed but grand manifestation of Urry's romantic tourist gaze. What might we deduce from the spirit bear's appearance in this video, together with the choice of "Super, Natural" as slogan? As Lester notes, visual images "rarely seem to be asking outright for the viewer to make complex connotative connections, although as communicative acts embedded within social, cultural and political contexts, this is exactly what they are always doing. It is this dual role of appearing to denote what is while also symbolizing what might be that provides them with a central place in mediated environmental politics" (Lester 2010, p. 140).

The Great Bear Rainforest and spirit bears were also featured in campaigns by the Canadian Tourism Commission (CTC). In its annual report for 2013 the CTC highlighted a "debut" collaboration with Aboriginal Tourism BC to promote a "Canadian Signature Experience" called Spirit Bear Lodge, a Kitasoo–Xai'xais First Nations enterprise (CTC 2014, p. 25). Elsewhere in the report (CTC 2014, p. 37), the CTC described itself as having "joined National Geographic Travel on the 50 Places of a Lifetime campaign to build emotional connections with Canada"

(CTC 2014, p. 37). "Canada's 50 places of a lifetime" (see Bellows 2013) included the Great Bear Rainforest (Kennedy n.d.), and this was the travel feature that appeared at the top of the list when I searched for the Rainforest on National-Geographic.com. Here, the information provided about the protection gained for the forest in 2006 was positioned at the bottom of the article next to the subheading "Fun fact". Next to the subheading "Accommodation" was a link to "signature experience" Spirit Bear Lodge (n.d.), where a video on the business's homepage declared the Rainforest's vulnerability to unspecified "threats that come with encroachment of the modern world" (Roscovich 2010). And although the "50 places" *National Geographic* feature's Rainforest copy ignored the pipeline, next to a "Helpful links" subheading the unobtrusive words "*National Geographic* article" linked through to the online version of the article "Pipeline through paradise" (Barcott 2011a), and the words "*National Geographic* map of the area" linked through to an online version of the map of the proposed pipeline and oil tanker routes that had been part of the original printed pipeline story. Indeed, the thumbnail image of the spirit bear that appeared in the search results next to the link to the "50 places" feature about the Rainforest and as the hero shot for the article itself was from Paul Nicklen's photography for the "Spirit bear" feature (Barcott 2011b) that had appeared in the same issue of the print edition of *National Geographic* that had run "Pipeline through paradise". It was also related to the video story of his visit to the Rainforest that appeared with a spirt bear thumbnail at number 8 in the search returns, where he voiced his own concerns about the pipeline proposal.

In addition to the three images of the spirit bear in the Rainforest search results and its prominence in the "50 places" travel feature that was first in the list of those results, the spirit bear and past activism against logging in the rainforest (but not the pipeline) were mentioned in the written text of the travel item listed at number 9 (Tsui 2007). The spirit bear even made an appearance in the copy (but not the visual images) of a news article sponsored by Shell entitled "British Columbia rethinks its pioneering carbon tax" (Schultz 2012) that appeared at number 10 in the British Columbia search returns and referred to the province as the home of the spirit bear. In this instance, the bear was framed as a sign of governmental naiveté, a response that nevertheless suggested an authorial awareness of its symbolic power.

Conclusion

In Chapter 5, I explored ways in which elite public relations practice, elite networks and competition among sources for publicity could reduce the likelihood that challenger frames from non-elite sources or dissenting voices from within government would be mediated by travel journalists during times of environmental conflict. In the example of BBC *Wildlife Magazine*, the production of supplements in partnership with a state tourism office redressed less flattering representations that had appeared in the publication some years earlier and much more recently in the news media. Reviewing the search results for Alberta presented in this chapter,

I found brand-aligned material that had received unspecified support from a provincial tourism office achieving a similar outcome via the hierarchy of search engine returns. The more travel media organisations allow their brands to be aligned with the brands of government and quasi-public tourism organisations the more likely it seems that information bubbles will occur in searches of individual websites, either simply increasing the salience of brand-aligned frames or simultaneously pushing non-aligned items out of the top results, adjusting or submerging discourses that authorities find problematic.

It is of interest, however, that among examples discussed in this chapter I unexpectedly found an instance of a travel feature free of references to contemporary environmental conflict nevertheless creating opportunities for the flow of cosmopolitical discourses. "Great Bear Rainforest" (Kennedy n.d.) was one of *National Geographic Travel's* list of "50 Canadian places of a lifetime", a campaign in partnership with the CTC, yet it facilitated the ongoing circulation of the multipurpose symbol of the spirit bear via its prioritisation at the top of the results of my NationalGographic.com search for the term "Great Bear Rainforest" and the opportunities this afforded for the cross-signification of similar visual images from multiple genres. The brand-aligned travel article also contained hyperlinks to material that explicitly discussed the pipeline project – evidence that the hypertextuality of the Web (Berglez 2013, p. 113) can open the gates to alternative representations.

References

Alberta Venture staff 2014, "Bruce Okabe: Alberta's 50 Most Influential People 2014", *Alberta Venture*, 1 July, viewed 6 December 2014, http://albertaventure.com/2014/07/bruce-okabe-albertas-50-influential-people-2014/

Arvidsson, Adam 2006, *Brands: Meaning and Value in Media Culture*, Routledge, Abingdon.

Barcott, Bruce 2011a, "Pipeline through paradise", *National Geographic*, August, pp. 54–65.

Barcott, Bruce 2011b, "Spirit bear", *National Geographic*, August, pp. 34–47.

Bellows, Keith 2014, "Canada's 50 places of a lifetime, *National Geographic Travel*, viewed 16 September 2014, http://travel.nationalgeographic.com.au/travel/canada/places-of-a-lifetime/

Berglez, Peter 2013, *Global Journalism: Theory and Practice*, Peter Lang, New York.

Canadian Tourism Commission (CTC) 2014, *Helping Tourism Businesses Prosper: Canadian Tourism Commission 2013 Annual Report*, Canadian Tourism Commission, viewed 10 September 2014, https://en-corporate.canada.travel/sites/default/files/pdf/Corporate_reports/final_2013_annual_report_en.pdf

Cobb, Andy & Damanskis, Mike 2013, online Vimeo trailer video, in Amanda Stephenson, Calgary Herald and Bloomberg News 2013, "Travel Alberta demands anti-oilsands film trailer be yanked from YouTube", *The Calgary Herald*, 26 August, viewed 16 September 2014, www.calgaryherald.com/travel/Travel+Alberta+demands+anti+oilsands+film+trailer+yanked+from+YouTube+with+video/8835259/story.html

DeWitt, Julia 2010, Beyond the Edge: Sea Kayaking British Columbia: Islands at the Edge of the World, National Geographic Adventure, blog, 9 August, viewed 8 October 2014, http://adventureblog.nationalgeographic.com/2010/08/09/sea-kayaking-british-columbia-islands-at-the-edge-of-the-world/

Destination British Columbia 2014, *The Wild Within*, video, Destination British Columbia, viewed 23 November 2014, www.destinationbc.ca/

Evans, Andrew 2013a, "Digital nomad: Andrew in Alberta", blog with embedded video, *National Geographic* (Travel), 3 September, viewed 8 October 2014, http://digitalnomad. nationalgeographic.com/2013/09/03/andrew-in-alberta/

Evans, Andrew 2013b, "Digital nomad: The Alberta story: Welcome to Calgary", blog with embedded video, *National Geographic* (Travel), 19 August, viewed 8 October 2014, http://digitalnomad.nationalgeographic.com/2013/08/19/the-alberta-story-welcome-to-calgary/

Genier, Eric 2014, "British Columbians, Albertans differ wildly on Northern Gateway Pipeline project: Poll", *Huffington Post Canada*, 7 April, viewed 5 January 2015, www.huffingtonpost.ca/2014/07/04/northern-gateway-pipeline-british-columbia-alberta_n_5557870.html

Handwerk, Brian 2011, Pictures: Satellite views of Canada's oil sands over time, *National Geographic* (News), 22 December, viewed 8 October, http://news.nationalgeographic. com/news/energy/2011/12/pictures/111222-canada-oil-sands-satellite-images/#/alberta-tar-oil-sands-satellite-pictures-1984_46159_600x450.jpg

Hindman, Matthew 2009, *The Myth of Digital Democracy*, Princeton University Press, Princeton.

Jennings, Trip (director) 2011, *SPOIL*, viewed 30 August 2014, http://commonsense-canadian.ca/documentary-spoil-enbridge-great-bear-rainforest-2/

Kennedy, Taylor n.d., "Great Bear Rainforest", *National Geographic* (Travel), viewed 8 October 2014, http://travel.nationalgeographic.com/travel/canada/great-bear-rainforest-british-columbia/

Krishnamurthy Harini 2013, "Photo contest 2013: Athabasca glacier", *National Geographic Traveler*, viewed 8 October 2014, http://travel.nationalgeographic.com/travel/traveler-magazine/photo-contest/2013/entries/218079/view/

Kunzig, Robert 2009, "The Canadian oil boom: Scraping bottom", March, *National Geographic*, pp. 38-59.

Lester, Libby 2010, *Media & Environment*, Polity, Cambridge.

Linnitt, Carol 2013, "Alberta forces tar sands comedy pitch video for Indiegogo off YouTube", Desmog Canada, 14 August, viewed 11 December 2014, www.desmog.ca/2013/08/14/alberta-forces-tar-sands-comedy-pitch-video-indiegogo-youtube

Lury, Celia 2004, *Brands: The Logos of the Global Economy*, Routledge, Abingdon

National Geographic 2014a, "About Us", viewed 31 December 2014, www.nationalgeographic.com/about/

National Geographic 2014b, National Geographic 2013 Annual Report, viewed 29 October 2014, www.nationalgeographic.com/explorers/support/annualreport13/finance. html

National Geographic 2012, "National Geographic Shows 30.9 Million Worldwide Audience via Consolidated Media Report", press release, 24 September, viewed 27 January 2015, http://press.nationalgeographic.com/2012/09/24/national-geographic-shows-30-9-million-worldwide-audience-via-consolidated-media-report/

National Geographic n.d., *NationalGeographic.com: The Website for the Action Class*, media kit, viewed 20 November 2014, www.nationalgeographic.com/mediakit/pdf/ng-com/NG Com_Media_Kit.pdf

Newman, Josh & Evans, Andrew 2013, "Digital Nomad Alberta", *National Geographic Traveler* and Travel Alberta, online video, 3 September 2013, viewed 24 September 2014, http://digitalnomad.nationalgeographic.com/2013/09/03/andrew-in-alberta/

Nicklen, Paul n.d., "Where currents collide: The marine life of Vancouver Island", *National Geographic* (Environment), viewed 8 October 2014, http://environment.nationalgeographic.com/environment/habitats/wild-tides-vancouver/

Reiff, Ivan 2014, "Photo contest 2014: Twilight in the Great Bear Rainforest", *National Geographic Traveler*, viewed 8 October 2014, http://travel.nationalgeographic.com/travel/traveler-magazine/photo-contest/2014/entries/245238/view/

Remillard, Chaseten 2011, "Picturing environmental risk: The Canadian oil sands and the National Geographic", *The International Communication Gazette*, vol. 73, no. 1–2, pp. 127–143.

Roscovich, Twyla 2010, *The legend of the spirit bear and the land and people it came from*, embedded video, viewed 26 September 2014, www.spiritbear.com/

Schultz, Stacey 2012, "British Columbia rethinks its pioneering carbon tax", *National Geographic* (News/Energy), 3 May, viewed 8 October 2014, http://news.nationalgeographic.com/news/energy/2012/05/120503-british-columbia-reviews-carbon-tax/

Spirit Bear Lodge n.d., home page, viewed 14 September 2014, www.spiritbear.com/

Stephenson, Amanda, Calgary Herald and Bloomberg News 2013, "Travel Alberta demands anti-oilsands film trailer be yanked from YouTube (with video)", Calgary Herald, 25 August, viewed 16 September 2014, www.calgaryherald.com/travel/Travel+Alberta+demands+anti+oilsands+film+trailer+yanked+from+YouTube+with+video/8835259/story.html

Takach, Geo 2013, "Selling nature in a resource-based economy: Romantic/extractive gazes and Alberta's bituminous sands", *Environmental Communication: A Journal of Nature and Culture*, vol. 7, no. 2, pp. 211–230.

Travel Alberta 2014, "Bears in Banff National Park - Travel Alberta", video presented by Andrew Evans, YouTube, 1 April, viewed 17 January 2015, www.youtube.com/watch?v=uO17A2v_1d4

Travel Alberta 2011, "(remember to breathe – Travel Alberta, Canada)", YouTube, 23 October, viewed 6 December 2014, www.youtube.com/watch?v=ThFCg0tBDck

Tsui, Bonnie 2007, "British Columbia: Canada's newest preserve", *National Geographic Adventure* (Trips), viewed 8 October 2014, www.nationalgeographic.com/adventure/adventure-travel/north-america/british-columbia.html

WWF n.d. a, "Stand with Canada: We did it! 20,000 people are standing with science", viewed 9 January 2015, www.wwf.ca/conservation/oceans/greatbearsea/stand_with_canada/

WWF n.d. b, "The Great Bear Sea: No place for an oil pipeline", viewed 9 January 2015, www.wwf.ca/conservation/oceans/greatbearsea/

9 Running with the lists

The salience of environmental communication in the media is determined in part by hierarchies of presentation associated with the item in which it appears. In print media, this is a function of layout – the size of headlines and images, the number of the page on which the item appears, whether the page is on the right or the left, how far down the page the item is situated etc. Another hierarchy of presentation that has gained enormous popularity in the digital age is using lists as "scaffolding for stories" in an effort to attract the largest possible audience on social media and the greatest number of "shares" (Shepherd in Fernando 2013). This is an example of social analytics influencing the very structure of journalism.

The list was always popular in travel media but it has attained exceptional prominence since the genre went digital and social. Gazing along shelves of travel publications in newsagents, scanning the home pages of travel media or checking them out on Facebook or Twitter, you could be forgiven for thinking lists were all there was. Most will be "places to go" or "best-of" rankings – best bars, hotels, pubs, towns, family holidays, holidays with pets, ecotours, wilderness lodges, ethical destinations, cities, regions, islands, beaches and countries. These tourism rankings, in turn, are cognitively and digitally networked into the hierarchies that populate 21st century media, ceaselessly distributing and redistributing salience: Worldwide Web searches and searches of individual websites, as discussed in the previous chapter, but also drop-down menus on websites, local, national and international news headlines online and in social media, surveys, opinion polls, place brand indexes. Even lists of films, books, authors, plays, celebrities, food, wine, designs, sportspeople, furniture and events are related, because all come from someplace, meaning there is literally no end to the list of the lists that travel journalism lists can help place-branding exploit.

Sam Shepherd – a blogger and communicator who went from People for the Ethical Treatment of Animals to news-aggregator and entertainment site Buzzfeed – turned image-heavy lists into a journalism phenomenon. He believes that, far from being a lazy form of composition, hierarchies are fundamental to the way we construct all good stories (Shepherd in Fernando 2013). This may be true, but Matthew Hindman's (2009, p. 19) assessment in relation to search engines that "hierarchies are not neutral with respect to democratic values" applies equally to lists of travel destinations. Innumerable places are consigned to obscurity on sometimes questionable or unstated criteria. Meanwhile, the tendency of travel journalism lists to condense place image into one photograph and a single paragraph of brand-aligned text, together with their very strong propensity to be shared on social media, makes them exceptionally valuable branding tools for the winners. Time and again in my research for this book I encountered examples of a place's success in a travel list reported in media releases from government or quasi-public tourism offices and in local media. In February 2014, for example, Travel Alberta circulated a media release publicising Alberta's presence in lists by *The Guardian*, *The New York Times* (NYT), *USA Today*, *Vacay.ca* and *National Geographic*'s Digital Nomad blogger Andrew Evans (Travel Alberta 2014; see Chapter 8). And in my Tasmanian research, among a catalogue of successes on Tourism Tasmania's "Accolades" page in 2009 that had been published in the first decade of the 2000s were eight from *Travel + Leisure*, five from *Condé Nast Traveler/Traveller* and three from *National Geographic Traveler* (Tourism Tasmania 2009). Sometimes it even attracted a media release from a tourism minister, as was the case when Tasmania made the *New York Times* (NYT) list of "44 places to go in 2009" (Sherwood and Williams 2009; see Chapter 5). But in 2014 something unusual happened: the Icelandic Ministry for Environment and Natural Resources (ÚtgáfaUmhverfis- og auðlindaráðuneytið 2014) issued a media release about a *negative* review in a prominent travel list, the NYT's "54 places to go in 2014" (Pergament 2014). It was not the first occasion in its (then) nine-year history that the NYT's annual list had included this frame, but it was a particularly striking example. This led me to wonder if the consumer appeal of lists might provide opportunities for "brand-sensitive cosmopolitan concern" to do considerably more public sphere work than would initially seem possible in such an abbreviated form of journalism.

Many items in travel lists for which journalists or consulted panellists express concern are perceived to be under pressure from rampant tourism, but every so often the issue that attracts the reviewer's attention is associated with climate change, resource extraction, energy production or the transportation of fuel. In a 2012 London *Times* list of 11 "Places to go before they disappear" (Schmidt 2012) still accessible from its "Travel" page at the beginning of 2015, climate change was implicated in concerns for three of the destinations identified as endangered, though referred to directly only in one. Other environmental concerns mentioned were pollution, agricultural run-off, siltation, mining, deforestation, poaching, erosion and seismic damage. In a separate list of eight places published by *The Times* (Rivalland 2014), climate change was also implicated in concerns for three of the destinations identified as endangered, though again referred to directly only in relation to one item.

In this chapter I have chosen a number of examples of "brand sensitive cosmopolitan concern" (see Chapter 5) in travel-list items to highlight three aspects of the frame's circulation and reception. The first case demonstrates both the efforts of destinations to shield local publics from criticism and the ability of journalistic agency to challenge this, if only to a limited extent. In the subsequent case I consider the possibility that "brand sensitive cosmopolitan concern" in lists can stimulate local debate. Finally, I ask whether travel lists might encourage the formation of imagined communities of global risks.

Journalistic agency: Holding destinations to account?

In literature on place-branding, destination branding is a term used to refer specifically to its tourism component. By contrast, when Jonathan Tourtellot established the National Geographic Society's Center for Sustainable Destinations he intended the term "destination" to encompass more than the tourism component of place (Tourtellot, J 2009, pers. comm., 24 October). In addition, he distinguished between ecotourism and geotourism, preferring the latter because it refers to the sustainability of a place's entire geography rather than only the "nature niche", "where nature is potentially a small part of the equation" (Tourtellot, J 2009, pers. comm., 24 October). The concept grew out of Tourtellot's interests while he was working as a travel journalist for *National Geographic Traveler*. With editor Keith Bellows' support (Tourtellot, J 2009, pers. comm., 24 October), Tourtellot was able to progress his Sustainable Tourism Initiative into a centre within the National Geographic Society; other parts of *National Geographic* including *National Geographic Traveler* collaborated with the Center for Sustainable Destinations on "projects and programs with allied organizations, both global and local" (National Geographic Center for Sustainable Destinations 2010).

National Geographic Traveler magazine brands itself as having pursued "sustainable travel before it was cool", distinguishing between tourism and travel, stressing "the inquisitive not the acquisitive" and "eschew[ing] fashion and fluff in favor of articles that offer a strong sense of place, inspiring narratives that make readers take trips, and solid service information to help them plan those trips" (*National Geographic Traveler* 2015). In 2004 the magazine published an article by Tourtellot presenting the results of a "Destination Scorecard" produced by what was then still the Sustainable Tourism Initiative in collaboration with England's Leeds Metropolitan University. The scores were the result of a survey of more than 200 "specialists in sustainable tourism and destination quality" (Tourtellot 2004), approximately half of whose names were provided in a list on the website (*National Geographic Traveler* 2004b). The Scorecard ranked Tasmania equal third in the top five of 115 destinations. In the printed version of this article (Tourtellot 2004), Tasmania only appeared in the Scorecard list, where it was awarded the top rating ("good") for its environmental conditions and social and cultural integrity but was given a warning for its outlook. By going to the website (*National Geographic Traveler* 2004a) it was possible to learn that the warning related to its forestry practices and commercialisation in and around protected areas – concerns that had been the cause of conflict in Tasmania itself. The website entry for Tasmania on this webpage, which was described as a "glimpse" of the views of the panellists and not the view of the National Geographic Society, described its logging industry as "out of control" (*National Geographic Traveler* 2004a).

At the time that the Scorecard was published, the tourism sector was able to capitalise on the ranking locally by successfully directing attention towards

National Geographic Traveler's praise (Lovibond, 2004; Tourism Tasmania 2004). In its related article, Hobart newspaper *The Mercury* celebrated the accolade with the lead "Tasmania continues to weave its magic on the international travel market and has been rated in the top five international tourist destinations" (Lovibond 2004). There was no mention in the *Mercury* article of *National Geographic Traveler*'s warning or the panellists' comments provided on its website. The Tourism Council Tasmania chairman, Simon Currant – at the time also a board member of Tourism Tasmania and advocate of commercial development in and around national parks – was quoted as saying that "we need to do more to maintain and protect our magnificent World Heritage Area, our parks and our heritage buildings". Such sentiments about public assets that were already protected had long been part of Tourism Tasmania's and the Tourism Industry Council Tasmania's discourse of accessible nature and there was no indication in *The Mercury* that Currant might have been responding to criticism by *National Geographic Traveler* or the panellists when he made this comment. On the contrary, the report emphasised that the accolade "strengthen[ed] Tasmania's position as a must-see destination in terms of a clean environment" and, paraphrasing Currant, "proved the strength and value of Tasmania's brand" (Lovibond 2004). In the same article *The Mercury* reported an accolade in *Travel + Leisure* it had already reported in 2000, added a 2002 accolade from *Condé Nast Traveler*, and prominently positioned a recent award for one of the state's lagers in the World Beer Cup. In 2005, however, Tourtellot reprised the Scorecard criticism in an interview with Tasmania's second biggest newspaper, Launceston's *Examiner*, during a visit to the north of the state as a guest of Ecotourism Australia to attend another ecotourism conference Tourism Tasmania supported and expected to deliver the state strong positive publicity (Department of Tourism, Arts and the Environment 2006, p. 27). In an alternative example of local media interpreting the international reception of the brand, the *Examiner* reported the criticism (Van den Berg 2005). The article was headlined "Logging a Concern for Travel Writer". Although Tourtellot's expert status was only established in the article by his association with *National Geographic*, his own agency and expertise were acknowledged by *The Examiner*'s inclusion of his observation that he was surprised by Tasmania's high ranking in the survey in view of its forestry issues. The negativity of this quote was undercut to some extent by his reference to the high percentage of Tasmania's environment that was protected. In the newspaper, this comment was provided without the qualification Tourtellot added during his interview with me, in which he made the observation that "the higher scoring destinations tend to have populations that basically give a damn about the stewardship of the place, and the fact that there are some pretty shrill arguments about how forestry is managed in Tasmania is a good indicator, because there aren't any in Borneo, and look who's lost most of their forests" (Tourtellot, J 2009, pers. comm., 24 October).

Elsewhere in *The Examiner* article the newspaper reported Tourtellot's comment that Tasmania's arguments about logging were akin to those taking place in North

America, thereby positioning environmental conflict as part of the human condition but also situating Tasmania's citizens as members of imagined communities of global risks (Beck 2011). Interestingly, the ubiquity of environmental disputes was one of the arguments offered by Flinn for his decision *not* to report on Tasmania's forestry conflict (see Chapter 5), but that was unusual within the bounds of my Tasmanian case study. Most interviewed travel journalists who, like Tourtellot, referred in our conversations to environmental conflict in their home markets did so in relation to their inclusion of Tasmania's forestry conflict in their articles. In addition, former Tourism Tasmania public relations practitioner Nicholls recalled a comment similar to Tourtellot's made by a *National Geographic Traveler* journalist on a reconnaissance visit during which Nicholls had been unable to shield her from evidence of logging in the Styx Valley (Nicholls, D 2009, pers. comm., 9 March, see Chapter 5). Although it is not possible to determine from the interviews for my Tasmanian case study whether that journalist's experience on her visit was associated with the 2004 Scorecard assessment, Nicholls' description of the view of the Styx from the helicopter, the correlation between comments by the journalist on the helicopter recci and Tourtellot about logging also being an issue in the United States, and the earlier comments by *National Geographic Traveler*'s then-editor at the World Congress on Adventure Travel and Ecotourism in Hobart in 1994 (see Chapter 4) suggest that the magazine felt entitled to hold Tasmania to account in relation to its "natural" branding. This was confirmed in 2006 when it published a piece of travel journalism by Tourtellot entitled "Greenish Tasmania" (Tourtellot 2006, p. 38), based on the 2004 Scorecard and a brief drive with Tourism Tasmania's international public relations practitioner following his attendance at the ecotourism conference in 2005 (Tourtellot, J 2009, pers. comm., 24 October). Indeed, in Tourtellot's view travel journalism had an obligation to report on what some travel journalists and travel editors regarded as side issues such as the state of the environment, regardless of the genre's soft reputation. In the following quote, firm genre divisions between news journalism and travel journalism (such as those supported within the scope of this case study by Doward's and Flinn's explanations of their understanding of travel journalism quoted in Chapter 5) are represented as inappropriately inhibiting travel journalists' ability to mediate environmental conflict:

> [T]ourism has become much, much too big and important a phenomenon to be relegated to the super-soft journalistic category, where it's all kind-of cheery and promotional and we don't really care very much. And this is a real problem in journalism. Because even those writers who would like to tackle it that way have no place to put it. Because most editors are going to say, "Oh, it's travel, we stick it in the travel section. Oh, but this is serious. The travel section is supposed to be appealing." So you can't get published. Or if you try to get in the front section, they say, "Oh, this is travel, it's not hard news," and again, you can't get it published. It's a real problem. And so getting some journalistic respect for the serious side of what travel and tourism is all about

and the enormous impact it has is a challenge that we both [Tourtellot and Harvard University's Elizabeth Beckett] think journalism has not met...the mindset that travel and tourism stops at the hotels and restaurants – and this is a mindset that holds within the industry as well as in other ways – is ignoring the fact if it is [a] touring-style tourism situation, or an R&R style situation – rest and recreation type tourism – the place is part of the tourism product. And so if the place has forests in it, that's part of the product. If the place is supposed to have forests but doesn't, that product has been altered. And I'm putting it in cold economic terms because that's sometimes the only way you get traction. But very often the industry forgets that its product is the place. That's beginning to change, but only recently.

(Tourtellot 2009, pers. comm., 24 October)

In his 2006 *National Geographic Traveler* text Tourtellot confirmed Tasmania's branding as "an ecotourism paradise" but with "one big 'except'": logging. He represented Tasmanians as caring about their forests, using the government's claim that 40 per cent of the island is protected as evidence. But he also reported that some old-growth forests were still threatened and ended his article with an overt call to action with clear cosmopolitical resonances: "Visit Tasmania, and help a logger find a job in tourism" (Tourtellot 2006, p. 38). The message of Tourtellot's article was that threats to Tasmania's forests were undermining its otherwise strong brand.

Encouraging local debate from afar?

In January 2014 *The Guardian* named 40 destinations in its "Holiday hotspots: Where to go in 2014" (Guardian writers 2014) and the NYT published "52 places to go in 2014" (NYT 2014). Among them, there was only one clear example of environmental "brand-sensitive cosmopolitan concern". Iceland, which appeared in both lists, was praised for its natural attractions in *The Guardian* but criticised for its environmental stewardship in the NYT. Scoring a mention in "52 places to go in 2014" should have been just another public relations coup for a destination already surfing waves of international publicity as a location for blockbuster films and television series. But instead of walking in the footsteps of Walter Mitty or seeking out landmarks from the *Game of Thrones*, the NYT narrowed its interest to the Highlands (Pergament 2014). Beneath the subheading "Natural wonders are in danger. Go see them before it's too late", travel journalist Danielle Pergament informed her readers of threats to fragile wetlands from proposed hydro development. With slightly more than a hundred words in her armoury, she donated an entire sentence to the chairman of the Iceland Nature Conservation Association, Árni Finnsson. Her account caused a flurry of indignation in Iceland, and was criticised by its Ministry for the Environment and Natural Resources in a media release in Icelandic (Umhverfisog auðlindaráðuneytið 2014). On the advice of Finnsson (in Kyzer 2014, p. 6), the NYT amended the online version to clarify how much of the country was covered by the wetlands (NYT 2014) but otherwise left the copy intact. Within weeks Finnsson was in the news again, this time in Iceland's irreverent English-language magazine *The Reykjavík Grapevine*, which was discussing Pergament's review (Kyzer 2014). Finnsson told the *Grapevine*, "It takes many millions to recover a loss of reputation…It's a huge resource, but it is so easy to destroy it" (in Kyzer 2014, p. 6). The *Grapevine* said he was speaking about "Iceland's image as a country whose nature is its biggest selling point" (Kyzer 2014, p. 6). According to the *Grapevine*, the wetlands at issue were not tourism attractions in their own right and were little known outside the country, but their protection was framed as contributing to Iceland's international image as a natural wonderland worth visiting and protecting:

> …it is noteworthy that an outlet such as The New York Times chose to highlight these issues on a more prominent stage, especially given that Iceland's breathtaking landscapes are often a driving force supporting its tourism industry. As Árni Finnsson wonders, "Who goes to Iceland to see power plants and power lines?"
>
> (Kyzer 2014, p. 6)

Pergament (in Kyzer 2014, p. 6) explained to the *Grapevine* that her reason for highlighting threats to the wetlands was to raise attention among her readers, who were aware of the country's natural attractions but not its environmental threats. The *Grapevine* argued that this was likely to have little impact on the outcome of the debate. It concluded that the government's decision not to confront the NYT, and to respond only with a media release in Icelandic, ensured the debate did not acquire the newsworthiness of a public battle between Iceland and the media organisation, and was thereby largely confined to the knowledge of the domestic population (Kyzer 2014, p. 6). The *Grapevine* article said its purpose was to correct the government's claim that the NYT paragraph was "paradoxical and wrong", but having done this it overtly rejected "the ecotourism solution" or bowing to international pressure, concluding instead that change would have to "come from within" (Kyzer 2014, p. 6). The article asserted national authority over environmental issues, yet there was, perhaps, implicit in its commentary, recognition that Pergament's "brand-sensitive cosmopolitan concern" in a high-profile travel list had at least briefly stimulated local debate.

Imagined communities of global risks?

Just as editors considering "brand-sensitive cosmopolitan concern" in travel features must weigh the risks and benefits to the media organisation's own brand and its relationship with potential advertisers or "partners", so must they constantly juggle competing claims for space on "Travel" landing pages. For example, on 1 January 2015 an item about Australia's Great Barrier Reef contained in a London *Times*' list of "8 places to see before they're gone" (Rivalland 2014) could be accessed from a text-only hyperlink on the "Travel" landing page. The very strong concerns expressed for the reef in this item included climate change, water pollution, tourism and fishing. There was no reference to the Australian Government's poor record on carbon emissions or protracted environmental conflict related to the reef but the small paragraph cited predictions by the Inter-governmental Panel on Climate Change that the reef could be gone within decades. By 4 January, the "Travel" landing page link to this list had itself dis-appeared, and a traditional travel feature about the reef had been hyperlinked in its place. A second hyperlink to another traditional feature about the reef had also been introduced nearby. Neither of the new items mentioned global warming, pollution, overfishing or too much tourism, and one included among its list of the six best Barrier Reef islands a recommendation entitled "best for ecologists". This gatekeeping decision to remove the link to the list incorporating "brand-sensitive cosmopolitan concern" and introduce instead links to favourable articles high-lights the commercial imperatives that are likely to diminish the appeal of negative lists to travel editors.

The Great Barrier Reef, ranked at number 5 in the list of "8 places to see before they're gone", was one of three items in the list in which climate change was implicated, though the issue was not mentioned by name in the paragraphs about Antarctica (at number 1) or Venice (at number 7). Nevertheless, I was interested to note that one of the four readers' comments following the list observed that by encouraging more people to visit these places *The Times* was probably contributing to the attractions' degradation (Arizonaman, 7 December 2014, 10.57am, com-ment following Rivalland 2014). There are many ways in which this reader's challenge to "the ecotourism solution" might be interpreted, but one way in which tourism has an impact on the environment is via the contribution of airline emissions to greenhouse gases. In 2008, the United Nations World Tourism Organization (UNWTO) reported that:

> [l]ong-haul travel by air between the five UNWTO world tourism regions represents only 2.2% of all tourist trips, but contributes 16% to global tourism-related CO_2 emissions…mitigation initiatives in the tourism sector will need to strategically focus on the impact of some particular forms of tourism (i.e., particularly those connected with air travel) if substantial reductions in CO_2 emissions are to be achieved.
>
> (UNWTO and UNEP 2008, p. 34)

Some of the interviewees for my case study of Tasmania who had written in their travel journalism about the impacts of climate change on vulnerable destinations in other articles (for example, Flinn 2002) or about environmental problems in Tasmania (for example, Fair 2000) were sceptical about the relative contribution of long-haul flights to greenhouse gases or the validity of airline carbon offset programs (Flinn, 2009, pers. comm., 1 March; Fair, 2009, pers. comm., 17 March).

At the other end of the spectrum was freelancer Paul Miles, whose comments revealed a deep ambivalence about the cosmopolitan potential of travel journalism in an age of climate change:

I think as news of climate change becomes increasingly worrying and the damage that we're causing – through, well, not just through flying obviously, but the damage that is happening to the planet is just becoming increasingly worrying – I just find it hard to rationalize promoting especially long-haul tourism, so I'm scaling back on that actually at the moment. And just doing local stuff, or trying to get away from writing about tourism. I'm writing less about tourism.

(Miles 2009, pers. comm., 9 March)

Despite having once published a mildly ironic piece in London's *Financial Times* about tourism's contribution to climate change that ended with a toast to international ecotourism (Miles, 2005), and an article about Tasmania's forestry dispute in *Condé Nast Traveler* written after a tour of the island funded by the state tourism office (Miles 2008), Miles was frustrated by his lack of control over the content of his travel writing for mainstream publications (2009, pers. comm., 10 March; see McGaurr 2013). As I have noted elsewhere (McGaurr 2014), Miles' decision to write less about distant destinations and largely confine his travel journalism to pieces about local tourism in environmentally conscious media exposes one of the enduring cosmopolitan paradoxes of the genre. For if travel journalists stop writing about distant destinations because they fear this will encourage tourism that makes an unacceptable contribution to climate change, they negate their own ability to witness and mediate distant environmental threats in ways that contribute to transnational connectedness.

In view of this finding from my Tasmanian research, I was interested to discover that debates about the environmental goods and bads of tourism are not simply academic but are already under way among readers who comment on travel lists. For example, among comments following *The Guardian*'s celebratory list of 2014 hotspots was a very long string initially engaging quite a few people but eventually narrowing to an argument between two. The first comment questioned the morality of *The Guardian*'s encouraging air travel if it accepted that the climate change consensus was correct (LoveisEternal, 3 January 2014, 10.35pm, comment following Guardian writers 2014). Another contributor argued in favour of tourism despite the environmental cost of its contribution to climate change because it increased cultural enrichment (Paul Underwood, 4 January 2014, 9.29am, comment following Guardian writers 2014), boosted developing economies and reduced xenophobia (Paul Underwood, 6 January 2014, 2.20am, comment following Guardian writers 2014). The same reader expressed no faith in the possibility of a global society (Paul Underwood, 5 January 2014, 10.41pm, comment following Guardian writers 2014) when this was proposed by another person. Others took Australia to task for its climate change policies, mining, coal-fired power stations and threats to the Barrier Reef (Agent Switters, 4 January 2014, 4.32pm; Stephen Herrick, 4 January 2014, 9.17pm ; Wobbly, 4 January 2014, 1.29am – all comments following Guardian writers 2014), and one person questioned the inclusion of Alberta in the list, in view of its bituminous sand-mining and a travel boycott of the province by environmental groups (JaneinAlberta, 4 January 2014, 2.04am, comment following Guardian writers 2014; regarding the Alberta boycott, see Takach 2014). A *Guardian* moderator ultimately deleted the entire string but it is an indication that even celebratory lists can prompt conversations about environmental risks among readers.

Conclusion

In Part 2, I identified a tendency by Tourism Tasmania and local newspaper *The Mercury* to publicise accolades from the travel media but ignore negative comment in international travel journalism features. This led me to conclude that travel lists could be used to crowd out "brand-sensitive cosmopolitan concern" in public discourse. The discussion of travel journalism lists presented in this chapter demonstrates, by contrast, that if the frame can itself gain access to such lists, it can achieve some limited progressive discursive outcomes. In the item critical of Iceland, access to the list was only achieved via the agency of the travel journalist concerned, while in the case of Tasmania, concerted work on the part of a journalist with high cultural capital was required to enable the frame to penetrate local media. In the example of Queensland's Great Barrier Reef, the potential power of cosmopolitan concern in a negative list was truncated when the hyperlink to the list was not only removed from its prominent position on *The Times* "Travel" landing page but also replaced by brand-aligned travel features about the same attraction.

In both examples discussed in this chapter in which "place-branded cosmopolitan concern" in a travel journalism list resulted in local media coverage, considerable elaboration was required to make the issue comprehensible. In the case of the *Wanderlust* list discusses at the end Chapter 7, which also gained local media coverage, the symbolic annihilation of contemporary Tasmanian Aboriginal communities in international travel journalism was briefly redressed by the list's acknowledgement of their claims to land in reserves in the bay's south. However, the publication then demonstrated the persistent limitations of such condensed narratives and the power of commercial tourism symbols by directing visitors to the Bay of Fires Walk tourism operation in the north of the bay without acknowledging Aboriginal claims to an already-existing national park traversed by that tour.

Unless travel journalists are willing to elaborate in other fora, it seems "brand-sensitive cosmopolitan concern" that does gain access to travel journalism lists risks being merely tokenistic – a loud call to consume in haste. How interesting then, to find that readers of *The Guardian*'s celebratory list of 2014 hotspots were themselves prepared to debate the ethics of promoting tourism for its ability to assist developing countries and improve inter-cultural connectedness in an era when air travel contributes to climate change. The combination of the list's multinational content, the media organisation's international reach online and the ability of climate change to speak for a wide range of local concerns are some factors that may have stimulated contributions to this particular comment string by readers from Britain and beyond. In Chapter 8, a public discourse of environmental risk was also evident in a caption to a photograph uploaded to NationalGeographic.com by a reader. Do any of these "small facts speak to large issues" (Geertz 1973, p. 23)? I am tempted to think it is possible, as Beck (2011) argues, that global risks create opportunities for the discursive strategies of place-branding to be unveiled transnationally in sites where traditionally those manipulations have been most effectively enacted (see also Dryzek 2006). I will return to this possibility in my concluding chapter.

References

Beck, Ulrich 2011, "Cosmopolitanism as imagined communities of global risk", *American Behavioral Scientist*, vol. 55, no. 10, pp. 1346–1361.

Department of Tourism, Arts and the Environment 2006, *Annual Report 2005–2006*, Government of Tasmania, Hobart.

Dryzek, John 2006, *Deliberative Global Politics: Discourse and Democracy in a Divided World*, Polity, Cambridge.

Fernando, Aneya 2013, "Why listicles are here to stay", 10,000 Words, 14 October, viewed 5 January 2015, www.adweek.com/fishbowlny/why-listicles-are-here-to-stay/264154?red=kw

Flinn, John 2002, "Bearing witness: Are Churchill's most famous residents on thin ice?", 22 December, *The San Francisco Chronicle*, 28 January 2015, www.sfgate.com/travel/article/BEARING-WITNESS-Are-Churchill-s-most-famous-2744033.php#page-1

Geertz, Clifford 1973, *The Interpretation of Cultures*, Basic Books Inc., New York.

Guardian writers 2014, "Holiday hotspots: Where to go in 2014", *The Guardian*, 4 January, viewed 22 February, www.theguardian.com/travel/2014/jan/03/holiday-hotspots-where-to-go-in-2014

Hindman, Matthew 2009, *The Myth of Digital Democracy*, Princeton University Press, Princeton.

Kyzer, Larissa 2014, "Fit for print: Did the New York Times get it wrong?", *The Reykjavík Grapevine*, issue 2, 7 February–13 march, p. 6.

Lovibond, Jane 2004, "Tassie in top five in world", *The Mercury*, 20 April, p. 3.

McGaurr, Lyn, 2014, "Your threat or mine? Travel journalists and environmental problems", in Folker Hanusch & Elfriede Fürsich (eds), *Travel Journalism: Exploring Production, Impact and Culture*, Palgrave Macmillan, Basingstoke, pp. 231–248.

McGaurr, Lyn 2013, "Not so soft? Travel journalism, environmental protest, power and the Internet", in Libby Lester & Brett Hutchins (eds), *Environmental Conflict and the Media*, Peter Lang, New York, pp. 93-104.

Miles, Paul 2008, "Tasmania's forest under threat", *Condé Nast Traveller*, March, p. 34.

Miles, Paul 2005, "One long guilt trip", *The Financial Times*, 28 May, www.ft.com/intl/cms/s/0/c626ea46-cf14-11d9-8cb5-00000e2511c8.html#axzz2TPCmJTc8.

Mocatta, Gabi 2008, "Bay of Fires, Tasmania, Australia", in *Lonely Planet's Best in Travel 2009: 850 Trends, Destinations, Journeys & Experiences for the Year Ahead*, Lonely Planet, Melbourne.

National Geographic Center for Sustainable Destinations 2010, "About the CSD", *National Geographic*, viewed 28 January 2015, http://travel.nationalgeographic.com/travel/sustainable/about_csd.html

National Geographic Traveler 2015, "About Traveler magazine", *National Geographic*, viewed 28 January 2015, http://travel.nationalgeographic.com/travel/traveler-magazine/about-us/

National Geographic Traveler 2004a, "2004 destinations rated: Destination scorecard – 115 places rated: Oceania", *National Geographic*, March, viewed 31 July 2011, http://traveler.nationalgeographic.com/2004/03/destinations-rated/oceania-text/1

National Geographic Traveler 2004b, "2004 destinations rated: Destination scorecard – 115 places rated: Meet our panelists", *National Geographic*, March, viewed 14 September 2012, http://traveler.nationalgeographic.com/2004/03/destinations-rated/panelists-text

New York Times, The 2014, "52 places to go in 2014", updated 26 January, viewed 22 February 2014, www.nytimes.com/interactive/2014/01/10/travel/2014-places-to-go.html

Pergament, Danielle 2014, "30. Iceland Highlands: Natural wonders are in danger. Go see them before it's too late", in *The New York Times* 2014, "52 places to go in 2014", updated 26 January, viewed 22 February 2014, www.nytimes.com/interactive/2014/01/10/travel/2014-places-to-go.html

Rivalland, Monique 2014, "8 places to see before they're gone", *The Times*, 6 December, viewed 31 December 2014, www.thetimes.co.uk/tto/magazine/article4285067.ece

Schmidt, Veronica 2012, "Places to see before they disappear", *The Times*, 27 July, viewed 28 January 2015, www.thetimes.co.uk/tto/travel/images/article3478220.ece

Sherwood, Seth & Williams, Gisela 2009, "The 44 places to go in 2009", *The New York Times*, viewed 21 January 2012, www.nytimes.com/interactive/2009/01/11/travel/20090111_DESTINATIONS.html?partner=permalink&exprod=permalink

Takach, Geo 2014, "Visualizing Alberta: Duelling documentaries and bituminouss ands", in Robert Boschman & Mario Tronto (eds), *Found in Alberta: Environmental Themes for the Anthropocene*, Wilfrid Laurier University Press, Waterloo, pp. 85–103.

Tourism Tasmania 2009, "Accolades and awards", Tourism Tasmania Corporate, viewed 4 April 2009, www.tourism.tas.gov.au/media/accolades

Tourism Tasmania 2004, *2003–04 Annual Report*, Tourism Tasmania, Hobart.

Tourtellot, Jonathan 2006, "Greenish Tasmania", *National Geographic Traveler*, March, p. 38.

Tourtellot, Jonathan B 2004, "Destination scorecard: 115 destinations rated", *National Geographic Traveler*, March, pp. 60–67.

Travel Alberta 2014, "Alberta making top travel lists", 5 February, viewed 22 February 2014, http://media.travelalberta.com/press-releases/alberta-making-top-travel-lists.htm

United Nations World Tourism Organization & United Nations Environment Programme 2008, *Climate Change and Tourism: Responding to Global Challenges*, viewed 28 January 2015, http://sdt.unwto.org/sites/all/files/docpdf/climate2008.pdf

ÚtgáfaUmhverfis- og auðlindaráðuneytið 2014, "Rangur fréttaflutningur New York Times", Útgáfa, 11 January, www.umhverfisraduneyti.is/frettir/nr/2532

Van Den Berg, Lucie 2005, "Logging concern for travel writer", *The Examiner*, 29 November, viewed 5 March 2011, www.examiner.com.au/news/local/news/general/logging-concern-for-travel-writer/958332.aspx

Wanderlust 2010, "Threatened wonders 2010", *Wanderlust*, February, viewed 8 October 2011, www.wanderlust.co.uk/magazine/articles/destinations/threatened-wonders-2010?page=all#

10 The (travel journalism) environment

In 2010, in the wake of the global financial crisis and severe European air-traffic disruptions associated with the eruption of the Eyjafjallajökull volcano, Iceland established a public–private partnership promoting tourism, culture, investment and trade (Íslandsstofa Promote Iceland n.d.). Three years later, a writer in the English-language tourism-oriented magazine the *Reykjavík Grapevine* hypothesised wryly that "the logic of marketing and branding has been permanently institutionalised to minimise the damage done by democratic processes, against which it currently has the upper hand. Meaning: Promote Iceland runs this shop. Iceland is a billboard" (Helgason 2013).

Simon Anholt considers the environment the most significant "hygiene factor" people take into account when deciding whether they admire a country (Anholt 2009a). Promote Iceland's official online gateway refers to the country as a place of fire, ice and "vast, unspoiled nature" (Iceland.is n.d.), yet by some measures its green credentials declined between 2010 and 2014 (Emerson et al., 2010, 2012; Hsu et al., 2014). This may be why, in July 2014, another *Grapevine* commentator took a particularly sceptical tone when reviewing a new Anholt index that rated contributions to the planet and humanity of 125 countries by drawing on 35 data sets. "As a marketing stunt it was brilliant, generating a few hundred thousand news articles around the globe," wrote Kári Tulinius (2014, p. 8), even though Iceland had once consulted Anholt on improving its competitive identity (see Anholt 2009b). Tulinius wrote that the *Good Country Index* (Anholt and Govers 2014) had ranked Iceland first for "contributions to planet and climate" despite the absence of Icelandic data for three of the five indicators in that category (Tulinius 2014, p. 8).

A few months after that critique was published, writers in the *Grapevine* offered an assessment of the tourism industry that refused to heap the usual accolades at the feet of place-brand gurus. Since the establishment of Promote Iceland, tourism had boomed, but in the *Grapevine* this was attributed to increased recognition associated with media coverage of the Eyjafjallajökull eruption as much as to successful place-branding (Gunnarsson 2014, p. 22; Helgason 2014, p. 22; see also Negroni 2010). With another volcano threatening to erupt, editors splashed the word "Yay!" in massive type across a cover shot of a gaseous plume. "As long as eruptions are not physically catastrophic," wrote Haukur Már Helgason (2014,

p. 22), "these days they provide Iceland with just the right titillation for successful nation-branding."

In the same issue of the *Grapevine* that discussed the publicity value of volcanic eruptions, there was a full-page photo of a puffin, stuffed and advertising souvenirs. "Puffinisation", one journalist called it (Gunnarsson 2014, p. 22): knickknack stores all over Reykjavík were the price the country had to pay for its magma-fuelled fame. But Icelandic puffins were not just stuffed and mounted in souvenir shops in 2014; they were also filleted and smoked. In *The Guardian* in January, *Huff Post Travel* in May and *Conde Nast Traveller* in September 2014, there was no hint of serious puffin breeding failures in the Westman Islands, possibly due to climate change (Náttúrustofa Suðurlands 2014; Powell 2013, 2014). Instead, consuming the bird in restaurants was recommended to "brave eaters" (Rexroat 2014), described as "pretty damn good" (JP in Church 2014) and excused by the observation that locals couldn't afford to be squeamish because Iceland had little other edible game (Pearson 2014, p. 86). Rather than referring to the hunting practice of catching them with nets on long poles and breaking their necks – something British restaurateur and television personality Gordon Ramsay (2011) describes as "sky fishing" – Harry Pearson in *Travel + Leisure* quoted a local resident recounting a story of inexperienced young puffins flying kamikaze-style into village lights. This enabled the journalist to recast the active practice of hunting as the normatively benign pastime of making good use of food that "drops into your lap" (2014, p. 86). Eating puffin was further depoliticised by the absence of photographs of live puffins in the article.

Minke whale was also on the menu in all three publications. In *The Guardian* it was declared "ten times better than the best steak" (JP in Church 2014), while in *Huff Post Travel* it was referred to as pleasantly surprising "local game" (Rexroat 2014). In *Conde Nast Traveller*, Pearson gave a cursory nod to a sign on one restaurant door declaring the establishment whale-friendly, but by then he was already on his way to listing minke and puffin among starters served elsewhere in the city (Pearson 2014, p. 84, 86). Pearson declined these delicacies himself, but only because he didn't like the taste of whale he'd eaten in the past, and because puffins, as it turned out, really were too cute for him to stomach (Pearson 2014, p. 86). Had Pearson chosen to contextualise the "whale-friendly" sign on the door of the Nora Magasin restaurant – a business he reviewed very favourably in his feature – he might have provided a more nuanced account of Icelandic identity. According to one report in 2011, 40 percent of tourists at that time ate whale assuming it was a traditional Icelandic dish, whereas only five percent of Icelanders regularly consumed it (*Discovery News* 2011). In 2014 Nora Magasin was one of more than 50 Icelandic restaurants promoted by the Icelandic Association of Whale Watchers (IceWhale) as whale-friendly (IceWhale n.d. a). Since 2010, IceWhale had collaborated with the International Fund for Animal Welfare (IFAW) on a "Meet us don't eat us" campaign, aimed at promoting whale-watching and whale-free restaurants in an effort to bring an end to commercial whaling (IceWhale n.d. b). In its four years of operation, the cosmopolitan project had attracted volunteers from 26 countries and claimed to have reduced tourist consumption of whale meat by half (IceWhale n.d. b).

Whether promoting whale-friendly restaurants and responsible whale tourism will reduce the number of whales slaughtered or achieve environmentally progressive policy change remains to be seen. Certainly, the whale-friendly "Meet us don't eat us" frame did not gain access to the travel features written by Pearson, Church or Rexroat, who chose instead to mediate place-branded traditional use. Anholt claims to have devised tools that governments can use to "help the world understand the real, complex, rich, diverse nature of their people and landscapes, their history and heritage, their products and their resources: to *prevent* them from becoming mere brands" (2010, p. 3; original emphasis). Yet his early enthusiasm for brand as metaphor (Anholt 2007, p. 23) is too often translated by practitioners into brand as rhetoric, brand as excuse, brand as strategic distraction. Working in a travel media environment of shrinking resources, precarious incomes and a tradition of cooperation with the tourism industry, travel journalists are familiar targets. As we have seen, factors that contribute to the dominance of brand-aligned discourses in travel journalism include crowded itineraries and attentive guides, the incorporation of travel journalists into elite discourse networks, source competition for access, explicit or perceived constraints associated with government salaries or grants, professional acculturation and personal preferences, blurred boundaries between editorial and marketing content in travel media, partnerships between government or quasi-public tourism offices and travel media organisations, the social-media affinity and news-journalism popularity of celebratory travel lists, and the gatekeeping function of digital hierarchies that amplify the other structural advantages already benefiting brand-aligned frames.

Place-branding shapes consumerist cosmopolitan discourses in ways that appeal to travel journalists and are consistent with the commercial constraints of travel media. This contributes to the circulation abroad of frames that depoliticise tourism attributes that may be contested in the news media. In addition, travel journalists sometimes build narrative strength through "place-branded cosmopolitan concern", a brand-aligned frame that positions readers as members of imagined cosmopolitan communities of environmentally conscious consumers, enhances the journalist's cultural capital and demonstrates environmental responsibility by governments, the tourism industry and the travel media. Even so, elite advantage is not unassailable. If governments lose control over place-branding during periods of environmental conflict, they are less able to influence the travel media's agenda and the way their brand messages are mediated in its journalism. This can afford travel journalism sources with interest-group sympathies, cosmopolitical travel journalists, and powerful travel media institutions that brand themselves as honest, environmentally responsible and/or discerning an opportunity to circulate alternative, politically charged meanings and symbols within a cosmopolitan discourse compatible with their participation in the tourism industry using the frame "brand-sensitive cosmopolitan concern" (see Chapter 5). Such interventions may be relatively rare, but the audiences they reach in their printed form can be numerically large and affluent. In addition, free online publication is still relatively common in big travel magazines and the travel sections of newspapers, which can greatly expand the reach and shelf life of such articles.

Many of the tactics that have been so well documented in relation to hard news coverage of environmental activism are evident in travel journalism source–media relations and production. The cultivation and deployment of powerful symbols (Chapters 4, 5 and 8), voices of potential side-effects (Chapter 6), tactical media (Chapter 7) and global networks (Chapter 7) are just a few of those in addition to framing highlighted in this book. More specific to travel journalism is the advantage challengers can gain from the flow of symbols between tourism and activism – wilderness (Chapter 4), spirit bears (Chapter 8) and glaciers (Chapter 8), for example. In addition, a place's inclusion in travel journalism lists for negative rather than positive reasons can piggyback on social media and news enthusiasm for "global" rankings to gain domestic as well as international recognition usually restricted to accolades (Chapter 9). And sponsorship of a challenger frame by travel journalists who also have high public profiles (for example, AA Gill in Chapter 6 and Richard Flanagan in Chapters 1, 4 and 7) can carry it to new constituencies (see Brockington 2013). Yet, for the most part these are rare and ephemeral victories for challengers in terms of their ability to apply pressure for change in the places being reviewed. Tourism public relations practitioners and travel journalists who believe politics has no place in the genre are likely to give little thought to the political interests that brand-aligned travel texts might serve, and even if a few journalists occasionally feel moved to report environmental conflict in tourism destinations they review, still fewer have the cultural capital, agency, opportunity and determination to usher challenger frames past the many obstacles they are likely to encounter before or after publication. In my own research, authorities were usually well resourced, well connected and agile enough to soon wrest back their traditional advantage. In the absence of overt calls to political activism, cosmopolitical concern expressed by high-status international travel journalists during their visits and in their published texts is more likely to provide feedback at the margins of the brand. This may be no small achievement, but more research would be required to establish whether it contributes to dissensus or a mood for change within and/or among government agencies and businesses.

When it is a reflexive attempt by cosmopolitical travel journalists to reconcile the competing norms and values of public relations and journalism, the frame of "brand sensitive cosmopolitan concern" does not necessarily indicate any weakening of the structural ties between mainstream media and the global tourism industry, but this does not mean travel journalism is irrelevant to the cosmopolitan public sphere. It is still possible that travel journalists' descriptions of very particular environmental conflicts thousands of kilometres from their home markets bring 'the global other' imaginatively into the midst of their readers (Beck, 2011, p. 1348). When travel journalism looks beyond the destination image projected by tourism offices (see MacCannell 2011, p. 210) to reflexively unveil distant environmental threats and conflict, it contributes to the mediation of a world where 'everybody is connected and confronted with everybody', whether or not they wish to know them on the deepest intercultural level (Beck, 2011, p. 1348). To varying degrees, international journalists I interviewed who chose to include environmental conflict in their travel features demonstrated in their conversations with me a sense that conflict is part of the human condition, the Earth is a shared, finite resource, the plight of local places of global value is of interest to distant audiences, and distant audiences experiencing similar conflicts will draw a sense of community from learning of others' battles. Such concern may conceivably form a bridge between disparate communities engaged in similar kinds of environmental struggle, helping create the conditions for bottom-up cosmo-politics. In contrast to Beck's vision of imagined communities of global risks being initiated by an awareness of shared vulnerability independent of compassion or normative intent (Beck, 2011), however, cosmopolitical travel journalism concerned with environmental problems tends to promote an 'ethics of care' (Szerszynski and Urry, 2002) by using the language of affect to build relationships between readers, distant environments and the other.

Climate change is the signature environmental issue of our time (United Nations Environment Program n.d.). As such, according to Alison Anderson, it deserves to be considered in the context of our "increasingly 'promotional' culture', highlighted by the rapid rise of the public relations industry in recent years and claims-makers who employ increasingly sophisticated media strategies" (Anderson 2014, p. 2). Travel media are one forum in which such an investigation of climate change communication could usefully be conducted. As discussed in Chapter 9, cosmopolitical travel journalists do, indeed, appear reluctant to question the future viability of the global tourism industry in light of the greenhouse gases emitted during long-haul flights to distant destinations (McGaurr 2014). However, my reading of travel features and lists during research for this book leads me to suspect that many travel journalists feel reasonably comfortable referring to the phenomenon of climate change directly or obliquely in relation to its effects on specific attractions such as glaciers, ice sheets, Antarctica, polar bears, small island states and other low-lying destinations. For example, although John Flinn considered Tasmania's forestry dispute an unsuitable subject for travel journalism (see Chapter 5), in a 2002 travel feature he quoted a climate scientist at length about the impact of climate change on the polar bears of Churchill in Manitoba, Canada. And in the same month as Pearson's 2014 Icelandic culinary travel feature appeared in *Conde Nast Traveller*, Oliver Berry published a feature about the country in *Lonely Planet Traveller* magazine in which he quoted the local who guided him on the Vatnajökull Glacier. It was only a sentence, but the message was clear: "For me, it's also our most precious landscape and, because of climate change, it's changing faster than ever" (Finnbogason in Berry 2014).

Simon Cottle (2013, p. 32) has observed that one way contemporary media play a role in transnationalising environmental issues is by "scaling them up by signalling 'local' concerns as 'global' issues; or scaling them down by rendering 'global' concerns as local issues". Does the borderlessness of greenhouse gases free travel journalists to discuss environmental concern more openly? Can the mediation of climate change in travel journalism initiate bottom-up cosmopolitanism by promoting awareness of our individual causal responsibility (Dobson 2006) or at least our interconnected vulnerability (Beck 2011) more effectively than representations of distant local disputes? How do generic representations of cause compete discursively with geographically identifiable representations of consequences? What are the implications for the framing of responsibility, particularly if the causes of climate change are decontextualised linguistically or by the use of symbolic or iconic images that, through repetition, "come to replace other possible representations, particularly those that locate and connect such issues in actual concrete processes such as global capitalism and consumerism" (Hansen and Machin 2008, p. 779)? To what extent does travel journalism's engagement with climate change simply "promote discourses suitable for branding and marketing" (Hansen and Machin 2008, p. 792)? Are there theoretical and practical insights to be gained from examples of readers scaling down global warming to local issues such as Australia's coal-fired power stations and Alberta's bituminous sands, or their willingness to engage in online debate about the very cosmopolitan climate-change paradox travel journalists seem keen to avoid (see Chapter 8)? These are important questions for scholars of environmental communication, for travel journalism is a valuable resource, time is short and the exploration has begun.

References

Anderson, Alison 2014, *Media, Environment and the Network Society*, Palgrave Macmillan, London.

Anholt, Simon 2010, *Places: Identity, Image and Reputation*, Palgrave Macmillan, Basingstoke.

Anholt, Simon 2009b, "Conversazioni", *Simon Anholt*, viewed 24 September 2014, www.simonanholt.com/Conversazioni/conversazioni-conversazioni.aspx

Anholt, Simon 2009c, "Planet and climate", *Good Country Index*, viewed 6 July, www.goodcountry.org/category/planet-climate

Anholt, Simon 2007, *Competitive Identity: The New Brand Management for Nations, Cities and Regions*, Palgrave Macmillan, Basingstoke.

Anholt, Simon & Govers, Robert 2014, The Good Country Index, viewed 6 July 2014, www.goodcountry.org/

Beck, Ulrich 2011, "Cosmopolitanism as imagined communities of global risk", *American Behavioral Scientist*, vol. 55, no. 10, pp. 1346–1361.

Berry, Oliver 2014, "The magic circle", *Lonely Planet Traveller*, September 2014, pp. 88–96.

Brockington, Dan 2013, "Celebrity, environmentalism and conservation", in Libby Lester & Brett Hutchins (eds), *Environmental Conflict and the Media*, Peter Lange, New York, pp. 139–152.

Church, Charlotte 2014, "Charlotte Church goes off-grid in Iceland", *The Guardian*, 25 January, viewed 1 January 22015, www.theguardian.com/travel/2014/jan/25/charlotte-church-off-grid-iceland-travel

Cottle, Simon 2013, "Environmental conflict in a global media age: Beyond dualisms", in Libby Lester & Brett Hutchins (eds), *Environmental Conflict and the Media*, Peter Lange, New York, pp. 19–33.

Dobson, Andrew 2006, "Thick cosmopolitanism", *Political Studies*, vol. 54, pp. 165–184.

Discovery News 2011, "Whale wars in Iceland", 20 July, viewed 25 January 2015, http://news.discovery.com/animals/iceland-whale-wars-110720.htm

Emerson, Jay, Esty, Daniel C., Levy, Narc A., Kim, Christine, Mara, Valentina, de Sherbinin, Alex, Srebotnjak, Tanja & Jaiteh, Malanding 2010, *2010 Environmental Performance Index*, Yale Center for Environmental Law and Policy, New Haven.

Emerson, John W., Hsu, Angel, Levy, Marc A., de Sherbinin, Alex, Mara, Valentina, Esty, Daniel C. & Jaiteh, Malanding, 2012, *2012 Environmental Performance Index and Pilot Trend Environmental Performance Index*, Yale Center for Environmental Law and Policy, New Haven.

Flinn, John 2002, "Bearing witness: Are Churchill's most famous residents on thin ice?', 22 December, *The San Francisco Chronicle*, 28 January 2015, www.sfgate.com/travel/article/BEARING-WITNESS-Are-Churchill-s-most-famous-2744033.php#page-1

Gunnarsson, Valur 2014, "The puffinisation of a country: Tourism today", *The Reykjavík Grapevine*, issue 13, 29 August – 11 September, pp. 22–23.

Hansen, Anders & Machin, David 2008, "Visually branding the environment: Climate change as marketing opportunity", *Discourse Studies*, vol. 10, no. 6, pp. 777–794.

Helgason, Haukur Már 2014, "A volcano bigger than Timberlake or: How we learned to stop worrying and love lava", *The Reykjavík Grapevine*, issue 13, 29 August – 11 September, pp. 21–22.

Helgason, Haukur Már 2013, "Come and meet the members of the brand", *The Reykjavík Grapevine*, 28 October, viewed 24 December 2015, http://grapevine.is/mag/column-opinion/2013/10/28/come-and-meet-the-members-of-the-brand/

Hsu, Angel, Emerson, Jay, Levy, Marc A., de Sherbinin, Alex, Johnson, Laura, Malik, Omar, Schwartz, Jason D. & Jaiteh, Malanding 2014, *The 2014 Environmental Performance Index*, Yale Center for Environmental Law & Policy, New Haven.

Iceland.is n.d., "The big picture: Where Europe meets America", viewed 24 September 2014, www.iceland.is/the-big-picture/

IceWhale n.d. a, "Choose whale friendly restaurants: Meet us don't eat us", viewed 24 January 2015, http://icewhale.is/whale-friendly-restaurants/

IceWhale n.d. b, "About IceWhale: Meet us don't eat us", viewed 24 January 2015, http://icewhale.is/about-icewhale/

Íslandsstofa Promote Iceland n.d., "About Promote Iceland", viewed 24 January 2015, www.islandsstofa.is/en/about

McGaurr, Lyn, 2014, "Your threat or mine? Travel journalists and environmental problems", in Folker Hanusch & Elfriede Fürsich (eds), *Travel Journalism: Exploring Production, Impact and Culture*, Palgrave Macmillan, Basingstoke, pp. 231–248.

Náttúrustofa Suðurlands 2014, "Viðkoma lunda 2014", viewed 21 September 2014, www.nattsud.is/frettir/?p=100&i=195

Negroni, Christine 2010, "In transit; From these ashes rises a boost in tourism", *The New York Times*, 3 October, viewed 31 December 2014, http://query.nytimes.com/gst/fullpage.html?res=9D00E6D8153EF930A35753C1A9669D8B63

Pearson, Harry 2014, "Natural remedies", *Travel + Leisure*, pp. 82–89.

Powell, Hugh 2014, "What does a puffin taste like? The answer is even worse than the question", *Slate*, 7 January, viewed 6 September 2014, www.slate.com/articles/health_and_science/science/2014/01/puffin_hunting_in_iceland_breeding_collapse_due_to_climate_change.single.html

Powell, Hugh 2013, "Little brothers of the Arctic", *Living Bird*, summer, pp. 20–33.

Ramsay, Gordon 2011, "Chef Ramsay goes sky fishing – Gordon Ramsay", The F Word, YouTube, 7 March, viewed 30 January 2015, www.youtube.com/watch?v=3gxWVo KHPSo

Rexroat, Kelsey 2014, "Daring foodie or leisure lover? Iceland has both covered", *Huff Post Travel*, 28 May, viewed 12 September 2014, www.huffingtonpost.com/travelzoo/daring-foodie-or-leisure_b_5406505.html?utm_hp_ref=iceland

United Nations Environment Program n.d., "Climate change: Introduction", viewed 24 January 2014, www.unep.org/climatechange/Introduction.aspx

Tulinius, Kári 2014, "So what's this I hear about Iceland being the 17th best country in the world?", *The Reykjavík Grapevine*, no. 10, 18–31 July, p. 8.

Index

actor-network theory 59–60, 69
advertising 16, 18, 45, 56, 58–9, 67, 93, 117, 153, 172
Afar 145, 147
Africa 8, 33, 39
agenda-setting 37–8, 55
agriculture 18, 69, 80, 88, 146
Ahluwalia, R 58
air travel 69, 173–4, 175, 182
Alaska 5
Alberta 4, 14, 101; bituminous sands 9, 65, 154, 155, 158–9, 174, 183; brand 5, 65, 160; digital searches 155, 156, 158–60, 162–3; Enbridge Northern Gateway pipeline, proposed 154, 155, 157, 158, 161, 162, 163; lists 167, 174–5; "remember to breathe" 5, 65, 160
Alps, D 96, 118, 119–21, 123, 124, 143
Americas 8, 33; *see also individual countries*
Amnesty International 9
Anderson, A 11, 30, 37, 45, 46, 132, 182
Anderson, B 29, 32, 42
Anderson, L 13
Anholt, S 3, 4, 60, 61, 62, 63, 66, 69, 71, 178, 180
annihilation, symbolic, 3
Appadurai, A 71
Arab Spring 57
Argentina 122
Aronczyk, M 60, 62, 135
Arvidsson, A 46, 62, 68, 101, 108, 153
Asia 8, 33
Ateljevic, I 39, 63
Atkin, M 2
Australia 7, 8, 9, 40, 52, 53, 55, 57–8, 89, 125; coal 1, 174, 183; Great Barrier Reef 172–3, 174, 175; Tasmania *see separate entry*
authenticity 46, 121, 126; tourist gaze and staged 40–2
autoethnographic elements 12–14
aviation 69, 173–4, 175, 182

Bacon, J 140
Bailey, S 141
Baker, Norman 95–6
Barcott, B 155, 158, 162
Barns, G 96
Barwise, P 58
Bauman, Z 29
Bay of Fires 124; Aboriginal land claims 128, 130, 175; Lodge 126–7; Walk 12, 103, 118, 124–30, 131, 175
BBC Wildlife Magazine 102–4, 105–8, 125
bears: polar 5, 182; spirit 155–6, 157–8, 159–60, 161, 162, 163, 181
Beck, U 6, 29, 30, 32, 36–8, 40, 41, 42, 46, 47, 71, 122, 170, 176, 181, 182, 183
Beecher, E 55
Bellows, K 162, 168
Benson, R 39
Berglez, P 163
Berry, O 182
Bianchi, R 33
blogs 7, 17, 58, 129, 160, 167
Bourassa, S 35
Bourdieu, P 38, 39, 41, 44
brand-sensitive cosmopolitan concern 113, 180, 181; challengers 135, 139, 148; digital searches 157, 160;

"ecotourism solution" and 104–5, 128; lists 167–8, 171–2, 173, 175; meaning of 101; travel media 117, 120, 128, 130, 131, 149

brands 3, 4–5, 6, 9, 16, 44, 46, 111, 180; anti-branding movement 62; brand-aligned cross-promotion 1; digital searches 153–4, 157, 160, 161, 163; informational capital of 62, 153–4; lifestyle 62; place-branding *see separate entry*; travel media 116–32, 168, 172

British Columbia 14; brand 5, 65, 161; digital searches 155, 156–7, 162; Enbridge Northern Gateway pipeline, proposed 154, 155, 157, 158, 161, 162, 163; "Super, Natural" 5, 65, 161

Brockington, D 181

Brown B 81, 85, 86

Buchman, G 85, 99

Burton, B 55

Busch, R 84, 85, 86

business news 56

Byrne Swain, M 63

Calhoun, C 30, 31, 32–3, 40, 42

Canada 2, 3, 8, 9, 182; Alberta *see separate entry*; British Columbia *see separate entry*; Enbridge Northern Gateway pipeline, proposed 154, 155, 157, 158, 161, 162, 163; First Nation communities 155–6, 161; national parks 64

Cannon, HM 40

capitalism 44, 62; corporate 43; neo-liberal 32

carbon tax 162

Caribbean 7, 39

Carvalho, A 11, 12, 84

Castells, M 17, 34, 46, 63, 69

Castles, G 89

celebrity 2, 45, 111, 129

challengers 135–9, 147–9, 181; tactical travel journalism 140–7

Cheah, P 31, 32

Chipperfield, M 125, 127–8

Church, C 179, 180

civil society movements 30

climate change 6, 29, 167, 172–4, 175, 179, 182–3

Cobb, A 160

Cocking, B 7, 16–17, 39

common heritage of mankind 81

compassion fatigue 38

competitive identity 61

Condé Nast Traveller 95, 116, 141, 143, 144, 167, 169, 174, 179, 182

connectedness, transnational 174

corporate capitalism 43

corporate elites, journalism and public relations 55–6, 57

cosmopolitanism 5–6, 29–31, 47, 63, 183; anti- 38; associated theoretical interests 42–6; banal 6, 34, 37, 47; brand-sensitive cosmopolitan concern *see separate entry*; commerce and 31–2; consumerist 30, 31, 33, 40, 41, 47, 84, 120, 126, 180; cultural 6, 31, 32–3, 47, 111, 120; eco- 35; environment and 34–6; faces of 31–4; Franklin River judgement 81; journalism and 36–9; place-branded cosmopolitan concern 101, 126, 130, 175, 180; political 6, 31, 44, 47, 111, 145; reflexive "second gaze" 41–2; thin and thick 35, 40; tourist gaze and staged authenticity 40–2; travel journalists and 39–40

Cottle, S 10, 37, 38, 57, 182

Couldry, N 59–60

Cox, R 3, 11, 79, 122

Cradle Huts ecotourism operation 82–3, 124, 125, 129–30, 131

Craven, G 140–1

critic role and travel journalists 54

critical discourse analysis 7

critical tourism studies 63, 68

Croome, R 109–10, 127

Crossley, L 80, 82

crowdsourcing 160

cultural capital 35, 39, 41–2, 47, 139, 148–9, 175, 180, 181

culture in brand strategy 9

Curran, J 55

Currant, S 169

Curwen, T 127, 128, 129–30, 131

Daily Telegraph 107

Davies, N 55

Davis, A 45, 55–6, 60

Daye, M 7, 35, 39
Deacon, D 13, 14
definition of travel journalism 14–18
democracy 14–15, 16, 178
Denholm, M 96, 100
destination branding 60, 168; *see also*
    place-branding
developing countries 33, 174, 175
DeWitt, J 157
difference, witnesses of 41
digital searches 153–63; conflict context
    159–62; methods 156; results 156–9
discursive strategies 11–12, 60–1, 71, 79,
    87, 101; framing *see separate entry*
"distanced brutality" frame 127–8, 138
Dobson, A 35, 183
Dore, L 6, 53, 58, 67
Dorney, S 52
Dovey, K 126
Doward, J 94–5, 97–8, 103
Dowty, R 93, 99, 128, 129
Dryzek, JS 85, 86, 176
Duncan, P 123
Dürr, E 65

eagles 104, 148
Earth Island Journal 144
Eastern Europe 8
ecological modernisation 84, 85
ecological romanticism 86
ecotourism 3, 79, 84–7, 99, 101, 102, 110,
    139, 168, 169, 171, 174; Bay of Fires
    Walk 103, 118, 124–30, 131, 175;
    Canada 155, 161; Cradle Huts
    operation 82–3, 124, 125, 129–30, 131;
    frame: "ecotourism solution" 84,
    104–5, 128, 130, 172, 173; Wilderness
    Society 102; World Congress on
    Adventure Travel and Ecotourism 84,
    170
emerging/developing countries 33, 174,
    175
Emerson, J 178
Emmett, ET 80
Enbridge Northern Gateway pipeline,
    proposed 154, 155, 157, 158, 161, 162,
    163
Englefield, B 129
Entman, RM 11

environment movement 4–5, 6, 9, 90, 97,
    110, 118, 139, 140, 148; Canada 161,
    162, 174–5; Franklin River campaign
    79, 81, 89; interface between places
    and flows 70; Tarkine National
    Coalition 146, 147; Wilderness Society
    81, 85, 96, 102, 137, 138, 140, 143,
    144
equity, reverse 83, 84
Ericson, RV 45, 55
Essick, P 158
ethics of care 5, 34, 182
Europe 8, 10, 33, 39; *see also individual*
    countries
Evans, A 158, 160, 167
Evers, N 82
Examiner 169–70

Fair, J 102–4, 105–7, 125, 128, 173
Fairclough, N 43–4, 84
Ferguson, E 103, 125
Fernando, A 166
Fickling, D 96, 97
The Financial Times 95, 141, 143–4, 147,
    174
Finnsson, Á 171–2
Flanagan, R 1, 2, 95, 96–7, 111, 112, 136,
    139, 145, 181
Fleming, K 1, 95
Flinn, J 108–11, 127, 170, 173, 182
Flyvbjerg, B 10, 43, 44
food 6; Iceland 179–80; and wine 2, 9, 18,
    96, 98, 100, 103, 118–23, 131, 142,
    144, 148
foreign correspondents 38, 52, 96, 141
forests in Canada 159; Great Bear
    Rainforest 155, 156, 157–8, 159–62,
    163; logging 155, 157, 161, 162
forests in Tasmania 1, 5, 79, 80, 88, 94, 95,
    108, 110–11, 129, 131, 144–5, 174,
    182; compatible sectors 79, 85, 87,
    103–5, 107; "distanced brutality" frame
    127, 128; Flanagan 1, 2, 95, 96–7, 112,
    136, 139, 145; Gill's 2007 assessment 2,
    128; logging 1, 9, 85, 95–7, 99–102,
    103–5, 106–7, 112, 113, 121, 128,
    135–9, 142, 143–4, 146, 168, 169–70,
    171; regulating staff 99–102; Ritchie
    111; wilderness, ecotourism and

recreational forestry 79, 84–6, 87; *see also* pulp mill
Foucault, M 44
foxes 98
framing 2–3, 5, 9, 11–12, 57, 59, 81, 110, 112, 143, 180; "compatible sectors" 79, 85, 87, 103–5, 107; controlling access to sources and frames 95–8; digital searches and environmental frames 153–63; "distanced brutality" 127–8, 138; duelling frames 102–8; "ecotourism solution" 84, 104–5, 128, 130, 172, 173; "warlike conflagration" 96–7, 112, 121, 131, 136–7, 144; *see also* nature; wilderness
Franklin River 79, 81–2, 84, 89, 104, 106, 107, 110, 125, 126, 136, 161
Fraser, N 42
free travel and accommodation 6, 13, 16, 37, 52, 57–8, 68, 111, 116, 136; ubiquity of 53–4, 70–1; *see also* visiting journalist programs
freedom 44, 62
freelancers 16, 54, 95, 117, 141, 144, 173–4
Frey, D 112
Freycinet Peninsula 86, 124, 125, 131
Friendly Beaches Lodge 86, 124
Furneaux, Tobias 125
Fürsich, E 7, 15, 53

Gamson, W 57
Gans, HJ 55
Garcia, D 57, 140
Gartner, WC 58
Geertz, C 10, 18, 176
Genier, E 155
geotourism 168
Germany 9
Gill, AA 2, 127, 128–9, 132, 181
Gill, S 32
Gillespie, I 6, 52
glaciers 5, 158, 181, 182
Glaetzer, S 1
global risks, imagined communities of 6, 30, 42, 47, 131, 168, 170, 172–6, 182
globalisation 7, 31–2, 36, 38, 42, 61
globalism, banal 34, 38, 47
government public relations 55–6, 70–1;

politics, travel journalism, the brand and 67–9; travel journalism and 57–60
Govers, R 29, 46, 58, 60, 61, 63, 69, 71
Great Barrier Reef 172–3, 174, 175
Great Bear Rainforest 155, 156, 157–8, 159–62, 163
Greece: national parks 64; travel magazine 7
green political parties 4–5, 9, 81, 100
green rationalism 85
Greenpeace 137
Greenwald, J 102, 144–5, 147, 148–9
Gross, AC 64
The Guardian 96, 97, 167, 171, 174–6, 179
guidebooks 18
Gunnarsson, V 178, 179
Gunns Ltd 96, 107, 118, 122, 128, 141, 143

Habermas, J 32, 42, 43, 44
Hajer, M 4, 85
Hall, S 44, 45, 55, 68
Handwerk, B 159
Hanna, D 103, 128
Hannerz, U 5–6, 30, 31, 32, 33, 34, 36, 37, 38, 39, 40, 41, 47
Hansen, A 3, 35, 65, 88–9, 183
Hanusch, F 6, 7, 8, 16, 17, 18, 39–40, 52, 53, 54, 55
Hartley, J 15, 16
Harvey, D 32, 38, 71
Heise, U 35
Helgason, HM 178–9
Herrick, S 174
Hickton, G 69, 71
Higgins-Desbiolles, F 33
Hilgartner, S 57
Hill-James, CR 2, 7
Hindman, M 112, 154, 166
history of evolution of Tasmania's discourse of accessible nature 79–90
Hochman, D 123, 125, 127
Hodgman, P 84
Holland, P 15, 18
Hollinshead, K 63, 68
Hollister, D 100, 103, 145
Holton, RJ 29, 31
homosexuality 9, 109–10, 127
Hsu, A 178

Huff Post Travel 179
Hunt, G 124–5
Hutchins, B 45, 46, 69–70, 71, 108, 111, 140
hydro-electric power 80–1, 89, 171
hydro-industrialisation 80
hyperlinks 163, 172, 173, 175

Iceland 2, 3–4, 8, 14, 167, 171–2, 175, 178–80, 182
imagined communities of global risks 6, 30, 42, 47, 131, 168, 170, 172–6, 182
impression formulation literature 58
Independent 125
indigenous peoples: Aboriginal inhabitants/community 80, 85, 86, 125, 127–8, 130, 131, 175; First Nation communities 155–6, 161
information, regulating flow of 93–5; controlling access to sources and frames 95–8; regulating staff 98–102
informational capital of brands 62, 153–4
integrity: cultural 168; journalistic 93, 95; travel magazines 116
International Fund for Animal Welfare (IFAW) 179
international relations 63–4
Internet 7, 12, 46, 54, 57, 123, 132, 139, 140–1, 149, 180–1; blogs 7, 17, 58, 129, 160, 167; digital searches 153–63; hyperlinks 163, 172, 173, 175; *Tasmanian Times* 129
Iraq 56–7, 67
Ironside, R 2
island factor 65, 89
Islands magazine 144–5, 147
isolationism 38

Japan 9
Jenkins, M 1, 5, 122, 135–9, 145, 148–9
Jennings, T 158
Jeong, S 34
Johnston, J 60
Jordan, S 146, 147

Kant, I 31
Kennedy, T 158, 159, 161, 162, 163
Kermode/spirit bears 155–6, 157–8,
159–60, 161, 162, 163, 181
King, Geoff "Joe" 109, 110, 128, 147
Knight, G 43, 44
Köhler, M 42–3
Kovach, B 15
Krishnamurthy, H 158
Kunzig, R 155, 158–9
Kyzer, L 171, 172

Lagan, B 2
Lake Pedder 81, 89
Lash, S 62
Latona, K 83, 86–7, 110, 118, 121, 124–5, 126–7, 128, 129, 130
Latour, B 59
Law, G 135–6
Lester, L 9, 11, 43, 45, 57, 70, 81, 89, 90, 125, 126, 137, 140, 161
Lewis, J 55, 56–7, 60, 67, 101
lifestyle journalism 6, 15, 57
Linnitt, C 160
Lisle, D 18
lists 1, 2, 12, 16–17, 18, 111–12, 130, 166–76, 180, 181
Livingstone, S 38
local or regional media 1–2, 16, 70, 71, 95, 111, 121, 129, 169, 175; World Congress on Adventure Travel and Ecotourism 86
logging: Canada 155, 157, 161, 162; Tasmania 1, 9, 85, 95–7, 99–102, 103–5, 106–7, 112, 113, 121, 128, 135–9, 142, 143–4, 146, 168, 169–70, 171; *see also* pulp mill
Lonely Planet 1, 12–13, 18, 125, 130
Lonely Planet Traveller 18, 116, 182
Lovibond, J 169
Lovink, G 57, 140
Lury, C 5, 46, 60, 61–2, 68, 69, 71, 101, 108, 153

MacCannell, D 41, 42, 126, 181
McColl, M 144
McCracken, G 11
McGaurr, L 3, 4, 5, 7, 9, 90, 146, 161, 174, 182
McGinity, M 124, 126
McKay, D 123
Mackellar, J 6, 53, 57–8, 67

Macnaghten, P 34–6
McNair, B 14–15
McRobbie, A 57
magazines, travel *see* travel media
marine wildlife tourism 105
Marks, K 130
Masterman, J 83, 86–7, 124, 125
media: local or regional *see separate entry*;
    travel *see separate entry*
Meikle, G 57, 140, 144
The Mercury 1–2, 86, 111, 123, 131,
    140–1, 169, 175
Metcalf, S 117–19, 120, 121–3, 131, 132,
    137, 145
methods and approach 9–12
Middle East 39, 57–8
Miles, P 95, 102, 141–2, 143–5, 146–7,
    173–4
military conflicts 56, 59, 67
Miller, D 45
mining 80, 155, 167, 174
minke whales 179
Mocatta, G 100, 128, 130
Moeller, SD 38
Molotch, H 44
Montgomery, B 2
Mooney, N 100, 102–3, 104–5, 108–9,
    110
Morgan, N 63, 67, 68
Moss, C 6, 14
Mowforth, M 38
multiculturalism 36
Murcutt, G 126–7
Museum of Old and New Art (MONA)
    9

nation-branding 60, 179; *see also*
    place-branding
National Geographic 136, 139, 149, 154–5,
    156, 157, 158–9, 160, 162, 163, 167
National Geographic Adventure 121, 128,
    155, 156
National Geographic Society 154, 168
National Geographic Traveler 85, 86, 99,
    116, 155, 156, 157, 158, 160, 167,
    168–9, 170, 171
NationalGeographic.com 149, 154–5,
    156–63, 176
national parks 4, 63, 64–5; Canada 157,

160; Tasmania 79, 80, 81, 82–3, 86,
    120, 121, 124, 125, 130, 131, 169
nationalism 29, 31, 32, 36, 38, 61
nature 3, 4–5, 6, 8, 9, 65, 71, 79, 81,
    89–90, 159; Bay of Fires Walk 126; as
    brand 87–9, 98, 99, 103, 104, 105,
    107–8, 110, 131–2, 138, 143, 145, 148,
    170; British Columbia 161; culture and
    34–5; ecotourism and geotourism 168;
    from accessible wilderness to accessible
    83–6; from wild to mild 86–7;
    romanticised 35, 65
Negroni, C 178
neo-liberal capitalism 32
network society 34, 46, 69
networks and professional judgement
    108–13
The New York Times 1, 12, 96, 111–12,
    167, 171–2; *Magazine* 125
New Zealand 8, 63; "100% Pure"
    campaign 5, 53, 65, 67, 68–9, 71
Newman, J 158, 160
news agenda 37–8, 55
news journalism 10, 15, 45, 55, 70, 97–8,
    110, 111, 130, 141–2, 143, 146, 147,
    170–1, 180
news, travel 17
Nicholls, D 83–4, 87, 99, 102, 109, 124,
    131, 142, 170
Nicklen, P 157, 158, 162
non-government organisations (NGOs)
    30, 37, 43, 56, 95, 140, 141, 142, 148
North America 8; *see also* Canada; United
    States

Observer 97–8, 103, 125
O'Byrne, M 111
Oceania 8
Okabe, Bruce 5, 65, 160
Otterman, S 111–12
Ottoman empire 31
Outside 1, 5, 79, 125, 135–9, 149

Palmer, A 81
paradox 174, 183
partnered or sponsored texts 17–18, 102,
    105–8, 157, 159, 162
Pearson, H 179, 180
Pearson, S 5, 9, 79, 139

People for the Ethical Treatment of
   Animals 95
Pergament, D 167, 171, 172
Perrottet, T 125, 127, 149
Phillips, G 123
pipeline, proposed Enbridge Northern
   Gateway 154, 155, 157, 158, 161, 162,
   163
Pirie, A 122, 123
Pirolli, B 7, 17
place-branded cosmopolitan concern 101,
   126, 130, 175, 180
place-branding 3, 5, 9, 29, 30, 46, 47, 53,
   54, 60–2, 70–1, 131, 176, 180;
   alignment of stakeholders 98, 123;
   autonomous/covert induced/induced
   promotion 58–9; brand-sensitive
   cosmopolitan concern *see separate
   entry*; digital surveillance and feedback
   153–4; environmental attractions and
   64–5; history of evolution of
   Tasmania's discourse of accessible
   nature 79–90; Iceland 178, 180;
   interface between places and flows
   69–70, 111; managing public opinion
   internally 111; media and 66–7, 98,
   124; networks and professional
   judgement 108–13; public relations,
   politics, travel journalism and the
   brand 67–9; publication's branding and
   116; tourism, public diplomacy and
   62–4; web and social media data
   153–4; *see also* challengers; framing;
   information, regulating flow of; nature;
   wilderness
Planet Ark 140
polar bears 5, 182
political contest model 45, 101–2
pollution 29, 65, 118, 127, 155, 159, 167,
   173
Portugal 7, 39
postmodernism 38, 64
Powell, H 179
printing press 32, 42
produsers 17
professional judgement and networks
   108–13
prosumers 17
public diplomacy 66–7; tourism,

   place-branding and 62–4
public relations 17, 52–3, 60, 61, 64,
   70–1, 102, 182; cooperation or
   contestation: journalism and 54–7;
   politics, travel journalism, the brand
   and 67–9;
   travel journalism and government
   57–60
public relations, Tasmanian 1, 84, 87, 89,
   94; accessible wilderness: harnessing
   PR power of protection 80–3; *see also*
   visiting journalist programs
public sphere 14–15, 32, 42–3, 44, 46
publishers 56
puffins 179
pulp mill 2, 95, 96, 100, 118–23, 128,
   129–30, 131, 132, 141, 142, 143–4
purposes of journalism 14–15

Qantas 140
Quarmby, D 80, 83

Raman, U 7, 17
Ramsay, G 179
refeudalisation of public sphere 43, 45
regional media/newspapers *see* local or
   regional media
Reiff, I 157
Reitsma, G 65
Remillard, C 155, 159
reverse equity 83, 84
Rexroat, K 179, 180
Ribbon, A 140
risks, imagined communities of global 6,
   30, 42, 47, 131, 168, 170, 172–6, 182
Ritchie, B 111
Rivalland, M 167, 172, 173
road construction 85, 100, 103–4, 145–7,
   161
Robbins, B 31, 32
Robertson, A 31, 32
romantic tourist gaze 161; and staged
   authenticity 40–2
Roscovich, T 156, 162
Rose, H 129
Ryan, C 3, 63, 65, 67
Ryan, J 64, 89

Sachs, A 121, 128

Saito, H 32, 36, 59
San Francisco Chronicle 108–9
Santos, CA 7, 11–12, 39
Schlesinger, P 10, 14, 45, 55
Schmidt, V 167
Schofield, L 123
Schudson, M 55
Schultz, S 162
Seagram, K 100, 118, 119, 121, 122–3,
 131
searches, digital 153–63
Seaton, AV 7, 53
Seligman, M 6
Shell 157, 159, 162
Shepherd, S 166
Sherwood, S 111, 167
Simon, J 6
Singapore 9
Smith, W 36, 38
social media 153–4, 166, 167, 181; lists
 166, 167
social movements 57, 85, 108
soft journalism 5, 15, 45
soft power diplomacy 64
source–media relations 43–5, 47, 55–6, 68,
 70, 181; controlling access to sources
 and frames 95–8
Spindler, A 125, 126, 127
Spirit Bear Youth Coalition 161
spirit bears 155–6, 157–8, 159–60, 161,
 162, 163, 181
sponsored or partnered texts 17–18, 102,
 105–8, 157, 159, 162
staff journalists, workplace acculturation
 of 97–8, 103
Stamou, A 7, 64, 85
Street-Porter, J 125
Styx Valley 96, 99, 102, 103–4, 106–7,
 135–8, 140, 170
The Sunday Times 2, 132
Switzerland 5
symbolic annihilation 3
Szerszynski, B 5, 6, 30, 32, 34, 35, 38, 47,
 182

tactical travel journalism 140–7
Tahune Forest AirWalk 99, 102
Takach, G 9, 65, 101, 160, 175
Tamar Valley: proposed pulp mill 2, 95,

96, 100, 118–23, 128, 129–30, 131,
 132, 141, 142, 143–4
Tarkine 85, 100, 107, 145–7, 161
Tasmania 8–9, 45, 52, 79–80, 89–90, 173;
 Aboriginal inhabitants/community 80,
 85, 86, 125, 127–8, 130, 131, 175;
 accessible wilderness: harnessing PR
 power of protection 80–3;
 autoethnographic elements 12–14;
 forests in *see separate entry*; from
 accessible wilderness to accessible
 nature 83–6; from wild to mild 86–7;
 island factor 65, 89; lists 130, 167,
 168–70, 175; methods and approach
 9–12; Museum of Old and New Art
 (MONA) 9; nature as brand 87–9;
 regulating flow of information 93–102;
 Tourism 21 98; visiting journalist
 program (VJP) 9, 83–4, 87, 93–5, 96,
 99–104, 107, 108, 119, 121, 128,
 141–3, 148, 174; whole-of-government
 approach 3, 79, 85, 98, 99
Tasmanian devils 97–8, 108–9, 145, 147,
 148
Tasmanian tiger 88, 108–9, 127, 138
Teasdale, A 18
Telegraph 125, 128, 130; *Magazine* 96
The Times 2, 128, 132, 167, 172–3, 175
tourist gaze and staged authenticity 40–2
Tourtellot, J 122, 168, 169–71
Travel + Leisure 116, 118, 123, 125, 132,
 167, 169, 179
travel lists 1, 2, 12, 16–17, 18, 111–12,
 130, 166–76, 180, 181
travel media 116–18, 163, 168, 172, 180,
 182; brand value of brands 124–30;
 circulating concerns through brand
 extensions 118–23; power 116–17, 144,
 147; *see also individual publications*
Travel Trade 86
Tsui, B 123, 162
Tuchman, G 15
Tulinius, K 178

Underwood, P 174
UNESCO 89
United Kingdom 8–10, 12, 52, 80, 95–6,
 108, 125, 128; Africa 39; Caribbean 7,
 39; government issues management:

branding and public diplomacy 67;
Leeds Metropolitan University 168;
military conflicts 56; public relations
56; Tourism Concern 33
United Nations 9; World Heritage List
64–5, 79, 81, 82–3, 89, 169
United Nations World Tourism
Organization (UNWTO) 4, 33, 173
United States 7, 8–10, 12, 16, 52, 125,
128, 155; Alaska 5; Ethical Traveler
33, 144, 147; government issues
management: branding and public
diplomacy 67; manatees, endangered
110; military conflicts 56–7; national
parks 64; Portugal 7, 39; Society of
American Travel Writers 18, 147
Urry, J 33, 40–1, 89, 161

Van den Berg, L 169
Van Ham, P 29, 61, 63–4, 66, 67
virtual mobility 7
visiting journalist programs (VJPs) 16, 53,
57–60, 67, 71; "issues" or "experiences"
95; Tasmania 9, 83–4, 87, 93–5, 96,
99–104, 107, 108, 119, 121, 128,
141–3, 148, 174
Voase, R 39

Waisbord, S 122
Walker, M 80
Walterlin, U 102
Wanderlust 130, 131, 175
"warlike conflagration" 96–7, 112, 121,
131, 136–7, 144
water quality 69
Waters, Alice 123, 132

Weir Alderson, J 6–7
whales 179–80
Wheeler, M 109, 125
Wheeler, T 125
White, J 55
Whiteley, S 137, 138–9
wilderness 5, 9, 79, 89–90, 99, 119, 125,
126, 139, 143, 148; from accessible
wilderness to accessible nature 83–6;
from wild to mild 86–7; harnessing PR
power of protection: accessible 80–3;
social construction 82; Tasmanian tiger
88, 138
Wilderness Society 81, 85, 96, 102, 137,
138, 140, 143, 144
wine and food 2, 9, 18, 96, 98, 100, 103,
118–23, 131, 142, 144, 148
Wineglass Bay 86
witnesses of difference 41
Wolfsfeld, G 19, 45, 57, 59, 95, 101–2,
117, 148
Wood, L 7, 53
Woodward, I. 33, 34, 36, 38
Woolf, M 96
World Congress on Adventure Travel and
Ecotourism 84–6, 170
World Heritage List 64–5, 79, 81, 82–3,
89, 169
World Intellectual Property Organization
141
worldmaking 63, 68
WWF 140

YouTube 5, 160

Zeiher, C 1

For Product Safety concerns and information please contact our
EU representative GPSR@taylorandfrancis.com Taylor & Francis
Verlag GmbH, Kaufingerstraße 24, 80331 München, Germany